IDENTITY

For over 25 years, John Sweetman worked as a Detective Garda attached to the Garda Technical Bureau in Garda Headquarters, Phoenix Park. He qualified as a Fingerprint Expert and later as a Security Document and Handwriting Expert and has spent the bulk of his career examining crime scenes and scenes of crime exhibits for the purposes of presenting expert identification testimony in Irish Courts.

As a dedicated member of the Technical Bureau, John was involved in numerous serious crime investigations over the years, up until his retirement from An Garda Siochána in 2023. A keen artist, with an excellent eye for detail, John put his talent to use in the meticulous and exacting field of forensic comparison and individualisation, using the skills he acquired during his service as a valued member of the Garda Technical Bureau.

John lives with his family in North County Dublin. *Identity: Murder, Fraud and the Making of a Garda Forensic Expert* is his first book.

IDENTITY

MURDER, FRAUD
and THE MAKING of a
GARDA FORENSIC EXPERT

JOHN SWEETMAN

HACHETTE
BOOKS
IRELAND

First published in Ireland in 2024 by HACHETTE BOOKS IRELAND

1

A CIP catalogue record for this title is available from the British Library.

ISBN 9781399735872

Typeset in Sabon LT Std by Bookends Publishing Servies, Dublin
Printed and bound in Great Britain by Clays Ltd, Elcograf S.p.A.

Hachette Books Ireland policy is to use papers that are natural, renewable
and recyclable products and made from wood grown in sustainable
forests. The logging and manufacturing processes are expected to
conform to the environmental regulations of the country of origin.

Hachette Books Ireland
8 Castlecourt Centre
Castleknock
Dublin 15, Ireland

A division of Hachette UK Ltd
Carmelite House, 50 Victoria Embankment, London EC4Y 0DZ

www.hachettebooksireland.ie

CONTENTS

Dedicated to my Da, Seamus Sweetman, 1945–2020

PROLOGUE

Pages and pages of a handwritten, anonymous letter lie across my desk. A concerned garda from Athlone in County Westmeath has submitted the letter consisting of 23 lined A4 pages containing depraved threats of extreme sexual violence and murder.

There's no preamble. From the very first page, the author writes of his 'plans to abduct female students'. 'Sexual torture', 'slow, drawn-out death' and vows to 'abduct, torture, rape and kill' are among the phrases used. He relates his ambition to be 'a new serial rapist and killer' and tells of his 'sound-proof and escape-proof torture den', where he will kill one teenage girl a week and will have 'ultimate power and control' over his victims.

Reading on, the detail he goes into is unnerving. He lists equipment he claims to have amassed in his torture den: 'cable ties, handcuffs, superglue, blindfolds, mouth gags, dog leash and chain, whips, plastic bags (for over girls' heads), breast-clamps and jump leads (electric shock device), tape recorder (to record girls' screams), ankle clamps, syringe (to inject semen), leg spreaders, rubber gloves, meat hooks'.

He refers to the murder of 29-year-old Jill Meagher from Termonfeckin, County Louth, who was killed in Australia in 2012 and 24-year-old student nurse Karen Buckley from Cork, who was abducted and beaten to death with a foot-long wrench by a man called Alexander Pacteau in Glasgow in April 2015. The letter-writer states that what had happened to Karen 'would only be mild suffering compared to what I would have done to her'. Line after line of this letter is twisted and callous.

He rambles on, mentioning girls whose photos he has cut out of newspapers and a list of sick fantasies that he planned to carry out involving them. The material is so extensive that I am satisfied that the writing is not disguised. It's very difficult to maintain a consistent level of intentional disguise in writings of such volume. The blue-ink-pen writings are reasonably fluent in script and block style, and some pages have newspaper clippings and pornographic material attached to them. However, the garda from Athlone has no suspect, no clue who the writer could be.

It's 18 November 2015. I've been part of the Garda Technical Bureau since 1997, examining thousands of fingerprints and hundreds of handwriting cases. Unfortunately, these kinds of vile anonymous letters aren't unusual. But occasionally, something stands out with a piece of writing, and the rage expressed in this letter concerns me.

My old wooden desk holds a scattering of paper, pens, my ancient magnifying lens and a simple networked computer. It's only two feet from the neighbouring desk. But over the years, I've assembled my own ramshackle privacy wall, surrounding myself with a few shelves and other discarded bits and pieces. I've piled books and other work-related belongings around me, and my trusty giant stereo microscope sits on the bench behind my chair. Although only a half dozen of us are working in the

Documents and Handwriting Section (D&HW), we're all housed within one office area, so there is always banter. The sound levels rise as a garda arrives delivering new exhibits for examination. The sounds of people and activity in adjoining offices also bleed into our room.

However, once I lower my head to examine these letters, it's almost like I am alone. My corner of the office is where I'm happiest. It's my little island in D&HW, a small section tucked away in a dilapidated office in garda headquarters in Phoenix Park.

I filter out the ambient noises and get 'into the zone', immersing myself in the material. Once I start on a case, I need to be fully attuned to whatever I am doing. Making notes. Sketching letter formations. Letting the letters guide me.

I examine every facet of this anonymous writer's writing, the height, width, size and consistency of each individual letter, paying close attention to any unique flourishes, dots and loops. I check the baseline – do the words lie above, below or upon the lines of the A4 pages?

I make my notes and sketch a chart, capturing the variations in letter constructions that the author employs. Then I begin searching through the Documents and Handwriting records and reviewing old case files.

I'm searching for a while before I come across another case from the midlands that involves handwriting and sexual violence. It's from over a decade ago, February 2004, more than three years before I joined the Handwriting Section. Schoolboys playing in a wooded area in the Meelaghans near Tullamore in County Offaly stumbled across a 'hide' containing a wheelie bin buried in a furrow and surrounded by plastic sheeting. I read how a pointed shovel, handsaw, hammer and ropes were also found at the scene.

A biscuit tin sealed with Sellotape is found in the bin. The report says the tin contains extensive handwritten notes and cut-outs from pornographic magazines. The notes are similar, sadistic and graphic. I see that DNA tests carried out at the time only revealed they were from a male.

But as soon as I leaf through the photocopies of the handwritten material found, I recognise the writing. It has been written by the same person whose letter is on my desk. One entry reads, 'My sins. Summer Plan … I will go out, mainly on Saturday evenings, driving around or hunting for my prey.' Again, the writings are disturbing in their detail. He has written out lists of locations, described as his 'hunting areas', complete with distances and allotted travelling times. He outlines his fantasy of seeing 12-year-old girls naked. Again, I see his rage and obsession with schoolchildren: 'I want to rape and destroy their sexy bodies. I want to pound them to death and cut their bodies into little pieces.' Sick fantasist? Or potential murderer?

I call the garda in Athlone and let him know of the Tullamore case from 2004. Within two weeks, two more cases are submitted from two gardaí in two different stations in the midlands – one from Birr and another from Tullamore. As soon as I open the exhibits from the new files, I recognise the same author's hand.

It doesn't take a psychiatrist to know that whoever is crafting these letters is volatile and unpredictable. The latest exhibits continue in the same vein as the 23-page document received a fortnight ago. More obscenities. More threats. More fury. If anything, the content grows even more chilling. There are also sick claims made regarding the unsolved disappearance of an Irishwoman.

Sorting genuine threats from empty ones is a complex and time-consuming task, and unfortunately, there are instances where warnings or indicators are missed or not taken seriously enough until too late. Without any suspects or lines of inquiry, these letters could easily be filed and forgotten. However, I am determined this case is not going to be forgotten. This man is dangerous and has to be found. It's a gut feeling that proves to be one of those defining occasions in my career as a garda.

1

GENESIS

It has been said that there is no fool like an old fool, except a young fool. But the young fool has first to grow up to be an old fool to realise what a damn fool he was when he was a young fool.
Harold Macmillan

Kevin strode to the door of the neat suburban house and rang the doorbell while I hung back. Kevin was a seasoned member of An Garda Síochána, so I was more than happy to let him take the lead. He always had everything under control, and this was just another routine call for us on a leafy estate in Malahide in north County Dublin. I can't even remember what the call was about – only what happened next.

As the door opened, a fury of snarling hair and teeth rushed past Kevin and launched at me. I only got a glimpse of glistening fangs before they sank into the arm I'd raised in defence and, suddenly,

I was wrestling with a huge German shepherd. As Kevin and the owner roared and tried to prise his jaws from me, I desperately flailed around, grappling with my free arm to get my baton out. Even in all the chaos, I remember feeling indignant. Why had this dog ignored my colleague and flung himself at me?

There's no scientific evidence to suggest that dogs inherently hate people in uniforms. Some say they pick up on cues from owners who distrust or dislike people who wear them. But I often questioned why that dog swerved around Kevin, also in uniform, to go for me. Had it sensed my weakness? Walking away that day with a torn navy jumper sleeve, I asked myself, not for the first time, if a career in the guards was right for me.

I have a good memory. I can clearly recollect many events from my childhood and adolescence. Sometimes, people marvel at how I recall the tiniest details about things that happened many years ago. Yet, try as I might, I cannot remember why I joined An Garda Síochána. There was no vocational calling. No eureka moment. The clouds never parted. The skies never lanced me with light beams of inspiration. I never had a sudden moment of clarity – 'Jesus H. tapdancing Christ! I want to be a guard!' It just sort of … happened.

I was born in 1972, the second of four kids for Seamus and Anne Sweetman. I have an older brother, James, and two younger sisters, Mary and Bernie. Nobody in my family, on either side, had been in the force.

All my life, I've lived in a small townland called Piercetown, just outside Skerries in north County Dublin. As Da was a farmer, I spent my youth out and about in the fields, exploring around the seaside and cliffs of nearby Loughshinny.

I finished my Leaving Certificate in 1989 and can remember I came home, flung off my uniform and swore I'd never wear one again. I had a vague aim to pursue something art-related. Art was the only subject I liked and was good at, so I wanted to go to the National College of Art and Design (NCAD) in Dublin or maybe work for a company like Sullivan Bluth, making animated movies. The late 1980s and early 1990s were a boom time for the animation industry in Ireland. My best friend Sean and I submitted our art portfolios to NCAD and other colleges, fully expecting to be welcomed with open arms. We hadn't realised the applicant numbers were huge, and many had taken special courses to prepare their portfolio. I was royally pissed off when the colleges turned us down. I was only 17 but didn't want to wait another year for a shot again. As with countless other times, Mam and Da gave me the direction I needed.

They saw a newspaper advertisement for a fine arts, animation and graphic design diploma at the Fitzwilliam Institute. The course would help me prepare a portfolio of all the disciplines needed to apply to art college, and it was only six months long. Finances were tight for any north Dublin farmer and market gardener like Da, but my folks paid for my enrolment in the course that autumn.

However, within months of starting the course, I landed my first job. The animation company Murakami-Wolf came headhunting, and I was among the lucky ones selected to become a cel painter at their Harcourt Street studio in the city centre. A cel painter applies the colours to the individual frames or 'cels' used in the animation industry, and Murakami-Wolf was a big name, producing the hit *Teenage Mutant Ninja Turtles* cartoon. I was in full-time employment by my eighteenth birthday, earning decent money.

However, it didn't last long. Murakami-Wolf lost the contract for the *Ninja Turtles* about a year after I started, and the work slowed down. Meanwhile, my folks saw a recruitment ad for An Garda Síochána during the summer of 1991. Believing a career with the police force would be more stable than the unpredictable animation business, they encouraged me to apply.

I had no burning desire to be a guard, but I had a bizarre dream around this time where my cousin Ken and I were motorcycle cops – like the guys in the American TV show *CHiPs*, a hit series that had ended years earlier. I dreamt we were on duty in Loughshinny, decked out in leathers and shades and riding big fuck-off motorcycles because Ronald Reagan was coming to visit our seaside village. That fantasy of leathers and motorcycles must have been in my head when I filled out the application.

The guards called me for an aptitude test on 1 September, and I made my way to Inchicore in Dublin with hundreds of others to sit the test. That same week, 66 of us in Murakami-Wolf were made redundant. We were painting away on some cels when we were all called to a meeting and told, effective immediately, we were out of work. Within days, my girlfriend also dumped me. It was not a good week.

Many Murakami-Wolf colleagues sought work in other studios, but I'd had enough. I didn't relish commuting daily on the unreliable, over-packed train to a new job in the city. I often wonder what would have happened if I had continued in that line of work.

In the meantime, however, I was content to work on the farm

for Da and Uncle Francis. As I had grown up on the farm, it didn't seem like work to me, and I enjoyed being outside all the time, cutting cauliflowers, pulling parsnips and tilling land. Of course, Da and I knew it would never be a long-term option, as it was only a small farming concern that made just enough for the family to get by. But for the time being, I worked on the farm, dabbled in art and even exhibited with established artists. I let my hair and beard grow long and dishevelled, so I looked like any rough-and-ready farmer's son.

Early in 1992, I was called to Skerries garda station for an informal chat with the local sergeant after passing the aptitude test. I filled out the necessary forms, and he measured my height. Back then, male gardaí had to be at least 5' 9", and females had to be 5' 5". I was an acceptable 5' 11". (An Garda Síochána abolished these height restrictions in 2001.)

The following month, Da arranged for me to go on a ride-along with a garda friend stationed at Santry garda station. Maybe he saw my reluctance about joining the guards and thought this might encourage me. Kevin was in the Task Force unit, which patrolled the district and responded to calls from the Command and Control dispatch centre. Unlike regular patrol car crews, they used unmarked cars and sometimes wore plain clothes.

I spent the night in the back of the car as Kevin and his partner responded to calls, even buckling up for a few high-speed responses. During the shift, Kevin and his partner arrested a few 'social deviants' and plonked them in the back of the car beside me for transport to the nearest garda station.

That night was my first exposure to the garda-speak and the gallows humour I became accustomed to in the years that followed. 'Scrotes', 'gougers' and 'scumbags' were standard labels then. Even official Ireland referred to 'deviants', 'juvenile delinquents' and old-fashioned 'criminals' rather than 'individuals with criminal convictions'. Not politically correct, but that was the way it was. God knows, those 'social deviants' had plenty of names for the guards, and none were complimentary either.

My night with the Task Force in 'the H District' – Santry, Whitehall and Ballymun – was an exciting insight into manning a patrol car. I didn't realise it then, but it didn't represent the bulk of police work, which comprises more of writing charge sheets, reports, statements and compiling files and court preparation.

I had an interview with the local chief superintendent in Balbriggan station in June 1992, and two weeks later I had a final interview with a panel of senior garda officers in Harcourt Square. They must have been impressed by my neat hair and clean-shaven face (compared to the unkempt, hairy-faced farmer who appeared in my application photos) because soon after, I was informed only one hurdle remained – the garda medical.

For the rest of the year, I worked on the farm, socialising with the lads and knocking out the odd bit of art while waiting my turn to be called for the medical. The day after my twenty-first birthday in February 1993, I was called for my medical at garda headquarters, Phoenix Park.

That morning, I headed to the Depot hospital towards the rear of the garda HQ campus. Headquarters seemed vast, full of imposing old buildings, many dating back to its origins in 1842 as headquarters for the Irish Constabulary. When the newly formed An Garda Síochána took over in early 1923, they used the place as a combined headquarters and training centre known as the Phoenix

Park Depot. It's still referred to as 'the Depot' today.

Around 20 of us were called for medicals that day, and the various examinations would take hours to complete. All applicants, male and female, were told to change into dressing gowns and assemble in a waiting room. The dressing gowns were a tad short, and even though I was wet behind the ears, I had the common sense to leave my boxer shorts on. Those unfortunate enough to sit opposite the lads who didn't keep their shorts on had an unobstructed view of their family jewels.

One by one, we were called. A nurse measured me again for height and weight. We had tests for lung capacity, hearing and eyesight. There was also a test for colour blindness. Failing the colour blindness test did not mean failing the medical, but it meant not being able to drive a patrol car.

I completed each test and waited my turn until I was called into the surgeon's office for my final examination. I knew the garda surgeon's decision regarding my fitness would be final, so I nervously entered the little room, its walls lined with medical books and journals. The surgeon himself was old and stern. Very stern. Especially when he told me to drop my shorts and cough while he cupped my balls in his hand. I always wondered if it was possible to fail this test.

I was informed by the surgeon that I needed to lose some weight, which I duly did over the following weeks, before returning to the Depot hospital for a second medical. As I'd previously passed all of the medical tests, I only had to be re-weighed on this return trip. My efforts had paid off and on 23 June I received official notification that I had been successful in my application to An

Garda Síochána. I was to present myself for induction at the garda training college in Templemore, County Tipperary, at the end of August.

I was nearly overwhelmed by the news. Suddenly, it seemed very real. It had been two years since I had applied and now, here I was, with two months of normality left before my life would change forever. Gulp.

2

TIPPERARY TATOOINE

If there is a bright centre to the universe, you're on the planet that it's farthest from.
Luke Skywalker describing his home planet Tatooine in the movie Star Wars: A New Hope

A long time ago, in a county far, far away ... The little town of Templemore lies in County Tipperary in the south-central portion of Ireland. For me, it might as well have been the far side of the moon or, to borrow from *Star Wars*, in the Outer Rim. On the morning of 23 August 1993, I loaded my overstuffed suitcase into the car and Mam, Da and I hit the road for the long drive to Templemore. My first journey to the Garda Síochána College took place before they built the M50 and most motorways and bypasses. We had to drive to Dublin city before heading out the Naas Road.

I clearly remember sitting in the back of the car, listening to the sound the tyres made on the surface of the Naas Road as my home and county slipped away behind me. Every few hundred yards, the tarmac sections were joined in little ridges, and the tyres driving over them made a rhythmic *du-dum* sound. It was like an ominous heartbeat. It reminded me of the music from *The Terminator*. *Du-dum, du-dum, du-dum. Templemore is out there. It can't be bargained with. It can't be reasoned with, and it absolutely will not stop. Ever. Until you are a guard. Du-dum, du-dum, du-dum.*

The route to Templemore would become permanently ingrained in me over the following two years. From the Naas Road, we drove on through Kildare, Monasterevin, Ballybrittas, Portlaoise, Mountrath, Borris-in-Ossory, Roscrea and then that last stretch into Templemore. We arrived after midday, and as we turned onto Church Avenue in the town, I got my first glimpse of the imposing pillared entrance to the Garda College.

With its central block and clock tower lying beyond, the Garda College was an impressive sight and even bigger than Garda HQ back in Dublin. The British constructed the earliest buildings as an army barracks on a 57-acre site in 1815. A soldier garrisoned in Templemore wrote to his mother in 1847, describing the barracks as 'splendid, with two large squares and buildings three storeys high', while adding that the town was 'a wretched place'.

Student gardaí met each recruit and the families, giving us a quick tour of the college and our accommodation blocks called Oisín and Cúchulainn. My room was on the first floor of Oisín. It was small but bright and clean, with a single bed, a desk and chair, a large wardrobe and a sink that soon became known as 'the en-suite'. There were showers and toilets at each end of the corridor on every floor, all immaculately clean.

We had a whistle-stop tour of other parts of the college – the classrooms, main lecture theatre, the rec hall, coffee shop and canteen. There was also a gym and a 25-metre swimming pool, which was closed for renovations during phase one of our training.

At the rear of the rec hall was a firing range and 'Tac Town' – a mocked-up street complete with a bank for firearms and tactics training. Outside the main walls of the campus was a nine-hole golf course, basketball and tennis courts and full-size playing fields for GAA, soccer and rugby. The college also housed two squash courts and a handball alley. Of course, none of the sports facilities meant anything to me because I hadn't, and still don't have, a single sporting bone in my body.

Then, it was time for the recruits to say goodbye to the families. I still remember watching my folks walking away and disappearing around the accommodation block. Those doubts about my career choice resurfaced and, for the first time, I experienced a pang of homesickness.

That same day, we were allocated our garda registration numbers – unique identity numbers for our entire career and retirement (if we made it that far). My number was 25926H, which was temporarily prefixed with an 'S' as a student garda. This number meant that I was the 25,926th male garda since the founding of An Garda Síochána in 1922. The female members were still being allocated numbers in the 700s under a separate numbering system, a practice which was dropped later.

After my folks left the campus, I was glad to spot the familiar and friendly face of a lad I'd met at my second medical. Aiden, from a garda family in Portlaoise, was to become my best mate throughout training and beyond. He was allocated the preceding number, 25925, so we ended up in the same class and sitting beside one another. Another chap, Liam, who I'd met during the medical, was also in our class.

At the end of the first day, I rang home even though I'd only seen my folks hours earlier. The college had a few scattered payphones, which everyone queued to use – it was still years before mobile phones. To round off the evening, a crowd of us squeezed into the packed Polly's pub, which is conveniently located just outside the college gates, for a few pints – the first of many to come during training.

As a junior phase one student garda, I faced six months of training in Templemore. Phase two would be a six-month attachment to a garda station, followed by phase three, a further three months back in the college. Then, if everything went to plan, we would be sworn in as gardaí.

However, the training would continue: phase four would comprise nine months in a garda station before phase five – which entailed several more weeks back in Templemore for our final exams and passing-out parade. Garda management had implemented this phased training programme only a few years earlier, in 1989.

My early days in Templemore involved lots of form-filling and what would become the most frequent activity throughout training – drill. I was too busy to experience any more of my early doubts. We racked up hours and hours of drill practice in the large parade ground during our time there. The intimidating drill sergeant barked orders in Irish to march, size off, slow march, mark time, stand to attention and be at ease.

I remember one of the recruits throwing in the towel at the end of that first week. He was a quiet lad, and it probably didn't help that the training sergeant had made him the butt of a joke. The college training staff begged him to take the weekend to rethink his decision to quit. However, he insisted he'd made up his mind, and he signed the release papers. That Sunday evening, he arrived back at the college, no doubt under orders from his parents, but he was refused entry. He had signed away his career in the guards before it even started.

We continued with countless drill classes and physical education classes. We also spent hours in the classroom with Irish classes, legal studies and policing studies. In legal studies, we had to learn about the endless acts detailing criminal offences. Policing studies was about garda rules, regulations and procedures as detailed in our new garda code books, each as thick as a telephone directory.

We also had lectures on forensics, psychology, self-defence, report-writing, typing and even German. I found I was quite good at taking fingerprints, which would come in handy a few years later. They showed us how to use now antiquated phones and fax machines and their prehistoric computer system. We practised using walkie-talkies and rehearsed mock courtroom situations and scenes-of-crime investigations. Wednesday afternoons were designated for sporting activities, and since I had no interest in such pursuits, and the various activities weren't supervised, I would usually spend the afternoon in bed.

Throughout phase one, we had to undergo fitness tests of sit-ups, press-ups and a timed run. The run was a mile and three quarters (five times around the front square), which had to be completed in under 11 minutes and 45 seconds. On my first attempt, I scraped through with four seconds to spare but continued to shave more off each time we had to do it. They also took us on runs along the many country roads surrounding Templemore.

It was mid-September before the college bused us to garda headquarters to get our long-awaited uniforms, complete with batons and whistles. We paraded about, thinking we were the bee's knees in our new rig-outs. I even brought mine home that weekend to show my family. Fully fledged gardaí usually wear their district numbers on their shoulders. As we were only student gardaí, we had to wear yellow patches, giving rise to the derogatory nickname 'yellow packers'. In later years, they replaced them with better-looking blue patches showing the college crest.

For the duration of phase one, I took the train home and back to Templemore every weekend. The trains were packed with recruits, and on our return on Sundays we got off and headed to Polly's for our last weekend pints. And that was the way it went as the months crawled by: lectures, drill, physical education and copious pints in Allen's, Murphy's, Maher's, Collier's, the Templemore Arms and, of course, Polly's. We also had a bar in the rec hall, so we were never in danger of dying from thirst. A lot of drink was involved.

One of our 100 or so recruits had a peculiar party trick where he liked to drop his pants and jocks and belt out one of Tom Jones' hits, 'It's Not Unusual' or 'Delilah', I can't remember which. He 'performed' in the corridors of the accommodation block and even on the packed Sunday-evening train. And then we had the infamous 'Tom Jones incident' in Allen's pub one night when he bared all and then stuffed a poor girl's head under his t-shirt. That performance was to have repercussions.

We all signed out at the guardroom at night and had to pretend to be sober when we signed back in. I had none of the stamina that some had for the consumption of gargle. Some guys (and girls) could consume gallons of porter, have a quick casual vomit outside the gates, and sign back in with no problem.

Even after a couple of weeks, fellas and girls were pairing off. Most of these relationships would run their course, but a few resulted in marriage down the line. That September, I started going out with Orlagh, a girl I met in the Black Raven pub in Skerries one weekend. We saw each other every weekend and wrote letters to each other the rest of the time as it was too expensive to make payphone calls. Also, it was difficult to find an available payphone with so many other doe-eyed boyfriends and girlfriends waiting in line.

Once we had our uniforms, we had weekly parades where the college chief superintendent would stride up and down the ranks, inspecting our dress and haircuts. If things weren't up to scratch, we got a tap on the shoulder and were ordered to smarten up before the next inspection. Regulations stipulated that for men the back of our hair had to be a minimum of two fingers' width above our collars. Our locks could not come down further than half the length of our ears. If we had a moustache, the corners could not protrude further than the sides of our mouths. Beards, of course, were a complete no-no, and tattoos had to be completely concealed. I rebelled against all this in later years, but by then, regulations had relaxed anyway.

Room inspections took place after each parade. Floors had to be hoovered, desks cleared, the bed neatly made, and the auld 'en-suites' had to look pristine.

After three months, we became 'senior phase ones', and we were ordered to entertain a new crop of juniors with a concert. I was tasked with videotaping the show from the rec hall balcony, so I was sober (one of few) as the concert began. As a car wreck of a show continued, 'Tom Jones' stepped onstage and motioned to unbutton his trousers. I was about to pass out in horror but, thankfully, others saw the carnage about to unfold and, following a brief onstage scuffle, 'Tom' was bundled off.

Near the end of phase one, the college invited us to list four garda stations where we'd like to spend our six months' placement in phase two of training. In order of preference, I listed Santry, Coolock, Ballymun and Raheny – all stations near my home. They gave me Santry – the same station where my Task Force friend Kevin worked when he took me for that ride-along. I couldn't have been happier.

We held an enormous party celebrating the end of phase one on Thursday, 20 January 1994, and everyone attended apart from 'Tom Jones'. Unsurprisingly, the girl whose head he shoved under his T-shirt in Allen's pub made a formal complaint, and the college sent him packing.

It was only six months, but phase one seemed to go on forever. It was half a year away from home, and I think being away from the sea affected me most. I had grown up within a stone's throw of Loughshinny and Skerries beaches and missed the sea air.

I was glad to see the back of the place for a while. The day after the party, my folks and sister Bernie came down in the car to bring me home. Phase two was to start in Santry garda station in a fortnight, so I'd soon see what being a garda was all about.

3

WELCOME TO HOTEL ALPHA

The man who has everything figured out is probably a
fool.
Jerome Lawrence, Inherit the Wind

My first day in Santry garda station coincided with the morning
after a party for a garda. I'll never forget it because my very
first call was to collect the guard concerned from hospital. After
foolishly trying to drive home from the function, he'd put his car
through a wall. We picked him up in the patrol car from the A&E
department, all patched up and looking sheepish. Thankfully,
he'd hurt nobody else.

While garda members worked hard and diligently, many
partied equally hard, and there was a big drinking culture in the
job. I would be no different in the years to come. Drink-driving
regulations were more relaxed back then, and the legal limits for the

consumption of alcohol were much less stringent. Unfortunately, many of us took advantage of this and got behind the wheel when we shouldn't have.

Santry was part of the north division of the Dublin Metropolitan Area (DMA) with an assigned code name, Hotel Alpha (HA). The HA District remains a built-up suburb on Dublin's north side, home to Morton Stadium, the Omni shopping complex and many industrial parks. Dublin Airport also falls within its boundaries. Sited in the old Chrysler-Talbot car factory on Shanowen Road, the station's adjoining warehouses were used for archiving and storing seized vehicles and recovered stolen goods.

It was 6 a.m. on the morning of my 22nd birthday when I started at Santry station. As part of my phase two training, I would spend three months attached to the station there, followed by three months spread across other district units, including the Task Force, the Juvenile Liaison Office, the Detective Unit, Neighbourhood Police and the garda station at Dublin Airport.

During this time, I had to maintain a diary and submit a project about a relevant topic in my district. (I focused on security in Beaumont Hospital.) Training also included a two-week social placement with a local agency involved in, for example, providing youth services, or assisting the elderly. Phase two training also entailed attending classes one day a week in Harcourt Square. During training, An Garda Síochána would pay me £50 in old Irish punts per week, which was quite a reduction compared to my old salary in Murakami-Wolf.

Fully trained gardaí were assigned to trainees to expose us to as much regular policing work as possible. My tutor, Dave, was the official motorcycle driver on the unit, which limited the time I could spend with him. That didn't matter, as the rest of the crew took me under their wing. Joe, the official patrol car driver, Andy, Katrina and Joan were in my Santry unit. I had my sergeant, Mick, and a second sergeant, Ronan.

After collecting the garda from the hospital, I also had the eye-opening experience of travelling with the car crew to Mountjoy Jail to deliver a prisoner on my first day. I can still hear the clang of security gates as we entered the jail and handed over custody to the prison guards. Not a nice place, but then, it's not meant to be. I would spend more time in the bowels of Mountjoy some years later when I attended the scene of a fatal assault.

The regular roster involved eight-hour tours of duty back then. The dreaded changeover took place at certain intervals during a four-week roster. On a changeover, we finished a late tour at 10 p.m. and had to be back in at 6 a.m. the following morning. It was a killer, especially if you got stuck with a prisoner late into the shift. These times and rosters would change as new EU regulations stipulated a minimum number of hours of rest between shifts.

My first week on night shifts in Santry was a difficult one because I've never been one to sleep late. I'd get home from work around 7 a.m. and go to bed, but I'd find myself wide awake by midday before going back to work at 10 p.m. The adrenaline would keep me going on busy nights, but I struggled to keep my eyes open when things were quieter.

During those three months, I experienced much of the bread-and-butter calls and daily activities of gardaí. Santry was a quieter district than most others in the DMA, and some days I would sit in the back of the patrol car wondering if the Command and Control dispatch centre would ever have a call for Hotel Alpha One, the code for the Santry car.

Dave did his best to expose me to other aspects of the work and took me to body identifications (BIDs) at Beaumont Hospital when formal identifications of a deceased have to be made by a family member in the presence of a garda – always very sad.

As part of my training, I got to sit in those little booths with garda immigration members in Dublin Airport as they checked arriving passengers' passports. Dave even brought me to an arriving plane, where I spoke to the cockpit crew. Of course, this was before 9/11 and the ring of steel that surrounds pilots nowadays. I had to spend time in the station's public office, witnessing dozens of passport applications, answering phones and filling out traffic accident report forms.

Dave brought me to the District Courts, which at the time were located beside the Bridewell garda station on Chancery Street. To me, the courts were particularly daunting. It was all hustle and bustle, with gardaí, judiciary, solicitors, accused persons and witnesses milling everywhere. I couldn't keep track of everything going on, but even in the confusion, it became clear that the cogs moved quite slowly during court proceedings.

Often when the court clerk called a case, the prosecution or defence had some problem, such as lacking a witness or the defendant being sick. The delaying tactics went on and on. I feared I'd never get the hang of this craic when the time came for me to present my own cases. Over the years, I've given evidence in every tier of the Irish courts: Coroner's Court, Civil, Central Criminal, Special and High Court, but the District Court was always the most hectic and unpredictable. For those first few years on the job, court terrified me.

There were also surreal types of calls, like the time the Kellogg's warehouse in one of Santry's industrial parks received a bomb threat. I found myself wandering inside the immense building, gingerly peering into boxes and behind pallets. It occurred to me that this was crazy. Shouldn't there have been a call to the army's explosive ordnance disposal (EOD) team? What was I supposed to do if I found a suspicious device? Wave my baton at it? Joe shrugged it off, saying false bomb threats were a regular occurrence, so there was no point in calling out the specialists.

For my two-week 'social' placement, I had hoped to link in with a youth club or care home in my district. However, a classmate in Coolock garda station and I drew the short straw because we were sent to Coolure House near Castlepollard in rural Westmeath.

Back then, Coolure House was a cold and damp country house operating as an adventure getaway for kids. Young offenders on community service were often used to staff the place. Living in 'the boonies' and entertaining kids day and night was not my idea of fun. For me, the highlight of those two weeks was shovelling manure in the stables. I don't know what this placement achieved, apart from a capacity for dealing with shit, which I suppose has come in handy over the years.

We didn't even manage a few pints in Castlepollard, which was probably just as well. A garda recruit who was previously on placement in Coolure was walking back from the pub one night when he accepted a lift from the young offenders he worked with. Only when the guards stopped them did he discover they had stolen the car. Even though the poor recruit was oblivious to the theft, he was done for being a passenger in a stolen vehicle. I counted down the seconds until my two-week placement was up.

Back in Santry, I went out in the car one night with Joe and Joan, patrolling one of the many housing estates in the district. Everything seemed quiet as we slowly cruised around. Then, we spotted three lads removing what appeared to be tools and other builder's equipment from the side door of a parked van. As soon as they copped us, the lads made a break for it, running off in different directions. Immediately, Joan was out of the car and after one of them, so I took her cue and set off after another one.

I vividly remember the racket I made running in my garda shoes. During phase one, many of us had put steel caps on the heels of our shoes to stop them from wearing down from all the drill we had to do. Now, as I pegged it after the absconding youth, the click-clack, click-clack of my shoes resounded through the housing estate. There was no fear of being able to sneak up on anyone. The young lad turned a corner just ahead of me, and I followed. Then I abruptly stopped because he was nowhere to be seen.

It was only by listening carefully that I could make out someone breathing, or rather, panting, in the darkness. I couldn't see anything, but the heavy breathing came from the front garden of the corner house beside me. I called out 'gardaí!' along with a few colourful oaths. To my surprise, the young lad emerged from his hiding place in the bushes.

As a student garda, I had no power of arrest, but luckily, he didn't know that. I kept a firm grip on him until Joe and Joan arrived after apprehending one of the other would-be thieves. Joan arrested my captive, and with both in the back of the patrol car, we headed back to the station to process them. I felt pretty chuffed. On my first week of nights, I managed to catch my first 'gouger'.

I had started to pick up the lingo within the job and learnt terms like 'mules', 'skippers', 'cigs' and 'hawks'. A 'mule' is a garda, usually a lower rank, and it's how members of the force refer to themselves and others in the 'polis'.

A 'skipper' is a sergeant, and a 'cig' is an inspector, taken from the Irish *cigire*. The typical conversation between two members could be:

'How are tings?' (Very important to drop the 'h'.)

'Do you know John?'

'Yeah. Is he a mule?'

'Yep. He's in the polis. He's a skipper in Santry.'

'Right, I heard his cig is a bit of a bollix, but he has a few good hawks.'

A 'hawk' is any sort of service that a mule can get cheaply or even for free. A typical 'hawk' was the age-old tradition of picking up the next day's newspaper for free directly from the printers in the city centre. Many a night, I picked up a free *Irish Independent* from the printing press on Abbey Street. A standard hawk was getting cheap grub from a chippy or café within the district. Unfortunately, we always ran the risk of any employee who didn't like the gardaí adding extra 'ingredients' to our snack boxes.

Of course, you had to look after a hawk if you didn't want it to dry up. You were expected to be on hand and patrol the hawk's area regularly if needed. You also had to watch out for the odd mule who would tear the arse out of a good hawk and ruin it for everyone. Or watch out for mules from neighbouring districts encroaching on the same patch.

The months flew by, and soon I was heading back to Templemore for phase three of training. It had been a largely enjoyable time in Santry, but I already had a niggling feeling deep down that maybe this wasn't the job for me.

Being a guard meant navigating the confusing court system and dealing with the public. The prospect of court terrified me, and I also found dealing with the public daunting. I was a quiet sort of fella and more than a bit socially awkward.

I tried to put it out of my mind, hoping I'd grow into the job, but I was keenly aware that my days as a student were ending. Time was running out if I wanted to change career direction. In three months, I was to be sworn in as a fully fledged garda.

4

ASSIMILATION AND PROCRASTINATION

I was a little excited but mostly blorft. Blorft is an
adjective I just made up that means 'completely overwhelmed but proceeding as if everything is fine and
reacting to the stress with the torpor of a possum'.
Tina Fey, Bossypants

After three more months of drill and lectures in Templemore,
attestation day had arrived. On 27 October 1994, we all filed into
the new gym building as student gardaí in full uniform to declare
the oath.

Holding a bible in my right hand, I stood to attention and
recited the lengthy garda oath in Irish. I had learnt the oath by
rote, pretty much phonetically, so I didn't have a clue what I was
saying. It might as well have been in the Klingon dialect. We then

ceremoniously removed the yellow patches from our shoulders, and there was much applause, but no throwing our caps in the air or anything like that. Then, we left the gym as sworn members of the force. And that was it. I was assimilated into An Garda Síochána, just like the Borg in *Star Trek*. Resistance was futile.

I remember taking a quiet moment afterwards to ponder what had just happened. Here I was, fresh off the production line, officially a guard, albeit still on probation for another 18 months. Only a few years previously, I had left school and sworn I'd never wear a uniform again. I was an artist. I had a creative drive. Was being a garda really being true to my nature?

A fortnight earlier, there had been much excitement as we crowded into the lecture theatre to learn where we were going for our nine months of placement in phase four. We all hoped not to be sent to the border or some other godforsaken backwater. It was less stressful for those of us considered 'Dubs' as we usually got a city station. A Limerick chap beside me whispered he had pulled a few strings and would get somewhere close to home. His name was called, followed by his destination, Blacklion, and he turned to me to ask where it was. I told him I didn't know. I didn't have the heart to tell him it was a border station in Cavan. So much for pulling a few strings.

When it came to my turn, I fully expected to be sent back to Santry or maybe Coolock or Ballymun. I was chuffed when they said I was going to Malahide. The lovely seaside village was only about 15 minutes' drive from home. Of course, some lads reckoned I was given a 'cushy' station because I had 'rope' or knew someone, but this wasn't the case. I wasn't even aware that Malahide was in the DMA then, so it was completely off my radar.

Another colleague, Helen, got Malahide as well, but it wasn't such a pleasant surprise for her as she was from Ballinasloe. My mate Aiden got Naas, which he was delighted with, but another good pal, Dec, from Kildare, got Castleblayney, another border station. Anyway, regardless of which stations we got, we all went for pints to celebrate or drown our sorrows.

I drove home from Templemore the next day, stopping on the way at Malahide station to submit my transfer documentation. The following day, at 10 a.m., I started my first day's duty. Malahide station was sited in a double-storey Georgian building, a stone's throw from the harbour and marina. Our sergeant, Seamus, was a real gentleman. The others on the unit were Jerry, Paul, Kevin and John, all fairly seasoned mules. I also met a young guard from another unit in the station called Glenn, who I would become close friends with down the line. Even though we were now sworn gardaí, all the former recruits met up at classes once a week in Harcourt Square. We also had to keep a diary and prepare a dissertation to be submitted as part of our final exams in phase five.

The town of Malahide wasn't as built-up then as it is now, so it was quiet compared to the two other stations in the 'R' district, Coolock and Swords. It had no problem areas, and most of the calls and complaints we dealt with concerned public order offences or alarm calls. It was an entire month before I made my first arrest. While out on patrol, we came across a blind drunk fella lying in the middle of the road, and we prosecuted him for public intoxication.

Judge Delap, who was very pro-garda, heard our cases at Swords District Court, which lessened the trepidation I experienced going to court. Things were so quiet in Malahide that I only had a handful of court proceedings during phase four anyway.

Although the district was relatively free of serious crime, I still had plenty of duties to keep me occupied. As well as station orderly and observer in the patrol car, I did regular beats around the village and nearby Portmarnock, calling into most shops and businesses to get acquainted with the locals. On Saturdays, we also took turns doing a four-hour overtime beat from 10 p.m. to 2 a.m. to be visible in the town centre when the pubs closed and the streets filled. It was a handy few extra quid.

Another regular duty was to attend the nearby quarry in Feltrim when the explosives were being delivered. The van carrying the munitions had an armed garda escort. Once delivered, the escort left, while the local member had to stay until the explosives were placed and detonated. Sometimes, I assisted the explosives foreman and placed them into the deep bore holes in the rock face of the quarry. It was interesting stuff.

And yet, those doubts remained. I didn't want to deal with people if I didn't have to, so even if it was boring, I was happier doing a beat away from the town centre. I had plenty of time to think about my plight during the long night shift as the station orderly or when doing the special beat near a local government minister's house.

Although outwardly I may have come across as carefree and as capable as any young man in the job, in truth those early years were frequently miserable. The reality was that I suffered from a crippling lack of self-confidence. I dreaded answering the radio when calls came in. I feared any sort of conflict, not because I was scared of being hurt or injured, but because I didn't know how to interact with people in the professional yet emotionally detached manner expected of a garda.

I felt like a fake. Sometimes I'd prefer to reason with a troublesome kid than detain him, but then, in the same shift, I could bawl out a few kids who only needed a quiet word. I felt my instincts and demeanour were wrong for a garda and feared being a liability to my colleagues.

A few things happened that enlivened the long spells of boredom but also led me to question my career choice again – like when that feckin' huge German shepherd launched itself at me and took a big bite of my garda jumper.

Another time, Kevin and I went to a call in Portmarnock where some fella had cut loose in a house. In his frenzy, he could not be reasoned with, and we had to call for assistance, eventually taking four of us to subdue him. We brought him by ambulance to St Ita's mental hospital in nearby Portrane, as I sat astride his struggling form. When we finally wrestled him into a padded cell in the hospital, the doctors had to dose him with enough sedatives to knock out an elephant.

I struggled on, working on my dissertation on video piracy and racketeering and completing a short sports project. Feckin' sports. I would have much preferred doing a project on the *Star Trek* convention held in the Grand Hotel that summer. I tried to keep my diary up to date, but it was difficult to fill it with anything worthwhile as my beats and tours of duty were, in the main, uneventful.

Everyone in the unit was sound, though, and we also got a new inspector, who sensed that I was green around the gills and did his best to boost my confidence. He also came to my rescue when I needed it most.

I was the station orderly when the staff of a fast-food place in Portmarnock called one night to say they had a drunken customer who had driven to the outlet. They were doing their best to delay his food so gardaí could stop him from getting back in the car. They gave me the car registration number.

The patrol car crew had just returned to the station, and when I told them about the call, Paul made a decision: 'Right, Sweets, let's get you a Section 49.' Nearly all of us had nicknames: Horse, Kaner, Slev, Jingles, Shrek, Buck, Bento, Baldy – the list was endless. We all took pride in our nicknames, and they stuck with us throughout our careers and beyond.

Of course, the last thing I wanted to do was go out and arrest a drunk driver, but Paul drove us out on the coast road towards Portmarnock. Like any alleged offence, certain criteria must be met before invoking the power of arrest. With drink-driving offences, the person has to be observed in the act of controlling a vehicle. When we arrived, we spotted the car in question and pulled our car around the side of the kebab shop so the purported offender would not see us. We noticed what appeared to be fresh damage to the side of the car, possibly from scraping off a wall or maybe another vehicle.

After a few minutes, we saw a man leave the fast-food outlet and get into the car. He pulled out of the car park and headed down Strand Road. Paul and I followed, and a few hundred yards down the road, we put on the blue lights, signalling him to pull over.

The driver rolled down the window so I could speak with him, and there was an unmistakable whiff of alcohol on his breath. He admitted he had been drinking. Satisfied that he had consumed an intoxicant likely to affect his ability to drive, I arrested him under Section 49 of the Road Traffic Act. Kerbside breathalysers weren't yet prevalent, so the man had to be brought back to the station, where a doctor would be called and the man would be asked to provide a specimen of his blood or urine for analysis.

Paul drove this gent back to Malahide in the patrol car, and I followed in the car of the arrested man. He was polite and cooperative during his detention, and once he had provided a blood sample, we dropped him home. I was relieved. Everything had gone smoothly despite my nervousness.

However, I wasn't prepared for what happened next. I stayed with the patrol car for the rest of the shift, and Paul and I ended up assisting the Coolock car at a checkpoint. While we were there, a garda member approached me about my 'Section 49er'. News travelled fast, and it turned out that the man I arrested had connections within the force.

The garda suggested I should do this man a favour. However, I was still a probationer and wanted to do things by the book. Literally. I told the guard I'd already written up the incident in the Section 49 book back at the station. Still, he continued to pressurise me. This was at a time before they launched the garda Pulse system, and most records were still handwritten in occurrence books.

Thankfully, the inspector heard about the arrest and must have anticipated the trouble ahead. He called to the station shortly after my prisoner was released and signed my entry in the Section 49 book. Once he did this, nothing could be done, and I wasn't pestered any more. As predicted, the sample showed a high amount of alcohol in the bloodstream, so I proceeded with the case.

Not long after, the man was disqualified from driving for several months in Swords Court. He was always cooperative and fully admitted his wrongdoing. And thankfully, I was never put in such a tricky situation again. While I can understand where the other members were coming from, it was unfair to put a brand-new probationer under pressure for correctly following procedures.

The remainder of phase four passed relatively uneventfully. I still couldn't shake the cloud of uncertainty but hoped that by the time I finished phase five and got back to Malahide, I could work on my self-confidence. Maybe I would even grow to like the job. My unit was very supportive of me, and I felt lucky to be stationed in such a nice district. If I could overcome what I perceived to be my many shortcomings as a guard, perhaps I could really make a go of this policing lark.

Fate, it seems, had other plans for me.

5

IN (AND OUT OF) CONTROL

If you would be a real seeker after truth, it is necessary
that at least once in your life you doubt, as far as
possible, all things.
Descartes

It was during the next phase in Templemore that things became
darker for me. After particularly bad days, I began nicking myself
with a blade in the quiet of my room. Just a light cut and a trickle
of blood was a way to release some of the negative feelings that I
was carrying around, calming my anxiety. Cutting myself sort of
'depressurised' me.

I was always careful to make any cuts on parts of my body where
they wouldn't be seen. It wasn't that I felt a sense of shame about
doing it, it was more like 'my little secret'. I knew if anyone found
out, I would be turfed out immediately. These spells would always
pass, and there was no way I would tell anyone what I was doing.

Phase five training started on 10 July 1995 and comprised several more weeks in Templemore for our final exams and passing-out parade. They were long weeks filled with seemingly endless drill rehearsals for our big day and I found myself in these inexplicable foul moods. On days like that, I'd finish the day's classes and just want to go to bed. Not because I was tired; I just didn't want to do *anything*. On other days, I felt such anxiety that I'd self-harm. I didn't know it, but I was suffering from depression. It would be several more years before I recognised it for what it was.

One night, after pints down the town, I went to bed in a funk. The other lads didn't understand my humour either and were ribbing me and banging on my door. My ground-floor window was open as it was a warm night, and Aiden climbed in the window for a laugh. He didn't laugh as much when I furiously chased him from my room with my baton.

Much of the problem was the realisation that my training was nearly finished, and I would soon return to my station and the next 30 years of service as a member of An Garda Síochána. It was a prospect that I was not looking forward to.

As well as the usual legal and policing classes, we also had a week of tactics training, which was a welcome change from the norm during those interminable weeks in Templemore. We got to wear plain clothes and were each given a .38 revolver and holster. Of course, the guns weren't loaded, but the intention was to get us familiar with carrying a firearm.

We were expected to be mature and responsible at all times, but needless to say, as soon as we returned to the accommodation block, the place was filled with imaginary shootouts.

We also got to spend time on the firing range, where I discovered I was a good shot with live rounds too. We trained in tactical manoeuvres around Tac Town, clearing rooms, and went up the nearby Devil's Bit mountain to search for imaginary Provos.

The day before the final legal exam, we were told to assemble in the lecture theatre. It was common practice then for several probationers to be transferred to the Command and Control centre in Harcourt Square after training. It was a stupid idea, as being sent there essentially put a stop to any on-the-job learning that a fresh recruit needed.

We filed into the room, and they read out the names of the unlucky recruits. My class was the senior group, so the list started with us. As each name was read out, it was accompanied by gasps and muttered curses.

The brass just skipped down to every third or fourth name on the list: 'Buggy O'Reilly, Ryan ...' and then the inevitable, 'Sweetman'. All the blood in my body seemed to pool in my feet, and I remember hearing Helen exclaim, 'Oh no!' from behind. I was lightheaded, and it felt like the wind had been knocked out of me. Aiden and Dec didn't know what to say to me. My nice handy station, 15 minutes from home, had just disappeared like a fart in the wind. I would be sitting behind a desk on the far side of the city for years.

That evening, I phoned home in a rage, telling my folks what had happened. I rang Malahide. I rang Orlagh. I cursed everything. Fuck this shit. And they sprang this news on us on the fucking day before the most important exam! Well, I thought, what was the point in doing any more study? I'd been hobbled before I could even find my feet. I went down the town for my dinner in Murphy's pub and stayed out for pints – no more study for me.

Regardless, I got good passing grades in the exam. The final two weeks of drill practice ticked by, and on a blistering hot day on 17 August, we had our passing-out ceremony. Mam, Da, James, Mary, Orlagh and my uncle Billy travelled down for it. The Garda Band played while, sweltering in full wool uniform, we marched back and forth in formation for our families and the garda commissioner, who then presented us with our diplomas.

So that was it, the end of training. I put a brave face on, but it really had ended with more of a whimper than a bang for me. That weekend, I spent my last day's duty in Malahide, sulking around the station. The inspector who looked out for me during phase four took me out for one last beat and tried to raise my spirits. He said he would do his best to get me back to the district. I knew, however, that I was facing at least a couple of years of answering phones and dispatching cars.

A few days later, on 22 August, I drove to Harcourt Square to meet my new superintendent and hand over my official transfer form, my D20. In return, I got my new shoulder number, B218. The very next day, as a form of protest, I went to a grubby little tattoo parlour on Capel Street and got my first tattoo. It was the first of many I would get over the years, my way of rebelling against the rigid system that I had somehow chosen to be part of.

Command and Control was on an upper floor of the building complex that housed Dublin Metropolitan Area headquarters. It encompassed one large room with several call-taking desks where garda members answered 999 calls from the public and inputted the details into computers. The incidents then popped up on the dispatchers' screens. We rotated as call takers and dispatchers on four-week rosters. Dublin city and suburbs were split into northern, north-central, south-central, south and east regions – each with their own dispatch desks. The traffic units and the armed response unit had their own dedicated dispatch desks too.

Control turned out to be both a blessing and a curse. As I said, it wasn't the place to learn about policing. The commute was also a bitch, and I was always trying to find parking, particularly after the Criminal Assets Bureau was set up in an adjoining building. However, all I did was answer phones and dispatch cars, and I had no investigation files or summonses. Even making statements was rare and only usually requested in serious cases. One such instance was the brutal torture and murder of Mark Dwyer in 1996.

I was on an early shift on the northern dispatch desk when a call came in to say two men had been found tied up on waste ground in Finglas. One of them, Mark Dwyer, had been shot dead. 'Cotton Eye' Joe Delaney, a big-time drug dealer, was arrested for the murder. Delaney had blamed Dwyer for the loss of a large stash of ecstasy tablets, so he had Dwyer tortured and beaten with iron bars before having him shot and dumped near Scribblestown Lane.

I had to make a statement and give evidence in the subsequent murder trial, detailing the time that I dispatched the local patrol car to the scene. Although my involvement in the case was minimal, it was still daunting getting up in the witness box in a packed Central Criminal Court with the accused staring at me. Joe Delaney was sentenced to life for murder, the first time the state won a murder conviction against a gangland leader.

I also remember another occasion, late one night, when I took a 999 call from a young woman in an extremely distressed state. She said that she'd been raped. I kept her on the line, trying to calm her down while assuring her that the patrol car was on the way. I spoke to her as a person, not a garda, as I still didn't consider myself one. She was terrified, ringing from a payphone on some dark street near to where the alleged incident had occurred. Thankfully, the gardaí didn't take too long getting to her, and she even thanked me before hanging up.

We had long periods of relative quiet, during which I ploughed through dozens of books. Then I had bursts of frantic activity, like when there was a vehicle pursuit in progress and the dispatcher had to keep mobile units updated on the location of the vehicle being chased. Also, as the desks had to be manned at all times, we often had to take over a second desk when someone went on their meal break. It meant juggling twice as many calls and cars and keeping up with new incidents popping up on your screen. New Year's Eve and Halloween were the busiest nights, when you rarely got a quiet moment for the entire shift.

We worked in a foul physical atmosphere in the main control room. All the wiring from the banks of ageing computers and consoles was housed under a raised floor in the room. This meant that there was less space for air to circulate. The old foam-filled chairs were manned day and night, with more than a few potent mule farts absorbed in their innards. When starting a tour of duty, you eased yourself gently onto the chair; otherwise, all the gases left behind would envelop you.

Add in the fact that there was no air-conditioning, and at least a dozen staff members in the room at all times, and it was no surprise that the place was a breeding ground for colds and flu. If one member coughed and sneezed, it spread like wildfire. I became particularly susceptible to sore throats, and hardly a month would go by without me catching some sort of infection. Of course, it didn't help that I was smoking more than ever before. My frequent throat problems led me to see a specialist, and once I described my working environment, he suggested I seek a transfer. This was easier said than done. One did not simply ask to be transferred to a nice seaside station with oodles of fresh air. There was a strict protocol to be followed.

At that time, Control was staffed by garda members who fell into a few categories. There were the unfortunate probationers like me, and then there were members who had committed some infraction and were transferred to Control as punishment. Finally, there were members who hoped to transfer to stations closer to home. They applied for a transfer to Control, and after a few years they were usually rewarded with a station that suited them. One such member was Joan, who had been in my Santry unit. She was from Cork and wished to transfer back down to that neck of the woods, so she had applied for Control and was happy to spend a few years there before getting a station closer to home.

I had less than two years served in Control, but the throat specialist forwarded a medical report to the garda surgeon outlining my history of throat infections. He suggested I would benefit from being transferred to a different environment. Any such report couldn't just be ignored by management, so a few months later, I got my wish. I heard I was getting transferred back to the DMA North Division but not to Malahide. Instead, I was sent to Howth, part of the 'J' District, along with Clontarf and Raheny. I was pleased enough. I was heading back to a seaside post on the city's north side. My superintendent in Control wasn't pleased but couldn't overrule the surgeon's recommendations.

I arrived in the 'J' on Valentine's Day, 1997, for the usual meet and greet with the super. I started days later, spending most of that first shift with the patrol car crew.

I had promised myself I'd quit smoking once I got out of Control, but by the end of that tour of duty, it began to sink in that I didn't have a clue about day-to-day policing and my stress levels were rising. I was as green as they come and realised I may have made a huge mistake. I had left an environment that wasn't good for my health, but it had insulated me from the real, tough work of a garda.

When the car crew pulled in for petrol at a service station in Howth, I went in and bought a pack of cigarettes. Cleaning up my act would have to wait.

6

OUT OF THE BLUE

We all change. When you think about it, we're all
different people all through our lives. And that's good,
you've got to keep moving, as long as you remember all
the people that you used to be.
The Eleventh Doctor, Doctor Who

Da used to say, 'John, you'll always land on your feet.' While this
held true when I was younger, by the time I was 25 and four years
into my fledgling career, I was floundering. Just as I was getting
close to throwing in the towel, fate stepped in, in the guise of a
broken pint glass in the face.

Some say that one man's misfortune is another man's gain.
I've pondered that over the years, on the road to a crime scene
or during long courtroom days waiting to give evidence. If that
pint glass hadn't been wielded that night, I'd never have had a

25-year career as a fingerprint and handwriting expert. The stepping stones that led me to the Garda Technical Bureau were laid on the night of a brutal assault that took place three months after arriving in Howth.

The three months before that event had reinforced how completely out of my depth I felt in policing. I had no problem dealing with people as John Sweetman the person, but I couldn't convincingly switch to 'garda' mode when needed. Years later, as a garda fingerprint expert, I took prints from bodies on a regular basis. Some people would recoil upon hearing that aspect of my job, but I always quipped I never minded dealing with the public once they were dead.

Of course, it wasn't all doom and gloom stationed in Howth. I was blessed with a good unit of colleagues, and we did find the time to have a few laughs, usually at the expense of one or other of us.

Your typical polisman, or mule (*Mulicus Slobicus Maximus*), is a peculiar type of individual. When gathered in groups or packs, they tend to regress into adolescent mischievousness. Perhaps it's summed up best by a remark I once heard: 'If a mule can't eat it, drink it or ride it, then he'll break it.' Whether chasing down a good *hawk* or downing pints in quantities to make a billy goat puke, the mule's tenacity is unrivalled, as is his capacity for getting up to no good.

It was customary on night patrol to disperse groups of youths who were being a bit too boisterous. If they were underage, we'd confiscate any alcohol on them for consumption back at the station before wrapping things up on a Sunday night. Another bit of contraband we came across was bangers – not just puny little things, but really good ones that packed a hefty wallop, almost akin to miniature sticks of dynamite.

One night, I retreated to a nice, quiet toilet for a relaxing sabbatical during my break. Howth garda station is located at the top of Church Road in the village, in a location known as Dunbo Hill. The old three-storey building always reminded me of the house behind Bates Motel in *Psycho*. The quietest loo was the one located upstairs behind the detective's office. So, off I went, film magazine in hand, for a few moments of quiet time.

Not long after I ensconced myself in the cubicle, I heard the outer door open, and someone came in. It was either Dan or Paul, the two District Detective Unit (DDU) members who worked alongside our unit. I thought nothing of it and continued to attend to business. A few seconds later, there was an almighty BANG! The impact literally frightened the shite out of me.

My first thought was that one of the detectives had discharged his firearm by accident or, God forbid, had turned the gun on himself. Incidents like that had happened on occasion over the years. Heart thumping, I hastily finished what I was doing, yanked up my trousers – nearly doing myself an injury with the baton stowed down the side of my uniform pants – and opened the door, fully expecting to be faced with some poor mule bleeding out from a grievous injury. Instead, I found the loo empty, save for the remnants of one of those feckin' bangers smoking away in the sink.

I returned to the public office to find three or four supposed mates doubled over with laughter. 'Yis fuckin' bastards!' I roared, but their laughter was contagious, and before long I was in stitches with them. It could have turned out a lot worse. They'd intended to lob the banger over the cubicle door, but it had bounced back and landed in the sink. Christ knows what sort of damage would have been caused if they had hit their target.

Despite the camaraderie, the doubts and insecurity continued. There's an old saying, *You can't cod a codder*, but that is exactly what I felt I was doing. I was codding myself. From the first day in Templemore, I knew deep down that I was in over my head.

This was plainly obvious when I attended a domestic incident at a house in the Howth sub-district where a man was being physically abusive towards the woman he was living with. When my colleague and I arrived at the house, the woman's mother was also there, and she was extremely upset. However, her daughter was over 18 and did not wish to make a formal complaint against her partner, so I had to tell her mother that there was nothing we could do. I remember standing outside in the front garden with the mother, crying her eyes out, and I felt furious and frustrated at my uselessness. All I could do was hug her.

I found it difficult to deal coolly and objectively with the many situations that a frontline garda encounters every day. I regularly felt lost, confused and trapped in a job governed by rules, regulations and procedures.

It felt like there was a big sign on my back, proclaiming me as a fraud. I couldn't figure out how my colleagues didn't notice my lack of ability. Surely, they could sense it? I feared putting a member of the public or my colleagues in danger. I didn't know how much longer I could go on pretending.

The event that was to change the course of my life happened on a night I was on duty as the station orderly, when the car crew was called to a village pub. One of the responding gardaí, Cyril, discovered some thug had thrust a broken pint glass in the publican's face. The man had been 'glassed' and needed medical attention, but the culprit had already fled the scene.

Cyril was a seasoned member of the force, excellent at his job. He took possession of the broken glass, being careful to glove up to protect any physical evidence present. He placed it in one of our brown evidence bags.

The following evening, I was the observer in the patrol car with Cyril. I enjoyed being around my senior colleague as he was easy to talk to and was one of the few people I'd confided in and shared my doubts about the job. We drove to garda headquarters in Phoenix Park to submit the pint glass for fingerprint examination in the Garda Technical Bureau.

The correct procedure was to log the exhibit in the Forensic Liaison Office during the day. However, that evening, we bumped into two detectives from the Fingerprints Section. While Cyril outlined the incident with the pint glass, I glanced around, distracted by the impressive layout of the section, particularly the Automated Fingerprint Identification System (AFIS) suite. The suite contained multiple workstations where the staff scanned in fingermarks from crime scenes and searched for matches on the National Fingerprint Database.

The suite was also modern, spacious and air-conditioned, a far cry from the old Command and Control centre where I had worked for two years. Garda HQ had only installed the AFIS system the previous year, so it was state-of-the-art equipment. The visit to the Bureau was a watershed moment for me. I had no idea that the Fingerprints Section was so cutting edge. Fingerprints was the biggest section of the Garda Technical Bureau, which also contained the Photography, Ballistics, Documents and Handwriting, and Mapping sections. The gardaí attached to these sections were called on to attend serious crime scenes all over the country, including murders, suspicious deaths, fires and drug seizures.

The detectives took our exhibit for examination, and as we left the section, my head was racing. The place had been a revelation. On the return drive to the Howth sub-district, I chattered non-stop to Cyril about the Fingerprints Section. I was excited because the work seemed to be everything that I wanted. It involved detailed comparative work and crime scene investigation and came with detective and plain clothes allowances. I'd found a place I could fit in.

Cyril agreed the section could be a good fit for me and suggested I contact one of the two guys we had just dealt with. So I contacted the detective sergeant, a man called Joe, to see if any vacancies were coming up. From that moment on, I was determined to join the Technical Bureau.

The months slipped by and I was no closer to settling in to day-to-day garda life. However, Joe had assured me the Fingerprints Section would take on more staff before the end of the year. That kept me going. I phoned him now and then and did my best to continue my regular duties.

Finally, the Fingerprints Section advertised vacancies towards the end of the summer. I wasted no time submitting my application, and a few weeks later I was called into Garda HQ for an interview with the superintendent of the Bureau and the inspector from the Fingerprints Section. A former Control colleague called Allen was also called for an interview. It helped that our inspector from Control, an ex-Bureau member, put in a good word for both of us.

The interview board was left with no doubt that I wanted to work in the section, and I left the room confident that things had gone well. All I could do now was wait. But that interview was the last roll of the dice for me. I knew if I wasn't successful, I would quit An Garda Síochána.

The weeks ticked on as my hopes dwindled and sense of discontent grew. Then, while in the Howth patrol car on 17 October, I received a radio message telling me to call to the district office in Raheny garda station. I had butterflies in my stomach on the journey over. Could this be the call I was waiting for? The sergeant in Raheny gave me the news I dreamt of – I was successful in my application. I had been thrown a lifeline and grabbed it tightly with both hands.

In the early morning of 29 October, I completed my final shift in Howth garda station and spent my last hours in the patrol car until 2 a.m. I said my goodbyes, thanked my colleagues and cleared out my locker.

I saw the reflection of my garda uniform in my bedroom mirror that night before I tore it off. For the second time in my life, I vowed never to wear a uniform again. Thankfully, I managed to keep the promise this time.

I'd barely spent eighteen months as a frontline garda and couldn't wait to escape. After a few hours' sleep, I headed into Garda HQ with my D20, and a new chapter in my career began.

7

REBIRTH

Values are like fingerprints. Nobody's are the same, but
you leave 'em all over everything that you do.
Elvis Presley

Fingerprints are unique. They are formed before birth and persist
throughout life, unchanged, until the skin decomposes after death.
Only a deep injury, such as a cut or a burn, can permanently alter
the structure of a fingerprint.

If you examine the skin surface of the palms of your hands,
from the base of your wrists extending to the tips of your fingers
and thumbs, you will see that it differs from the rest of your
normally smooth body skin. It consists of a rougher type of
skin, completely devoid of hair, which is made up of a system of
ridges, and furrows between the ridges. These ridges and furrows
assist our sense of touch and our ability to grip. These are known
as *friction ridges*.

The distinct patterns that these form on the palms, fingers and thumbs are collectively called *fingerprints*. The friction ridges run roughly parallel to each other but can change direction, stop or start abruptly, and divide into two. Any such deviation in the flow of the friction ridges is referred to as a *ridge characteristic*.

Although friction ridges and their characteristics are common to all hands, it has been established through research, investigation and by fingerprint experts worldwide that the ridge characteristics only appear in the same type, position and relationship to each other when they come from the same finger or palm. This *coincident sequence* has *never* been found in impressions taken from different fingers, thumbs or palms. Put simply, fingerprints are unique to each individual. It is this fact that forms the basis of fingerprint identification. Fingerprints are like a personal ID card written in the language of ridges on your skin.

These ridges and their characteristics can be recorded by applying suitable ink to the fingers and palms and lightly pressing them onto paper. However, they can also be recorded in another way. Along the tops of the ridges are pores, which emit sweat. If a receptive surface is touched, a mark in sweat from the ridges may be left behind as a latent or invisible mark. Applying a suitable developer, such as a fingerprint powder, may reveal this mark. If revealed, the mark can then be lifted or photographed.

In general, fingermarks at crime scenes have been left by sweat deposits. The sweat consists mainly of water, with some amino acids and some solids. Occasionally, the fingermarks may be made in dust, blood or other mediums. Sometimes, an impression of the friction ridges can be left behind on materials such as putty or clay.

The friction ridges and the various characteristics contained within them enable them to be compared to sets of inked fingerprints to determine if they share the same coincident sequence. To better understand how fingerprints form and why they are so unique to each individual, it is helpful to understand how the friction ridges form.

In the very early stages of foetal life, about six weeks, bulges known as volar pads begin to form on the tips of the fingers and the palms of the hands, similar to the paws of a cat or a dog. These volar pads increase in size until approximately 13 weeks when they cease growing and remain roughly the size you would expect them to be at birth.

At 16 weeks, areas of the ridge structure push upwards, becoming visible on the skin's outer surface and eventually forming their final fixed arrangements as fingerprints at around 24 weeks.

Even in the case of identical twins, the ridge structure of each of their fingerprints is individual and unique and remains fixed and unchanging throughout life.

Just to clarify, the skin on the toes and soles of the feet (or plantar prints as they are known) is the same type of friction ridge skin as seen on the hands and forms in the same way. Footprints, therefore, are just as unique and immutable as fingerprints and can be used for identification purposes if suitable comparable marks are available.

In my early days in the Technical Bureau I soaked all of this stuff up like a sponge, fascinated by the detail. I also had to learn drier subjects like the history of fingerprints as a means of identification and the law pertaining to the taking and retention of fingerprints.

Fingerprints have been part of Irish police investigations for well over 100 years. Two members of the Dublin Metropolitan Police set up the first Irish fingerprinting section in 1901. This section became part of the Garda Technical Bureau when it was formed in 1934. The Fingerprints Section moved to Garda HQ in Phoenix Park in the 1970s, sharing a building with the Forensic Science Laboratory and the Ballistics and Photography sections. (The Mapping Section was in Harcourt Square.)

My desk was in the office and admin area of the Fingerprints Section, which was located on the second floor of the Bureau building back then. The floor also contained the National Fingerprint Collection with thousands of sets of inked fingerprints, all safely stored within large fireproof revolving shelves.

Sharing that floor was the AFIS suite and its cutting-edge Printrak 2000 fingerprint system for the automated searching of fingermarks from crime scenes. The suite was also used for quality control and storing digital copies of the fingerprints from the National Collection.

Scenes-of-crime exhibits were also examined in a special chemical development unit on the ground floor. Using various processes, we searched for and developed latent or hidden fingermarks. A small photographic studio was located beside the chemical section, where fingermarks could be photographed for subsequent search on AFIS.

The Fingerprints Section worked different rosters from most garda members. We had a day shift from 9 a.m. to 5 p.m. and a late shift from 5 p.m. to 1 a.m. Allen from Control also landed a job in the Fingerprints Section and started the same day as me.

We worked with sergeants Myles and Declan, who oversaw much of our training. There was a lot to get through, and we were starting from scratch, but I was eager to learn.

We learnt how fingerprints formed and what made them unique to every person. We studied the history of fingerprint identification and its use as evidence in court. We had to learn how to classify fingerprints according to their patterns and, of course, how to take good-quality sets of prints.

We had to crawl before we could walk, so we wouldn't be working on crime scenes for quite some time. Instead, we quality-controlled the sets of fingerprints coming in daily, ensuring they were marked up correctly. We filed sets away in the collection, and under the supervision of more experienced section members, we worked in the chemical room, developing fingermarks on exhibits from crime scenes.

Every day for those first few months, I was learning something new. Every time I looked at a fingermark, I absorbed the visual information held within the friction ridge detail, reinforcing the scientific fact that every person who has ever lived, and every person yet to be born, has or will have unique fingerprints.

Although the advent of the new AFIS system meant that the National Collection no longer needed to be categorised under the old Henry system, I still needed to become familiar with the previous classification method. British-born Sir Edward Henry (1850–1931) was a police inspector general in the Imperial Civil Service in India. He devised a classification system which categorised fingerprints based on the patterns of loops, whorls and arches found on the fingers. This stuff was all very technical, but it was a fantastic way to learn the ridge patterns and their variations, even if the Henry system was discarded in later years.

Not long after joining the section, I began working in the chemical development unit. It was always busy, with scenes-of-crime exhibits coming in from garda stations, the Forensic Laboratory and the Ballistics and Documents sections. The chemical processes used in Fingerprints often destroyed or contaminated evidence types. So exhibits were often examined for DNA, drugs or firearm residue, blood, fibres or indented writing before coming to us.

We had many chemical processes for developing fingerprints, often depending on their surfaces. Porous surfaces, like paper, were treated with wet processes like Ninhydrin, Diazafluoren-9-One (DFO) or physical developer.

Fingermarks made in blood were enhanced using Amido Black, while marks on non-porous surfaces were usually treated with Cyanoacrylate Vapour (glue vapour). Fingermarks developed using this process could be further enhanced by applying a fluorescent dye and examined using the 'Quaser'. This is a fluorescent light source that uses a series of filters to illuminate fingermarks that can then be photographed. The Quaser could also help enhance marks made in blood by causing the background surface to fluoresce.

A myriad of other processes could be used, depending on the surface material and the condition of the exhibit: Sudan black, gentian violet, sticky-side powder and vacuum metal deposition.

A member of the Photography Section would then photograph developed fingermarks, and the marks would then be searched on the AFIS or through 'the bundles'. These were photocopies of physical sets of prints. They were separated into various regions and comprised copies of sets of fingerprints belonging to previously identified offenders.

Searching 'bundles' was a manual process, separate from AFIS, and was sometimes useful because before there were major motorways, criminals tended to stay within their own area. Also, AFIS was always pretty full of searchers so you might not get a free computer.

If I was assigned marks from scenes of crime in the Cork area, for example, I sometimes tried to narrow the search by going through the Cork bundle before queuing up and searching for marks on AFIS. If I had a good idea of what digit had made the mark (right thumb, left forefinger, right middle, etc), I would flick through the bundle just scanning that particular finger or thumb. It was a good shortcut, and I made many identifications or 'idents' that way. Manually searching through the bundles also helped me get my eye in.

Of course, if I didn't identify the print in the bundles, then I would search through AFIS. First, I'd nominate a finger to make it faster, but then without any nominated digit so as to cover all possibilities.

Sometimes, I spotted a particular fingermark with an unusual pattern or distinctive scar, and my subconscious recognised it from a previous search. I would go back to the bundle to find it. The bundles were abandoned after the nationwide construction of motorways as criminals travelled further outside their own area to commit crimes.

As well as working in the chemical section and doing quality control on fingerprints sets (or tenprints as they were referred to), I completed the standard scenes-of-crime course. This course taught us about collecting evidence from crime scenes. I also had to go to the scenes of burglaries around the city centre to hone my skills as a scenes-of-crime officer (SOCO).

Another regular duty was to go to the Dublin City Morgue or morgues in nearby hospitals to take fingerprints from dead bodies. It was a taster for things to come when I started attending murder scenes and suspicious deaths. When the bodies were intact, obtaining prints didn't prove too difficult. Occasionally, however, I was met with decomposed or burnt bodies, which presented their own challenges.

I had to learn the various tricks and methods needed to get a good set of fingerprints. Sometimes, I mixed a casting agent to take impressions from the hands. The impressions then had to be photographed and reversed left-to-right (or mirror imaged) to enable them to be searched. Very rarely, the skin, the fingers or the whole hand might have to be removed so that a more laboratory-controlled retrieval of the fingerprints could be carried out at the section. This could only be done with permission from the coroner.

None of this stuff bothered me. Again, I found it fascinating. I was in my element – every day was a school day, and I loved going in to work. Of course, it helped that my colleagues in the Fingerprints Section and the Bureau were a great bunch to work with. There was such a collective pool of experience between them that I was always picking up useful tips and tricks, and someone was always there to give me advice or a helping hand if I needed it.

I had found my niche. I was born again into the job and was determined to do everything possible to be a good fingerprint expert and crime scene examiner. It was a far cry from the previous few years when I was constantly doubting my abilities and always on the brink of quitting. To me, working in the Bureau was the best place to be in the whole organisation.

There was no juggling of files, summonses and charge sheets; no prisoners to deal with (unless you were called to take their prints); no awkward members of the public giving you grief for doing your job. Court was still daunting, but at least the evidence was all about one thing – fingerprints. I didn't need to worry about acts, sections and sub-sections (unless pertaining to fingerprints), and there was no feckin' uniform. From day one in the section, I became a *detective* garda. I was still only 25 and had a long, and hopefully rewarding, future ahead of me in the Bureau.

8

BEYOND THE TAPE

One does not simply walk into Mordor.
Boromir, The Lord of the Rings: The Fellowship of
the Ring

Suspicious Death – Shanballybaun, County Roscommon
There is nothing quite like the odour of a dead body. It's a sickly
smell, a mixture of decaying flesh, body fluids and gases that build
up inside the corpse. I always found it to be inescapable. At the
death scene, there's no way to mask it and it soaks into your clothes
and hair. I often returned home from a scene and people could still
get that whiff off me. 'What's that awful smell, John?' I never liked
to explain. But once you smell a decaying body, you never forget it.

By late 1998, I started accompanying Technical Bureau teams
to scenes of crime and suspicious deaths. My first foray into the
field was to Shanballybaun, an isolated townland outside Boyle in

County Roscommon. I was still only in training, so I went along as 'the boy' to assist the fingerprint expert and my sergeant, Declan. A ballistics expert also accompanied us. The scene was contained in a bungalow down the end of a dirt road. I remember the road was so bad, I had some trouble getting the crime scene van close to the house.

An elderly gentleman had been found dead with an apparent gunshot wound to his head. The deceased was tucked up in bed, and the heating had been left on, increasing the odour, which was the first thing to hit when we entered the scene, decked out in our white suits. At least the windows had been closed, so mercifully, there were few flies. There were also a couple of dogs in the house when he was found, but again, thankfully, they were unable to get into the bedroom. Hungry pets cooped up with a juicy corpse is not a situation you want to walk in on.

Once a body is found in suspicious circumstances, the scene is preserved until the Bureau team arrives. The photographer is the first of the team to enter to record everything in situ, and we entered once he'd done that. It was evident that the deceased had died from massive trauma to the head. One whole side of his face was gone, and the wall behind him was covered in brain matter. Lying on his chest was a large revolver, later categorised by the ballistics experts as a .357 Magnum. There were no signs of a struggle, and the man's pension book and a wallet containing cash were on the bedside table. It looked like a suicide, but that would be for the pathologist to decide.

A short time later, the relatively new deputy state pathologist, Dr Marie Cassidy, arrived at the scene. She completed her examination of the body, including taking the temperature (not with an oral thermometer – I'll let you picture the rest). We then assisted in the removal of the deceased from the scene, and a local undertaker took him to Roscommon University Hospital where the post-mortem would be carried out.

We searched the house, and I assisted the ballistics expert in gathering any pieces of skull that had been strewn around the bedroom. During our search, we managed to locate the bullet, which had ricocheted off the wall and landed in a cloth cap. John from Ballistics also showed me the gun's ammunition. He pointed out numerous marks on the sides of the bullet casings, which indicated that the firearm had perhaps been loaded, emptied and reloaded on several occasions. Maybe these were previous suicide attempts that weren't carried through.

It was all very surreal to me. For a year prior to this scene in Shanballybaun, I had continued fingerprint training, working between the chemical room and quality controlling on AFIS. Quality controlling, or QC, was a laborious process. It entailed going through each scanned finger from a set of prints. Often, a smudged or poorly taken set of prints would be marked up incorrectly by AFIS, so the person doing QC would have to erase the incorrect characteristics and mark in the correct ones.

Occasionally, you could come across sets of prints where the left fingers were in the location of the right ones, and these had to be corrected also. It was monotonous work, but whenever I felt bored, I reminded myself of the alternative. I could still be stuck out in a station and feeling miserable. Even though QC was dull work, it was still important. If the sets of fingerprints stored on AFIS weren't correctly recorded, then searches of inputted crime scene marks wouldn't 'hit' against them. Every aspect of the process was crucial, from QC all the way to searching and identifying marks.

Although during training I had to make the occasional trip to the morgue to take sets of fingerprints from bodies, the investigation at Shanballybaun marked the first time I had to attend the full post-mortem. I was nervous as we left the deceased's bungalow and followed his body as it was delivered to Roscommon Hospital. Observing a body at peace in a coffin or taking fingerprints from a cleaned-up corpse in a morgue is one thing. It is completely different dealing with a violent death and its aftermath. I was quickly learning there is precious little dignity in violent death.

Every post-mortem follows the same general routine. First, the body is undressed if clothed, and then the pathologist conducts an external examination before moving on to an internal one. The photographer is the most important member of the crime scene unit during a post-mortem. Their job is to make a visual document of the entire examination, so Ray from the Bureau continually snapped away and photographed anything Dr Cassidy pointed out as points of interest. These photos provide a detailed visual record for the pathologist to refer to if required to present evidence in court.

With no other injuries to the body, the bulk of the external examination concerned the wound to the head. Then, the full internal examination of the organs started, and Dr Cassidy used heavy shears to cut through the sternum and access the chest cavity. I thought I was coping quite well until the gases from the decomposition process were suddenly released into the rather small room. The sickening sound of air escaping from the body was followed by an even more horrendous smell. I had to step out for a few minutes to compose myself. Even though he was an old hand at this sort of situation, Declan followed. It was about this time someone realised that the air extractor hadn't been turned on. We went back in as they finally whirred into action.

Normally, the fingerprinting of a body is left until after the pathologist has completed their examination, but Dr Cassidy allowed me to take the prints while she finished examining the head, making her copious notes.

A dead body, even a relatively fresh one, is clammy to the touch, even damp, so I needed to dry the fingers with tissue before applying the fingerprint ink. Declan then assisted me in pressing the inked fingers and palms onto the strips of fingerprint cadaver paper.

I took care to get each print in the allotted box correctly, for example right thumb, right fore, right middle and so on. Again, this is sometimes awkward if rigor mortis has set in, leaving the finger stiff and unwieldy. On occasion, and only with the pathologist's or mortician's approval, the fingerprint expert can ask for the tendons in the wrist or the back of the hand to be cut, thus relaxing the digits.

With a satisfactory set of fingerprints taken, the ballistics expert asked me to swab the deceased's hands to retrieve any firearm residue. I did this but shied away from taking swabs from the poor man's destroyed face. It wasn't necessary anyway. Dr Cassidy was satisfied the death had been caused by massive trauma to the head as a result of a self-inflicted gunshot.

That was my first time at the gritty coalface of crime scene investigation involving a suspicious death. There would be many more to come.

I remember feeling pretty proud of myself as I drove the Bureau van back to Dublin after my first crime scene job. It had been educational, albeit sad and gruesome, but I had done what was required of me and had got through it without losing my nerve. Or the contents of my stomach.

The Murder of Marie Dillon

Marie Dillon, a widow in her early seventies, was found dead in the garage of her house on Beneavin Road in Finglas in November 1998. This time, there was no ambiguity about what had occurred. She had been murdered: brutally beaten to death.

The scene had been cordoned off with crime scene tape, and we had to give our details to the garda member whose duty was to preserve the scene. His job was to record the names of all persons entering and leaving the location. I ducked under the tape and made my way in to assist Mick, the fingerprint expert, and Declan, my sergeant, who was the crime scene manager. A guy from Ballistics was also on the team, and the photographer had taken his preliminary photographs.

I experienced a mix of emotions entering my first murder scene. I felt shocked at the violence of what had taken place, but also appreciated the privilege of watching crime scene experts investigate a murder. Most garda members wouldn't get past the tape, and any members with my relatively short amount of service would be lucky to get the job of minding the scene.

The deceased was lying face down beside her car in the cramped garage. She had blunt force trauma wounding to the head, and she was partially unclothed. Once again, Dr Marie Cassidy was the pathologist assigned to the investigation. The woman's body was removed to the old Dublin City Morgue on Store Street, and the scene had to be preserved for several days as there was a lot to search through. We arranged for Mrs Dillon's car to be brought to the garda garage at headquarters for a thorough examination. This was a few years before the special facility for examining vehicles was built at Santry garda station.

Before going to the mortuary, everyone from the crime scene, including Dr Cassidy, headed for grub in the Harbourmaster pub at Custom House Dock. I ate as heartily as anyone else knowing we had a long post-mortem ahead, so I was already exhibiting that ability of my colleagues to compartmentalise the work.

At the post-mortem, Dr Cassidy meticulously examined the body while the photographer recorded everything. The pathologist paid particular attention to the head wound. She suggested that Mick apply a small amount of black fingerprint powder to the damaged areas of the skull to provide a good contrast for the photographs. It was likely that the deceased had been repeatedly struck on the head with a heavy object, perhaps a piece of cement block that was found in the garage. The post-mortem went on well into the night, so it was the next day before we began examining the scene and the impounded car.

The scene yielded little in the way of physical evidence. I assisted Mick in applying fingerprint powder around the doors to the garage and on other receptive surfaces. We found fingermarks on the door, but these were quickly eliminated, belonging to the first garda on the scene. It is best practice to obtain elimination fingerprints from any persons who have access to a crime scene. Identifying and eliminating innocent persons from an investigation is just as important as identifying guilty parties.

Mick and I spent several hours back at headquarters examining the car, a black Fiat Cinquecento. Although the dark colour could make visible fingermarks hard to spot, the car had been parked up for some time and was covered in a layer of dust. We made out what appeared to be fingermarks made in the dust at several locations along the sides of the car. However, there were further fingermarks on the bonnet, and these appeared to have been made in blood.

Willie from Ballistics took swabs of the dried liquid, and it was confirmed as blood from the victim by the Forensic Science Lab. The fingermarks were photographed, and once we saw that the developed prints had captured the friction ridge details, we lifted them with fingerprint lifting tape and placed them on fingerprint lift cards.

I remember we were all nervously excited as we headed up to the AFIS suite in the Fingerprints Section to input the fingermarks into the search system. This murder was a relatively rare occurrence – a complete whodunnit. Most violent crimes are committed by persons known to the victim, but in this case, there were no suspects. There were also no witnesses, no CCTV and no apparent motive.

Declan and I flanked Mick as he carefully marked up the discernible friction ridge details of one of the scanned fingermarks taken from the car's bonnet. Enough of the mark was visible to enable him to nominate a digit and a pattern. It was a thumbmark.

Being able to discern the digit and pattern meant narrowing down the search that AFIS would perform as it trawled through the stored images from the National Fingerprint Collection. The AFIS system does not identify fingermarks; it only responds to the plotted points inputted on its system by the fingerprint expert. It then runs a search through the thousands of sets of fingerprints on file and displays a list of fingerprints that are the closest match.

The expert then looks through the respondents. If they see what appears to be a match, then the actual hard copy – the inked set of fingerprints – is retrieved from the National Fingerprint Collection, and a careful comparison is carried out. If they are satisfied that there is a match, their findings are verified by at least two other experts before an official identification is made.

AFIS only took a couple of minutes to bring back a list of thirty respondents and a numerical score for each one. It will always display a list, even if there is no match. The expert has to go through the list and determine if a match has been made.

In this case, we could see that number one on the list showed a promisingly high score. My heart was pounding as Mick brought up the two images side by side: the mark from the bonnet and the top respondent. The tension was unbearable, but we could see numerous agreements in the relative positions of the friction ridge details and no differences.

Mick then retrieved the hard copy of fingerprints from the collection at the other end of the section and made a meticulous one-to-one comparison. He was satisfied they were a match. Declan then carried out a comparison, and so did a third expert. It was 'an ident'!

As the crime scene manager, Declan informed the investigation team of the identification, and there was plenty of applause and back-slapping for Mick, but we still had a lot of work to do back at the scene. We didn't get finished until later that evening, and by the time we got back to headquarters, everyone from the section was in the bar celebrating the identification.

The following morning, the person identified, 17-year-old Richard Kearney, was arrested. When interviewed, he stated that he was trying to steal the car radio in the garage when Mrs Dillon disturbed him, and he attacked her while trying to escape. There was obviously more to it than that I felt, given the ferocity of the beating and the fact that she was partially undressed. Kearney was later convicted of murder and sentenced to life imprisonment. Mick's fingerprint evidence was a vital part of the prosecution's case.

It also emerged that Kearney had only recently been fingerprinted for the first time by a conscientious garda in Whitehall garda station who had arrested him for the theft of a leather jacket. If that member had not had the presence of mind to take a set of fingerprints, it is very possible that Marie Dillon's killer would never have been caught.

The Death of Francis Brooks

Francis Brooks died while in garda custody at Tallaght garda station in September 1998. Mr Brooks, who was in his early twenties, had been stopped by the gardaí under suspicion of drink-driving and had been conveyed to the Tallaght station to provide a sample of blood or urine. Gardaí noted that he was having trouble staying awake while in custody and were of the opinion that he was under the influence of drugs rather than alcohol. When they went to release him, he couldn't be woken. An ambulance was called, but on arrival at the station, the ambulance crew ascertained he was dead. It subsequently transpired that he had taken an overdose of methadone before being arrested. I was dispatched to the mortuary at Tallaght Hospital to print the body of the young man.

At Tallaght University Hospital, I took a seat in the viewing area of the mortuary while the inimitable Professor John Harbison carried out the post-mortem. He was the first state pathologist in Ireland and held that position from 1974 until 2003. He gestured to me to come in. I could get my bit done if I didn't get in his way.

Professor Harbison had a reputation for being somewhat eccentric. Still, on the few occasions I attended post-mortems conducted by him, I found him pleasant and possessed of a devilish sense of humour. As I was getting ready, I chatted with him. I had gone to primary school with his nephew, and we talked about what the chap was up to now.

After wiping the fingers with tissue to remove any moisture, they can be placed on a small glass plate inked with an ink roller, or the ink can sometimes be applied directly to the hands with the roller. It is important that the correct consistency of ink is used. Too much and the ridge detail will smudge, and too little ink makes the detail hard to see.

To help take Mr Brooks' prints, I used a cadaver spoon. This handy little tool has a concave end where you can slot in the strip of fingerprint paper and then press it against each finger in turn, capturing as much ridge detail as possible. Things were going swimmingly, and I just had the palm prints left to take. These can be tricky as the palms are padded with a lot of skin, and any inadvertent movement when pressing the skin surface to the cards used for palm prints causes a smudge.

As soon as I started to take the palm prints, Professor Harbison began to use a circular saw on the deceased's head so he could examine the brain. This had the effect of causing the hands to vibrate, making it impossible for me to get good prints. The high-pitched whine of the saw and the smell of bone dust in the air were also disconcerting. I was becoming more and more flustered. I didn't dare ask Professor Harbison to pause his work, and I was also afraid he would get impatient with me if I didn't hurry up and get the job done. Yet, I couldn't get palm prints that were even halfway acceptable while he continued with the post-mortem.

As I started to sweat, I glanced up to the viewing area and saw the garda photographer and the ballistics expert shaking with laughter. They were both seasoned campaigners and took great pleasure watching the 'newbie' struggle.

A Suspicious Death, South Circular Road, Dublin

The scene was a dilapidated Edwardian-style house on Dublin's South Circular Road. It was divided into numerous bedsits, each more squalid than the next. A 48-year-old man had been found dead, sitting in a chair in a small room on the first floor in May 1999. By the time the Bureau team was called to the scene, the body had already been removed to the Dublin City Morgue. I was at the scene as an assistant to the fingerprint expert, Aidan. When we entered the room, we were greeted by the largest amount of blood that I have ever witnessed. It appeared as if the man had completely bled out.

It was imperative to wear our face masks at all times. Unlike how it's depicted on television, blood dries relatively quickly and becomes brittle and flaky. The blood can easily become airborne. Even dried blood can be dangerous as some bloodborne viruses can stay alive and continue to be infectious for hours or even days outside of the body. The hepatitis B virus, for example, can live in dried blood for up to a week.

We saw no sign of a struggle, but Aidan and I had a lot of powdering to do, as several people had been living in the house. We concentrated on the doors, door frames, banisters, and receptive wall surfaces. Innumerable beer cans and bottles were strewn around the scene too, so we bagged some of these for examination back at the section.

While cans are quite good at retaining latent fingermarks, they are moveable objects and finding and identifying any fingermarks on them does little to prove anything other than a particular person has held them. With no functioning heating in the house, everywhere was cold and fingermarks were not developing. I picked up a handy trick from Aidan that day. Using a powerful light that the photographer had set up on a tripod, Aidan managed to warm the door surfaces, which made any fingermarks present easier to develop and lift. We lifted dozens of marks, but they were only of use as intelligence-gathering. None of them were in blood or on any implements that could have been used as a weapon.

It also turned out that we were a bit late to the party. The man had been found two days earlier and the scene hadn't been preserved. This was evident in the photographs taken by the local SOCO when compared with those taken by Joe, the Bureau photographer. Several items, including a television set, had disappeared from the scene prior to it being properly preserved. If a criminal investigation was to be instigated, it would have been very difficult to see it through the courts.

As it turned out, the pathologist, Dr Cassidy, ruled that the man's death was not suspicious. It was ascertained that he had had a quarrel with another individual with whom he was drinking and had sustained the injury because of being hit with a full can of beer. At Dublin City Morgue, she pointed out a small cut on the man's forehead, just between his eyebrows. Death had occurred because of massive blood loss from this small wound. The man had suffered from alcoholism. Instead of seeing to his wound, he had sat in his chair and continued to drink while bleeding out. Excessive consumption of alcohol can sometimes affect the blood's ability to coagulate or clot, meaning that even minor cuts can bleed excessively. Liver diseases can also have this effect on the body's circulatory system.

While satisfied that the man had not died a violent death, Dr Cassidy was still curious about some minor circular bruises on his face. She returned to the scene with us and noticed the round knobs on the cooker positioned right beside the chair. It was surmised that during his final drinking binge, the man had fallen out of the chair and hit his face against the cooker.

This job was an example of a Bureau team carrying out a lot of work for what ultimately turned out to be a non-suspicious death. It was also a salutary lesson for investigators – preserve the scene until all avenues of inquiry have been exhausted.

I also got to experience what is sometimes a necessary aspect of scene investigation – optics. As I said, the house was filthy inside, with cans and bottles and all sorts of rubbish strewn around the place. The senior officer would often be conscious of how it might look if exhibit bags weren't seen to be removed from the scene by the forensics experts.

There was also the possibility that some high-ranking member might query why certain items weren't removed for investigation from the scene. It was sometimes easier just to clean up and bag everything even if they were of no evidential value.

So we accrued several bags of these cans and bottles and piled them up in the front garden. Happily, the television cameras duly filmed the garda evidence bags out front.

When we finished at the scene, we loaded up the bags in the Bureau van. To onlookers and cameras, it looked as if the contents were off to be sifted through and examined. Instead, when we got back to base, we reversed the van around the back of the Bureau building and promptly dumped everything in the skip.

9

DISCOVERY

Every contact leaves a trace.
Dr Edmond Locard

I don't remember my first identification, but I do remember the rush when a fingermark from a crime scene got a 'hit'. I worked on fingerprint identifications either at the grey laminate tables in AFIS or at my simple wooden desk at the other end of the office. Our desks had dividers, separating us from neighbouring ones and providing us with a bit of privacy. The dividers also allowed us to hang Post-It notes and a calendar with our court dates, etc.

Most days, I'd put my head down behind the divider and zone out background chatter or the radio playing in the office. Of course, I couldn't zone out the early-morning sounds of the lions roaring and wolves howling from the nearby zoo as the sun came up. Sometimes, we'd also get the life frightened out of us when they test-fired their artillery guns in the army barracks next to HQ.

The actual identification was always made from the physical set of prints. For this, I used my old trusty hand magnifying glass, its handle yellowed with age. It bore a faded red sticker bearing the proprietary word 'JOHN' in black marker. I also had a pointer like the tip of a compass, used to keep track of the details that I was looking at.

The mark started to 'twitch' for me when I started to see matching ridge characteristics. As soon as I'd see that, I would become wide awake, scanning the crime scene mark and the corresponding print to see if all the details were in agreement. Very often, I would know within seconds that I had made a match, but I would always take time to ensure there were no discrepancies. Even after 10 years working in Fingerprints, regardless of the crime being investigated, I always got that dopamine buzz when a mark started to 'twitch' for me. I enjoyed that rush of euphoria and satisfaction as it became apparent that more and more ridge characteristics were in agreement.

Most of 1999 saw me continuing my fingerprints training as well as my chemical-room work and carrying out my QC duties. I also continued going out to burglary scenes and examining vehicles involved in various crimes. Vehicles could now be brought to and examined at a special facility beside Santry garda station. It was kitted out with all the equipment one would usually find in a mechanic's garage. It was also climate-controlled, providing ideal conditions for the retrieval of trace evidence. One section of the facility was essentially a large glue-fuming room, where entire vehicles or large exhibits were treated with cyanoacrylate vapour for the purpose of developing fingermarks. Over the years, the Santry examination facility was invaluable for the forensic examination of vehicles used in the commission of crimes.

Every member of the Fingerprints Section was issued with a scenes-of-crime kit containing all the equipment needed for fingermark retrieval. My kit contained fingerprint powders and brushes, lifting tape, lift cards, fingerprint ink and inking slabs (a second one used for the printing of cadavers), Mikrosil (a forensic silicone casting material) and cleaning equipment.

One of the fingerprint powders I most commonly used was aluminium flake – a grey, non-magnetic powder of tiny metal particles. It is typically applied to surfaces using a zephyr-style fingerprint brush with long, straight bristles that can apply powder over large areas. Only a small amount of powder is needed, so you lightly 'load' the brush, shake off any excess and apply it to the surface by constantly twirling the brush handle. This enables the SOCO to gradually build up a mark. Marks are then lifted using fingerprint tape and placed on black fingerprint lift cards to provide good contrast.

The rear of each card is then filled in with all the relevant details, such as date, time, place and crime type. A brief description of where the mark or marks have been lifted and a simple sketch should also be included. For example: *'Inverted at point of entry, left side of window'*. Including this information is vital as there may be dozens of lifted marks from any one scene, and being able to identify the significance of their locations can be very important. It is also very helpful to the fingerprint searcher when they are determining which digits are shown and their orientation. A simple arrow sketched on the card to show which direction is up is also beneficial. Any SOCO or fingerprint expert will deal with hundreds, if not thousands, of lifted marks over time, and it may be several years before evidence may be required in court, so having as much background information as possible recorded on the rear of the cards is invaluable.

Aluminium flake powder was great for developing fine detail in fingermarks. The minute particles could even capture tiny details, such as the sweat pores in crime scene marks. However, you couldn't use it on untreated surfaces or fine wood. The particles could become ingrained and were difficult to remove once the examination was finished. On a few occasions, I spilt the stuff on carpets, and it was a bitch to remove.

Thankfully, a second type of powder could be used, which was much easier to manage. Black magnetic fingerprint powder was excellent for developing latent or hidden marks on non-porous surfaces. It was made up of tiny metallic particles which would adhere to the residue in latent fingermarks. This powder was applied using a magnetic wand, which resembled a pen. One end had a narrow retractable magnet which could be 'loaded' with powder and gently moved around the area to be examined. Any excess or spilt powder was easily cleaned up with the wand. Fingermarks developed with black magnetic powder were lifted and placed on white lift cards.

As part of my training, I went to burglary scenes at business premises and private dwellings. My examination was usually concentrated around the area where the intruder had entered, or what SOCOs would refer to as the 'POE' or point of entry. If the homeowner or business staff were present, I would also obtain a set of their fingerprints for elimination purposes. These fingerprints wouldn't be entered onto AFIS and were only used for comparison against fingermarks found at a scene.

By this time, I was allowed to search AFIS for matches of marks from the burglary scenes and vehicles and made numerous identifications from them. As a trainee, any idents I made had to be verified by three fingerprint experts, and if any of the cases got to court, I had to hand over the case to a fully qualified expert who would present the evidence during court proceedings.

Fingerprint identification is not a numbers game, but unfortunately, in Irish courts, it is necessary to have at least *12 points* in coincident sequence between a crime scene mark and a fingerprint. All must be in agreement and none in disagreement before the identification evidence can be deemed admissible. There are convoluted exceptions to the rule, like if there were ten points in agreement in two marks from different fingers at the same scene. Or if two marks were made by the same finger at the same scene with an aggregate of at least 12 points between them. As I said, all very convoluted. Every case is different, as are the circumstances of fingermarks at a crime scene. A fingerprint is a two-dimensional representation of the three-dimensional surface of the friction skin. The skin's elasticity, the pressure applied in depositing the marks and the development medium used are just some factors that need to be considered.

I continued to get plenty of experience going to burglaries and became more skilled in making identifications. Occasionally, the fingermarks identified were made by the injured parties, but it was still good practice, as they were still idents.

At one particular burglary in the city centre, the damage to the door and point of entry for the intruder had already been repaired when I got there. I still carried out an examination and lifted some marks. Later that day, I inputted the marks on AFIS and got a hit, but it transpired that the fingermarks belonged to the glazier who had repaired the damage. He had been printed for some minor infraction almost 20 years before, and these prints were still in the National Collection. Although I wasn't able to identify the culprit for the burglary, at least all the marks were identified, and looking at fingermarks every day honed my experience.

After an intensive two-week period of training, I also passed the standard garda driving course in 1999. The course was mostly filled with regular garda members and mules from Traffic, who were mad for speed. I had had to put the foot down on a few occasions, but as a member of the Bureau, I envisaged little need to travel anywhere at breakneck speed.

We even stopped in Templemore for lunch one day during one of several long drives all over the country. It was my first time back in Templemore since passing out in 1995 and, mainly having bad memories of the place, it gave me the willies just being there again. I only returned once more a few years later on a detective training course. I was always happy to see Templemore in my rear-view mirror.

September was also memorable for me in 1999 because my girlfriend Orlagh and I got married, holding our wedding reception in the Grand Hotel in Malahide, only a stone's throw from my first station.

I went into the new year and the new millennium with fresh challenges ahead. Chief among these was attending the intermediate fingerprint course in the UK. Things were about to step up a notch.

10

BACK TO SCHOOL

Any fool can know. The point is to understand.
Albert Einstein

Two young children were brutally murdered in Argentina in June 1892. They were found with their skulls crushed in the hut where they lived with their unmarried mother, Francisca Rojas. On the evening of the murders, Rojas had run into a neighbour's hut and screamed that her children had been murdered by a man called Velasquez.

Velasquez was a labourer who worked on a nearby farm. He had wanted to marry Rojas and had proposed to her on several occasions. Rojas had spurned him and told him she was in love with another man. Rojas told the police that upon hearing this, Velasquez had flown into a rage and threatened both her and her children before storming off. Rojas alleged that when she came home later, she was attacked and her children were murdered.

Velasquez was detained, interrogated and tortured but maintained that he was innocent, even when he was tied up and left lying beside the children's bodies for hours. He admitted he had made threats but denied killing anyone.

A police inspector called Álvarez, who worked in a station outside Buenos Aires, was dispatched to assist in this murder investigation in the coastal town of Necochea. He quickly established that Velasquez had an alibi as he had been out with friends at the time of the murders. Álvarez also established that the man Rojas loved had been heard saying he would marry her if it wasn't for 'those two brats'.

Álvarez, who only arrived at the scene of the crime several days after the murders, spotted a stain on the bedroom door of the house. After careful examination, he realised that the stain was a fingerprint made in blood. Álvarez knew about fingerprinting from a colleague in his police station called Juan Vucetich, a statistician who had created his own system of fingerprint classification.

So Álvarez cut out the door section with the fingerprint and requested that Rojas be fingerprinted. He compared the mark from the door to Rojas' prints using a magnifying glass and identified it as made by the mother's right thumb. When this evidence was put to her, Rojas broke down and confessed to having killed her children so that she could marry her lover. She had killed them with a rock, which she later threw down a well. Although she had cleaned her hands and clothes after the crime, she failed to notice the small mark left in blood on the door.

Vucetich had faced opposition from his superiors, who were hesitant to adopt this new fingerprinting system to identify criminals. Until then, they used anthropometry, a pseudoscientific system that attempted to identify criminals by correlating facial and body characteristics to racial and psychological traits. For example, this system stated that murderers had prominent jaws.

The opposition to fingerprinting ended, however, after the Rojas murder case. The Álvarez investigation became the first known murder case to be solved using fingerprint analysis, and Rojas became the first criminal to be found guilty through fingerprint evidence. The court sentenced her to life imprisonment.

Fingerprinting may not have been widely used until the turn of the twentieth century, but mankind's awareness of fingerprints' importance dates back many thousands of years. Instances of petroglyphs or stone carvings have been found showing crude yet distinguishable images of hands with patterns incised into the fingertips. In China and the Middle East, ancient clay pottery shards have been recovered with the potter's fingerprint imprinted on the surface as a trade mark. Documents and deeds from ancient China have also been found to feature fingerprints to establish the papers' veracity and prevent forgeries. While it is not known if these people used fingerprints as a means of identification, it is clear that they were aware of the unique nature of the skin structure on the fingers and palms.

The first Europeans to recognise the value of friction ridge detail included Sir William Herschel (1833–1917), a British officer working in India in the 1850s. Herschel began using handprints and later fingerprints on contracts as a simple method of identification to prevent fraud among residents.

Another pioneer was Dr Henry Faulds (1843–1930), a Scottish physician and missionary in India and Japan who published an article in the scientific journal *Nature* in 1880 proposing fingerprints as a means of personal identification. In a letter that same year to eminent naturalist and biologist Charles Darwin, he noted that 'fingerprints can be classified easily and ridge detail is unique'.

Sir Francis Galton (1822–1911), a British anthropologist and cousin of Charles Darwin, later expanded upon these ideas. Galton established the uniqueness and permanence of fingerprints and devised a classification system for them. He published a book titled *Finger Prints* in 1892.

British-born Sir Edward Henry (1850–1931) was exchanging letters with Galton when he was appointed the inspector-general of police in Bengal in India in 1891. Fingerprinting had been used in India for identification purposes after being introduced by Herschel several years earlier but was not used by the police.

Henry devised a classification system which allowed fingerprint records to be organised and searched. His system helped fully realise the potential of fingerprints as a tool for identification and crime scene investigation. He was appointed the assistant commissioner of crime at Scotland Yard in 1901 and set up the Metropolitan Police Fingerprint Bureau the same year.

The foundation for modern dactyloscopy, the science of identification using the ridge patterns on the fingers and hands, was laid. Fingerprinting quickly became a cornerstone of forensics and police around the world.

We touched on the old Henry system of fingerprint classification during the intermediate fingerprint training course in England in

January 2000. The course took place in the Police Training Centre at Aykley Heads, Durham – the north-east region's version of Templemore.

Allen and I lived on campus for three weeks, doing some serious studying and practical searching exercises. We delved into fingerprint history and learnt about the contributions of Herschel, Faulds and Galton and the first successful conviction using fingerprints in Argentina with the Rojas murders case in 1892.

While this historical information was important, the real meat of the intermediate course was the actual searching and comparison exercises. The course modules also included theory and case law, but mainly we were engaged in endless fingerprint-searching exercises.

None of these searches were pushovers. We were in the bigger leagues now, as the assessors were experts themselves, so we had to give it our all. We were given packs to search, comprising several crime scene marks – usually photographs – and several sets of fingerprints. Our task was to identify the marks or, even more challenging, conclude that some of the crime scene marks were not to be found in the sets of fingerprints. We also had some mock courtroom practical exercises, but these skills would only be really tested on a later expert course.

Although the intermediate course was challenging, I enjoyed it. Only five of us attended it, and we gelled well, going out for grub and pints in Durham. It is a beautiful city, and I enjoyed strolling around and visiting the sights, including its impressive cathedral, which dates back to Norman times.

Both Allen and I passed the theory and practical exams with flying colours. I was chuffed reading the instructors' notes, which remarked: 'John completed all the searching exercises given to him without a single error.'

Back in Dublin, armed with even more knowledge, I became fully entrenched in my duties as a member of the Fingerprints Section. I loved my job and couldn't envision myself doing anything else. I was – to steal a quote from one of my favourite movies, *Predator* – 'dug in like an Alabama tick'!

11

THINGS THAT GO BANG!

In my defence, I was left unsupervised.
Anonymous

A massive haul of fireworks was discovered in a warehouse on the outskirts of Dublin just before Halloween in October 2000. As the seizure was getting plenty of coverage in the media, the local superintendent requested the services of the Technical Bureau. I was part of a Bureau team sent out to the Greenogue Industrial Estate in Rathcoole, where they found the haul.

In truth, there wasn't much for me to do as they had already arrested two people in connection with the discovery, and I wasn't about to look for fingermarks on the thousands of boxes of assorted fireworks. Instead, I assisted the ballistics expert in removing a portion of the haul for further 'testing' back at HQ.

All that day, a procession of patrol cars, vans and unmarked cars from the surrounding districts just happened to converge at the scene, and each one left weighing a tad heavier with their freshly acquired cargo. Mules have kids too, and the prospect of being able to put on an impressive display of pyrotechnics for Halloween was too tempting to pass up. I'm sure many of our warehouse callers that day had no kids at all, but had their own fascination with things that go bang. I was no different.

Of course, the ballistics guy claimed all the really serious exploding bits and bobs. The rest of us crammed as many boxes of fireworks as we could into the back of the Bureau van and divvied up the spoils when we returned to base.

The media estimated that the haul had a value of in excess of one million punts, which was the largest ever seizure of illegal fireworks in the country up to that time. I doubt this valuation would have been accurate by the time all those garda vehicles left the industrial estate.

My takings were meagre, and when I set them off down the field behind my folks' house a few nights later, it was a bit of a non-event. I heard that one mule, who had bagged some fireworks, later brought friends and family to a secluded spot to witness him orchestrate a magical and awe-inspiring pyrotechnical display. However, while making final preparations for the extravaganza, the smouldering ash of a cigarette dangling on his lips fell upon his pyrotechnics. It resulted in one almighty explosion of firecrackers, sparklers, smoke bombs, wheels, shell bursts and rockets, and the assembled crowd were treated to one hell of a show, albeit a brief one.

The fireworks from the seizure were destined for collection by army explosives experts and brought to a remote location for destruction. But I wonder how much was actually left for them to destroy. I'm sure that haul was nibbled on like dead buffalo floating down a piranha-infested river before it reached its final destination.

The Ballistics Section

During 'The Troubles' or the Northern Ireland conflict, the ballistic experts were seen as giants among men. (Like most specialised sections at the time, it was pretty much an all-male affair.) What the guys in the Ballistics Section didn't know about fires, guns, explosives and the like wasn't worth knowing. They were at the forefront of numerous major investigations, including the IRA assassination of Lord Mountbatten on 27 August 1979. The Provisionals blew up Mountbatten's boat at Mullaghmore in County Sligo, which also resulted in the deaths of three other people, including two teenage boys. To this day, the propeller from Mountbatten's ill-fated boat, *Shadow V*, is on display in the corridors of the Ballistics Section.

Such was the standing of the Ballistics Section in the polis that I have it on good authority that when Pope John Paul II was driven through the massive crowds in Phoenix Park in 1979, it wasn't armed Emergency Response Unit (ERU) members or close protection officers who were hanging off the sides of the Popemobile, but seasoned members of Ballistics.

The Ballistics Section was one of the first departments established when the Technical Bureau was set up in 1934. Over the years, the section has grown, and its members receive expert training in various disciplines in Ireland and abroad. The Federal Bureau of Investigations (FBI) in America also provides tactical training.

The duties of a member of the Ballistics Section are many and varied, with the bulk of the work involving firearms, ammunition and explosives used in the commission of crime or recovered from scenes of crimes. It also houses an extensive ammunition reference database used to link different crimes committed using the same firearm. To aid this task, they have a state-of-the-art digital stereo microscope for the detailed comparison of bullet striation marks and firing pin indentations.

At the rear of the Technical Bureau building is a purpose-built, fully enclosed and sound-proofed firing range where weapons can be safely discharged and spent ammunition can be retrieved for forensic analysis. They examine detonators, incendiary devices and hoax devices and explosives – from commercial to military and improvised devices. Other duties performed by the section include blood distribution pattern analysis, serial number restorations, fire and arson investigations, tyre and tool marks and footwear impressions.

When I began in the Bureau, the Ballistics Section was in a transitory period. The Good Friday Agreement of 1998 is generally regarded as the official end of the conflict in Northern Ireland, which had lasted for roughly 30 years. The Troubles provided many crime scenes involving firearms and explosives for the Ballistics Section to investigate, and they were held in high esteem as the top experts in these fields. Indeed, I worked with numerous members from Ballistics on various jobs over the years.

There were still some old-school Ballistics guys left in the Bureau when I started out as a greenhorn, and I found most of them to be founts of knowledge. However, I remember a couple of occasions where it occurred to me that a few could, in my opinion, 'get high on their own supply'.

The day after the huge fireworks seizure, I found myself flitting about between several garda stations in Monaghan and Louth. I was part of a Bureau team dispatched to assist in an investigation after suspected bomb-making equipment was discovered in the area.

We had to examine two private addresses in Louth, several cars and some exhibits recovered from these places. Items seized included a suspected incendiary device, which had already been rendered safe by the ballistics expert. Incendiary devices are little boxes around the size of a tape cassette, usually made out of plastic. They contain a timer, an ignition mechanism and some form of accelerant, and their sole purpose is to start fires.

Also seized were several sections of plastic piping, possibly for use in improvised explosive devices. I also took possession of numerous plastic bags, false registration plates, sheets of paper with lists of names and garda radio frequencies, and several issues of *The Sovereign Nation*, published by the Irish republican movement.

When we arrived, the Divisional Search Team was busy combing the houses for further incriminating evidence. I started to assist until I was rounded on by the senior ballistics expert, a seasoned sergeant. He reminded me that we were 'Bureau', and we should not be doing the task allocated to the other garda members milling about. I was a bit taken aback, as we weren't doing much else, but I did as I was told. To my mind, as Bureau members, we were part of the National Support Services and should have been at the disposal of gardaí investigating the crime and mucking in with the others. However, being a relatively junior member in the Bureau back then, I said nothing.

Even before I left the house, the ballistics skipper plonked himself in a living-room armchair and started to watch television. I could see members of the search team throwing us sideways glances. Who the hell did we think we were? I'm sure they were of the opinion that these Bureau big-shots from Dublin thought they were one step above buttermilk.

Some years later, I was at work when a call came in requesting the services of the Bureau after the discovery of a suspected car bomb. As explosives could be involved, a ballistics expert would be the team's lead investigator. It seemed the car could contain a large amount of explosives. Still, it couldn't be ascertained if the threat was real or just an elaborate hoax without the army's explosive ordnance disposal (EOD) team checking it out first.

It transpired that the EOD weren't available or were already engaged on a similar call, so what were we going to do? Well, following the advice of several ballistics experts, the sensible decision was made to hold off examining the car until the EOD could get to the scene.

Eh, actually, no. After experts in the Ballistics Section were consulted, it was decided that the Bureau team would be dispatched, and the ballistics guy would 'have a look' to determine exactly what we were dealing with. So, a well-seasoned ballistics expert, a photographer and I headed off in a Bureau car towards a Dublin garda station, where a tow truck had brought the suspected vehicle. Hang on a second, I thought to myself. The car had actually been moved? And brought into the rear compound of a garda station in a relatively built-up area surrounded by numerous private dwellings and business premises? Was I imagining this shit?

We arrived at the garda station and were pointed in the direction of the suspect car. I sheepishly got out of our car, but there was no way in hell I was going near the ordinary-looking vehicle sitting at the other end of the compound. The photographer was of the same mind as me, and we threw disbelieving looks at each other as the ballistics expert strode towards what could, if containing a viable explosive device, shred the rest of the cars strewn about the place into scrap metal and maybe even flatten the station itself.

The ballistics guy circled the vehicle, peeking in through the windows, and then, as I silently prayed like an atheist in a foxhole, he gingerly opened a front door for a better look. So far, so good. No flying body parts. With his curiosity still unsated, he then went around to the rear of the car and just popped the boot lid. Still no flying body parts. A few tense moments later, he beckoned us over, assuring us it was indeed a hoax but an elaborate one.

Suspicious wiring snaked out of the dashboard, ran through the centre console between the front seats and disappeared through the back seat. As I inspected the boot compartment, I saw the wire was fed through the rear seat and connected to several plastic bags full of granular material. Improvised explosives are sometimes made from certain types of fertiliser. The fertiliser must contain ammonium nitrate and be mixed with some sort of fuel. A detonator containing a small amount of an explosive compound is set off, causing the ammonium nitrate to vaporise, releasing large quantities of oxygen. The detonation wave and the oxygen ignite the fuel, and BOOM! – you have a bomb.

Whoever had put the imitation explosive device together had done their homework because it looked like the real deal. It turned out that the plastic bags were actually full of gravel.

Anyway, thankful my insides were intact and not splattered over the rear wall of the garda station, we continued with our examination of the car. But I still couldn't believe we had been put in this situation. When I got back to Fingerprints, my colleagues couldn't believe it either. I don't care who you are or what you know, some shit has got to be left to the specialists, no matter how long it takes them to get there.

It wasn't until I was safely back at my desk, where the worst injury I could sustain was a paper cut, that another thought struck me. Had anybody told the poor, unsuspecting tow-truck driver exactly what he was hauling through the busy streets? I think not.

12

EXPERIENCE, EXPERIENCE, EXPERIENCE

Just keep swimming.

Dory, Finding Nemo

The Murder of Niamh Murphy

Seventeen-year-old Niamh Murphy was the adopted daughter of a respected family from Knocknacarra, near Salthill in Galway. In her early teens she began to rebel, came to the notice of the gardaí and the Western Health Board and spent time in a facility for homeless teenagers. She eventually made her way to Dublin and quickly found herself homeless.

This was when she met Phillip Reddin, also living on the streets. The two of them ended up living in squalid conditions in a derelict house in the affluent Ballsbridge area of the city. Several other homeless people shared the house on Pembroke Road.

On the morning of 10 May 2002, Reddin alerted the gardaí that he had discovered Niamh's body in one of the upstairs rooms. He led them there, where he hugged her lifeless corpse and told the members at the scene that he wanted to help find her killer. Niamh had been strangled, and her throat had also been cut with garden shears.

When I arrived at the scene, Niamh's body had already been removed. I assisted fingerprint expert John, who had attended the post-mortem and taken her fingerprints. Now we had the task of going through the house for any useful fingerprint evidence to find the killer. The process would be time-consuming because the place was an absolute tip, filled with rubbish and signs of a rat infestation.

John concentrated his examination on the room where Niamh had been found, bagging the shears and other items of note. I went about powdering the doors and windows in other areas of the house. I filled 34 lift cards with fingermarks taken from various surfaces and bagged quantities of papers, plastic bags, beer cans and the like for further examination back at the Bureau. It took us two days to get through the scene even with Declan, the crime scene manager, rolling up his sleeves and getting his fingerprint brush out.

Back at base, John and I chemically treated the exhibits taken from the scene and ensured the developed marks were photographed. I handed over my developed marks and lift cards to John as he was the expert on the job, but I gave him a hand searching some of them. We didn't glean much in the way of incriminating fingerprint evidence from the scene. I think there were several prints from different persons on the shears.

Within a month, Phillip Reddin confessed to gardaí that he was the perpetrator of the grisly crime. He believed hugging the body would account for any physical evidence that might be recovered from it. He told gardaí that he and Niamh had rowed over one of his previous girlfriends, and, in what always seems to be common in such cases, he had just 'snapped' and found his hands around her throat. After strangling her, he said he panicked and grabbed the shears and drew them across her throat at least twice. He knew that the shears had been handled by several people with access to the house, and was attempting to cover his tracks. He also stated that Niamh had been pregnant at the time of her death, but Dr Marie Cassidy disproved this in the post-mortem.

Dr Cassidy also stated that it couldn't be ruled out that Niamh was still alive when the five-inch incision was inflicted on her throat. Death, she said, was due to the combined effect of manual strangulation and the cutting of the throat.

At Reddin's trial, about a year later, it took the jury less than two hours to return a guilty verdict. Reddin was given the mandatory life sentence, and he died in prison in 2010 from a suspected heart attack aged 31.

The case stuck in my mind for a number of reasons. It was a stark reminder of the conditions that many homeless people find themselves in. Even in a built-up and prosperous area such as Pembroke Road, poor unfortunates lived a pitiful existence. You would never know, if driving or walking along that road, that right across from the American embassy, people like Niamh were living in filth and absolute squalor.

I also remember how tenacious I became during the investigation. During the scenes-of-crime search, I found a piece of cardboard in a room, which contained what I believed to be a portion of a palm print made in blood. I bagged the exhibit and had the mark photographed back at the Bureau.

John was busy with dozens of other marks developed from the scene, so I took it upon myself to tackle this particular mark. By this time, we had the fingerprints of many of the people who had access to the house, so I started to methodically compare the mark in blood to each set of prints. I remember it took me nearly two days to determine the section and orientation of the palm to be searched. After many painstaking comparisons, I identified it was made by an individual who stayed in the house from time to time.

It was the beginning of a period of my time in the Fingerprints Section when I started to develop something of a reputation as the 'go-to guy' for identifying difficult palm marks.

By that time, I was pretty much searching files full-time and building up a good amount of idents. I also completed the detective training course.

Much of the five-week course that took place in garda head-quarters was classroom-based, featuring lectures on interviewing techniques, criminal profiling, photo-fits and subversive criminals. We had a fascinating demonstration by the Garda Dog Unit, who brought along one of their cadaver dogs. The dog handler buried small pieces of pork in grassy areas at the back of the Bureau building; then, the dog methodically began searching and sniffing out each morsel.

Professor Harbison gave us an interesting talk, accompanied by many slides from a multitude of scenes he had attended as the state pathologist. We also had a fascinating talk and slide show by Inspector Brendan McCardle of the Ballistics Section. Each slide showed a murder scene, with the body in situ, and we had to use the visual information available to build a profile of the type of homicide that had been committed: sexually motivated crimes, opportunistic attacks and pre-meditated murders. It was amazing how much information can be gleaned from a scene just by knowing what to look for.

The second week of the course was held in Templemore. We had an intensive week of tactical training, not unlike the tactical training during phase five, but dialled up by several notches. We were shown how to quickly remove a person from a car by reaching in and undoing the safety belt and then, with the same hand, grabbing the suspect by their belt or waistband and yanking them out to the ground.

We did room entry and clearance exercises in Tac Town using revolvers loaded with plastic pellets that gave you quite a sting when hit by them. We also traversed an obstacle course with the instructors firing Uzi submachine guns above our heads (loaded with blanks, of course). With sky-high heart rates, we then had to run to the firing range and shoot at targets using live ammunition. I had to fire off six rounds, quickly reload, and fire another six. I was pleased with only two misses.

On another day, we were brought to the Devil's Bit mountain to practise car stops. The instructors were in a van, playing the roles of armed criminals. Two cars, with two members in each, had to overtake and box in the van, and then we had to draw our weapons and demand that the 'criminals' surrender. Sometimes, they complied; other times, they came out firing with those little plastic pellets zipping everywhere. It was great craic. I left Templemore after the detective training course and, thankfully, never had to go back.

The Murder of Susan Prakash

On the morning of 17 December 2000, a man in blood-soaked clothes arrived into the public office of Portlaoise garda station. James Conroy had driven a half hour or so to the station, parked his red HiAce van in the car park outside and went in to tell gardaí he had just killed 26-year-old Susan Prakash at an isolated picnic spot in the Slieve Bloom mountains near Camross, County Laois.

The Bureau got the call, and I was sent along to assist fingerprint expert Eddie. When we arrived at Portlaoise station, Conroy's van was still in the car park, and we could see blood spatter across the front of it. We arranged for the van to be put under cover for examination and headed to the murder scene.

A popular spot for courting couples, the scene in the Slieve Bloom mountains was virtually inaccessible without a vehicle. It struck me as a very isolated and lonely place for someone to die. I remember it being freezing as we suited up in our white coveralls. Ms Prakash's body was already protected by a scenes-of-crime tent erected by the local SOCOs.

As usual, the photographer made a visual index of the entire scene. Eddie, the ballistics expert and I laid down metal plates to walk on at the scene so as not to inadvertently tread on any evidence in the vicinity of the body. I remember noting that Ms Prakash seemed very small, little more than the height of a 12-year-old girl. A blood-stained wheel brace lay near her body, and a large amount of blood had pooled underneath and around her head. We recovered very little, apart from the wheel brace and a few strewn condom wrappers and plastic bags. I took the wheel brace from the scene, gave it an exhibit number, and arranged for it to be taken to the Forensic Laboratory.

The local undertaker was called to take the body to Portlaoise Hospital, where the post-mortem would later take place. When removing a body from the scene of a suspicious death or murder, it is of paramount importance that every scrap of evidence on or around the corpse is recovered.

I don't want to sound heartless, but in the context of forensics, the body is also considered to be an exhibit, and is often the most important one in such scenes. There are special body bags for such purposes nowadays, but in some of these earlier jobs, the Bureau team used large pieces of plastic sheeting. The body was carefully lifted onto the sheet as we took note of and recovered anything found underneath it. Then, the remains were securely wrapped in the plastic and fastened with tape so nothing could fall out. The wrapped body was then usually placed in a metal casket and transported to wherever the post-mortem was to be conducted.

Professor Harbison carried out the post-mortem in this investigation. It was quite a long one, as most post-mortems involving violent deaths are, and went on from 4.30 p.m. that afternoon until nearly 10 p.m. that night.

The next morning, Eddie and I headed back to Portlaoise to examine the HiAce van. The van had been moved to a garage in a disused petrol station just up the road from the garda station, and we spent the day and part of the night going over it for any fingerprint evidence.

This was December, and the old garage had no heating. Even using the photographer's large lights to warm the grubby surface of the van, we found very little in the way of identifiable marks. We bagged and tagged anything we needed to bring back for examination in the chemical room. Meanwhile, the ballistics expert took samples from the blood spatter on the front of the van and sketched how it was distributed. It transpired that Conroy had attacked Susan near the front of the vehicle.

It would be almost three years before James Conroy's trial for the murder of Susan Prakash began. Conroy was pleading not guilty, even though he had turned himself in on the morning of the murder. Eddie and I turned up at the Central Criminal Court with a rather slim case file, as not much fingerprint evidence was garnered from the scene or the van. Even the wheel brace hadn't yielded any identifiable marks. It was just one of those frustrating cases where, despite all our efforts, fingerprint evidence was not going to help the state prosecution. However, they were armed with plenty of other physical evidence, including blood and fibre evidence. A jury had been sworn in, and the trial was all set to start, but by lunchtime the court was told that Conroy had changed his plea to *guilty*.

At his sentencing, the court was told he had picked up Susan, the mother of two young children, and driven her to the isolated picnic spot. He claimed the pair had already known each other. Susan started to ask sex offender Conroy about his criminal past as he had done jail time for assaulting two boys and a girl who were friends of his family. He said that she had asked him if he was a child rapist, and he just 'flipped' and hit her with his fists. Then, panicking and believing that Susan would report him, he dragged her out of the van and beat her about the head with the wheel brace. He then drove away, and Susan tragically suffocated in her own blood. James Conroy was jailed for life.

I heard, arguably, the best story about revenge in the fingerprints workplace during another training course in January 2001, when four of us from the Fingerprints Section were sent to the UK forensic training facility at Harperley Hall in County Durham.

I joined two other Skerries natives, Rodney and Terry, along with another new section member, Martin, and spent two weeks on a Fingerprint Evidence Recovery and Recording Techniques (FERRT) course. The four English people on the course were also a good bunch, including one called Simon who told us a story about a particularly hard-assed supervisor in Fingerprints where he worked in the UK. This guy made Simon's working day miserable, always relishing the prospect of finding fault in his work and forever checking up on him, seeking errors.

One day, a car came into his fingerprint examination facility, and Simon had to do the usual powdering for marks and gathering of exhibits. He went about his task, finding and developing marks and retrieving any items for chemical examination. When he finished, knowing that his supervisor would check if he had missed anything, Simon wiped the car clean and got to work on a bit of crafty comeuppance.

Sure enough, not long after he had completed his job, the supervisor turned up and, looking for any reason to give Simon a hard time, started to powder the car again, hoping to find missed fingermarks. He worked his way around the vehicle and found nothing until he began applying fingerprint powder onto the bonnet.

The supervisor was beside himself with glee when an unmistakable thumbprint began to develop, and then another one. And another.

He must have thought that he was going to have a whale of a time berating the officer about sloppy work, but the more he powdered, the more a pattern started to develop. Not so much a pattern as *letters*, seven of them to be exact, which neatly spelt out *FUCK YOU*, right across the bonnet!

Simon had laboriously constructed those words thumbprint by thumbprint. We all thought this was a work of absolute genius, an unambiguous message crafted in a way only a fingerprint expert could conceive.

Drugs

We never welcomed the approach of a scientist from the Forensic Laboratory who was dragging several bags of plastic wrappings behind them. When large amounts of drugs were seized, a portion of the haul would go to the Forensic Laboratory for testing, and they would pass the wrappings to Fingerprints.

Examining drug wrappings was labour-intensive. Controlled substances such as heroin, cocaine, ecstasy and marijuana or hash were usually contained in plastic wrapping for transportation or for individual deals. Powdered substances, like heroin and cocaine, were mainly sold in individual deals in small plastic bags and, in the case of heroin, typically put into the corners of plastic bags, which were then knotted or heat-sealed.

The little baggies would have to be flattened out, resulting in developed fingermarks being fragmented. They only occasionally yielded identifiable marks. You might get lucky if bales of cannabis were packed together in cardboard boxes, as these boxes were excellent for retaining identifiable marks.

The most common type of drug that I dealt with was cannabis resin. This black or brown substance is typically pressed into blocks and wrapped in vacuum-sealed plastic with an outer wrapping of more plastic and adhesive tape. Again, these types of material were good for developing marks, if any were present. The problem was, unless the bales of blocks or bars had been opened on arrival in Ireland, any fingermarks that developed, and especially any developed on the inside of the wrappings, would have been made at the point of origin, perhaps in Pakistan or Afghanistan, so you would never get a hit on AFIS from them.

A Bureau team was called to the scene of a large seizure of cannabis resin found in a lock-up in Navan in April 2002. We had three vehicles to examine at the scene, and I had several prisoners to be fingerprinted at Navan garda station. The lock-up was found to contain six large cardboard boxes, each packed with bars of cannabis resin contained in their usual plastic wrappings. In total, there were 624 individual bars, each with a street value then of up to €5,000 – quite a haul. Back at the chemical section, I examined the boxes and a selection of the wrapped bars. Only 11 fingermarks developed from the lot, and none were identified, but as I've said, this was not unusual in drug cases.

With all these wrappings being regularly received from the lab, remnants of powder or little pieces of resin would sometimes fall out, so you had to be careful about what you might be inhaling. In the days before the smoking ban, it may have happened that tiny pieces of cannabis resin made their way into an ashtray on the window sill of the chemical room. The aroma was nice, and we enjoyed seeing heads turn, noses twitch and the suspicious glints or amused grins of some visiting gardaí.

On one occasion, I have to confess, some of us in Fingerprints even abused the drugs we stored, though not in the way people might assume. Our drug use happened during a torrential rain storm one night on a late shift. With no let-up in the deluge, rainwater started pouring into the basement of the Technical Bureau building under the emergency exit doors.

At the time, the basement was used to store older case files held in paper folders in cardboard boxes. All were prone to water damage. Fingerprints, the Forensic Laboratory and the Documents and Handwriting Section all had files stored in the basement.

As it became clear the entire basement was in danger of becoming flooded, many of us donned our garda-issue wellies and did what we could to rescue as many cardboard boxes as possible. However, as the water began rising to knee height, many files became totally waterlogged. Even years later, with the files dried out and safely stored in the archives at Santry garda station, many important documents and fingerprint lifts ended up stuck together and damaged irreparably due to water damage that night.

We soon realised we had a bigger problem. The Forensic Liaison Office stored all their exhibits in a secure basement area. At that time, I remember the motorcycle used in the assassination of journalist Veronica Guerin was still down in that lock-up. But this area also had an emergency exit through which water was steadily leaking.

As well as hundreds of exhibits from crime scenes, that section of the basement also housed large quantities of drugs pending court proceedings. When such trials were completed, the area was also used to prepare the drugs for destruction. The drugs were packed into special cardboard containers and loaded into vans every few weeks or months. Then they would be brought to a secure site to be incinerated under armed escort. These trips were known as nice little earners as they were always at the weekend, so members usually got overtime and subsistence allowance. I was never lucky enough to bag these excursions, which seemed to be sewn up among a select few in the Bureau.

With water continuing to pour in, there was a real danger that many exhibits would get damaged. With nothing else for it, the decision was made to make use of the many bales of herbal cannabis being prepared for destruction. Herbal cannabis, also known as hash, hashish, weed, blow, pot, ganja and grass, is made up of the dried leaves and flowering parts of the female cannabis plant and is typically packed into blocks or bales resembling tightly packed herbs. Thankfully, for our purposes, these bales were highly absorbent.

So we began packing bale after bale of perfectly good weed head-high and several bales deep into the flood water. The power went as we battled the elements, and we continued our task with only emergency lighting. However, it did the trick. The weed began soaking up the water, and the rain started to ease. Total disaster was averted, and we even earned praise from our chief super for using drugs as a novel solution to the problem.

The only downside is that when herbal cannabis gets wet, it stinks to high heaven. Long after that rainy night, the basement was humming with a funk best described as a cross between good silage and bad dung.

13

GIVE THAT MAN A HAND

Often, the hands will solve a mystery that the intellect
has struggled with.
Carl Jung

A balaclava-wearing assailant brutally attacked a man called
Declan Gavin outside an Abrakebabra fast-food restaurant in
Crumlin Shopping Centre, Dublin, in August 2001. Gavin was
stabbed several times and fled inside the restaurant, where the
door was shut and locked behind him. His attacker pushed
against the door, which was stained with Gavin's blood, but
could not gain entry and fled the scene. Gavin subsequently died
from his wounds.

Detective Garda Chris O'Connor of the Fingerprints Section
identified the palm mark as belonging to Dublin criminal and
Gavin's former friend, Brian Rattigan, and he was charged and
eventually convicted for the crime. Rattigan tried to explain away

the presence of his palm mark on the door by saying that he had visited that Abrakebabra outlet some months previously, but it transpired that the glass in the door had only been replaced the previous week and was cleaned by the staff every few days.

In more recent years, the identification of palm marks from crime scenes has assisted many investigations. However, in the early years of fingerprint identification, inked prints were classified by the 10 digits only, and there was no dedicated training in the recognition and classification of palm prints or the friction ridge detail of the second and third joint areas of the fingers. Many early fingerprint examiners were intimidated when faced with palm marks from crime scenes, and quite often, these marks were never used in any comparisons at all.

When I joined the Fingerprints Section in October of 1997, the Printrak AFIS 2000 system had been up and running for about a year, but it could not search for palm marks recovered from a scene or exhibit.

When dealing with palm marks, the most important step in carrying out a comparison is *orientation*. If the correct orientation of the mark is not deduced, then it becomes very difficult to determine what part of the palm you are actually looking at. So, if you are looking at a mark and have incorrectly oriented it so that you are looking at it upside down, for example, then it will be next to impossible to match it to a corresponding set of prints.

Palm prints, however, contain many clues that can be analysed so that a searcher can determine the area and orientation of a palm mark from a crime scene. All palm marks display a broadly similar flow of friction ridges, and all palms can be divided into specific areas.

The first of these areas is the *thenar* or thumb side of the palm. The ridges flow from above the thumb joint, proceed downwards in a roughly semicircular pattern and exit at the bottom. This area can sometimes show abrupt changes in the flow of the ridges, forming right angles and even shapes like a square-nosed loop. These features are called *vestiges* and are usually only found in this part of the palm.

The next part of the palm is the *hypothenar*. This is the area on the little finger side of the palm, below the crease. This wide-open area contains ridges in an uninterrupted arching formation but also can contain various looping formations. At the bottom of the palm, where the thenar and hypothenar meet, is the area known as the *carpal delta*. The carpal delta can sometimes be located higher up on the palm, thus affecting the ridge flow around it.

The final major area of the palm is the *interdigital*. This is the area at the top of the palm, just below where it joins to the fingers. This area contains a wide variety of ridge flows and pattern combinations, but it is full of clues for the searcher to determine which hand, left or right, has made the impression. The areas below the fingers contain delta formations resembling the letter 'Y'. The direction in which the tails of these 'Y's flow, particularly the 'Y' below the middle and ring fingers, is a good indication of which hand you are dealing with.

Another helpful feature when determining what part of the palm is being looked at is the creases. Some of these creases are permanent and form at the same time as the friction ridge skin. Many other creases develop over time as a result of the ageing process, and these too are useful clues. These features are many and varied, with names such as 'bracelets', 'starbursts', 'cross-hatching' and 'crow's feet'. The areas of friction ridge skin on the second and third joints of the fingers also have specific types of ridge flows, enabling an examiner to zone in on particular areas when carrying out comparisons.

The old Henry system of classification entailed a lot of time classifying patterns and counting ridges. A mark would be examined, and then the examiner would have to search through the National Collection, all sorted under the old classification system.

The advent of the AFIS system did away with all that, being more automated. AFIS still needs correct input from the searcher, otherwise it won't make any positive 'hits'. We'd scan fingerprints into the system and plotted friction ridge minutiae on the computer screen before launching a search. In only minutes, the system would spit out results of what it calculated as being the closest matches. AFIS also had the added benefit of storing any unidentified marks, which would be automatically searched against any incoming sets of fingerprints, often resulting in identifications or 'reverse hits' after some time had elapsed since the commission of the crime.

The only drawback with this early iteration of AFIS was that it did not allow palm marks to be searched on the system. Detective Inspector Myles Fitzgerald of the Fingerprints Section created a novel solution to the problem. He devised a system that made searching palm marks on AFIS possible once a searcher nominated the area of the palm they thought made the mark. This was achieved by dividing palms into 10 smaller sections and splitting them up between the 10 numbered boxes normally used to denote the fingers and thumbs. This method had some drawbacks, mainly relating to the fact that palm prints vary greatly in size, from petite hands to big shovel-like hands. Still, it was better than not having any palm-searching capability at all.

I treated examination of a tricky palm mark almost like a crime scene itself. I looked for all the clues that would determine the correct orientation, allowing for factors such as the elasticity of the skin, the differences in the pressure exerted and the shape of the object that was touched. As my reputation grew as the best guy to go to with a difficult palm mark, they often asked me to examine the tougher ones. I loved the challenge that palm marks very often presented, and if I felt I was on the right track or the mark was starting to 'twitch' for me, I wouldn't give up until I'd either identified it or was satisfied that it did not match against the prints that I was comparing it to. If there was sufficient clarity in the mark, and the details hadn't been too badly affected by pressure, dirt or distortion, then every palm mark could be identified, providing you had the correct set of prints to compare it against.

Identifying palm marks continues to make a valuable contribution to prosecutions. During the investigation of the fatal shooting of Garda Colm Horkan in Castlerea in June 2020, Detective Garda Rachel O'Malley identified a left palm mark found on Garda Horkan's gun as having been made by Stephen Silver. During an altercation with Garda Horkan, Silver had wrestled his garda-issued firearm away from him and had shot him multiple times. Silver was convicted of capital murder and sentenced to serve a minimum of 40 years' imprisonment.

Over time, with the ever-improving technological advances in systems such as AFIS, palm marks have become much easier to search. Sometimes, though, especially if there are suspects in a case, you just can't beat tackling a tricky mark with a good ol' hand magnifier, a well-informed eye for detail and a nice serving of patience and tenacity.

14

YES JUDGE, NO JUDGE, THREE BAGS FULL JUDGE

There is a higher court than the courts of justice, and
that is the court of conscience. It supersedes all other
courts.
Mahatma Gandhi

The Shirley McKie Case

Marion Ross was found dead in her home in Kilmarnock, Scotland,
in January 1997. She had been stabbed multiple times. David
Asbury, a handyman who had worked on the Ross house, became a
suspect. The Scottish Criminal Record Office (SCRO) identified a
fingerprint belonging to the victim on a tin box containing money
following a search of Asbury's home. Another fingermark found
on a Christmas gift tag in the Ross household was identified as
belonging to Asbury.

The SCRO also went through other fingermarks from the murder scene in the house and identified one as belonging to Shirley McKie, a constable in the Scottish police. At Asbury's trial, McKie testified that she had been one of many officers surrounding the scene but was told not to enter the house. She insisted it was impossible that her fingerprint was in the house as she had never set foot inside. Over 50 other police officers working on the case confirmed they never saw her in the house.

Her testimony implied that the SCRO were capable of making errors in fingerprint identification, raising questions about the reliability of the fingerprint evidence linking Asbury to the crime. Nevertheless, Asbury was jailed for murder in June 1997.

In 1998, Shirley McKie was arrested and charged with perjury, but in May 1999, the High Court rejected the evidence of the SCRO, and she was unanimously found not guilty. Two fingerprint experts from the United States gave evidence that McKie did not make the fingermark found at the scene. They testified that they believed that the SCRO had 'invented' some of the supposed matching ridge characteristics and had also marked up features in the fingermark that weren't characteristics at all but actually caused by the surface it was lifted from.

Four fingerprint experts from the SCRO had concluded, wrongly, that the fingermark belonged to McKie. So, were they all wrong?

The so-called 'Scotch botch' fingerprints scandal rumbled on. McKie quit the force in 2002, citing ill health. Meanwhile, Asbury, who was jailed for murder in June 1997, was released from his life sentence the same year after an appeal court decided that the fingerprint evidence in the case could not be trusted.

As a cloud hung over the forensic community, Allen and I headed to Durham again for a three-week advanced fingerprint course shortly after Asbury's release. Fingerprint evidence was the cornerstone of forensics, and we knew any refutation of its truth would have serious consequences, especially in the courts.

The focus of the advanced course was on courtroom presentation skills. Up to this point in my career, giving evidence in court still scared the shit out of me. Even though I didn't have to worry about custody records, charge sheets, summonses and the like, I still found getting up in the witness box to be a very daunting experience. This advanced course would strengthen and polish my courtroom skills to the standard expected from a qualified expert giving identification testimony.

The other six on the course included five civilian trainees (four from the UK and one from Bermuda) and a police officer from the Mediterranean. I was a bag of nerves on the first day as we started straight into the mock court exercises. When the instructor asked who would like to go first, I volunteered. I reckoned the best thing for me would be to get it over with quickly rather than waiting and getting more and more nervous. My legs shook as I took the stand – a lectern at the top of the classroom.

In the UK, you stand while giving evidence. It can be daunting at first because you feel more exposed and are more conscious of your posture and what you do with your hands. In Irish courts, you sit, and the only visible part is your head and shoulders, so you can fidget away or nervously tap your foot without it being seen.

My first mock court exercise went quite well, and I was only asked to give my qualifications and a brief explanation about fingerprint identification. I was glad I had gone first because the cross-examinations of the other class members became increasingly tough as the day went on.

An important skill when giving evidence is sticking to what you know and what is vital to the case. For fingerprint experts, this is the evidence of identification. This is the reason you are in court, so you should always circle back to the identification. The last thing a defence barrister wants is for you to repeat that you've identified their client's fingerprints at a crime scene, so they will try to steer you away from that.

Courtroom scenarios were somewhat easier to Allen, the chap from the Mediterranean and me because, as police, we were much more used to giving evidence and being exposed to judicial lingo. Some others had had little courtroom experience, so it took them longer to get into the flow of things. One lad was an absolute fount of knowledge about fingerprints and their history. He knew everything about the formation of friction skin and was also a bloody good searcher. His only problem was that he couldn't shut up.

A smart defence barrister can sometimes throw out a random statement or remark and then pause, hoping you will take the bait and start digging yourself into a hole. In these situations, the right thing to do is to say nothing or maybe remark to the judge, 'Is there a question here?' The golden rule is to say, 'I don't know' when you don't know the answer to a specific question. Stick to what you know, and always find a way back to the meat and potatoes of your evidence: the identification.

The course instructors had a field day with this chap. They polished his ego for a while, remarking on how knowledgeable he was, and then they led him down the rabbit hole. Before long, he was talking about stuff that had nothing to do with his evidence. When he wound up explaining to the mock court what Darwin's knob was (part of the ear, if you were wondering), the instructors had to stop. They had led him a merry dance, and he was wandering further and further away from what he should really have been talking about.

We had many courtroom practicals over the three weeks, and with each one, we got better. Well, most of us did. I worked on my stance, doing my best not to move about too much yet not to come across as too rigid. I used my hands to explain how friction skin assists in gripping things and heightening the sense of touch. I used generic enlargements of fingerprints to explain friction ridge characteristics and patterns. I worked on my explanation of the methodology of fingerprint identification, trying to be as informative as possible yet keeping it digestible for the layperson. The instructors were all experts themselves, so you couldn't bullshit them. Or talk about Darwin's knob.

All of us were concerned about a few topics that could possibly derail our evidence if pressed to talk about them. Chief among these was a defence solicitor asking what we knew about wrongful identifications.

We knew the Scottish case was sure to be brought up by any canny defence barrister trying to cast doubt on our fingerprint evidence. We were worried about how to handle the topic if or when it was raised. As usual, we were advised to stick to only what we knew about the whole debacle: that we were aware of the case, that we had not seen or examined the marks in question, and that if the correct methodology is applied in any fingerprint identification, then that evidence will be reliable.

Finally, we should constantly reiterate that in *our* case before the court, the evidence is correct. Always circle back to the evidence.

As this was still a few years before the two public enquiries published their findings into SCRO's procedures, the instructors were reluctant to make any definitive statements about what they believed had gone on. However, they indicated to us that they'd heard, through the grapevine, that some skulduggery had taken place. It was likely that a lot of peer pressure was applied to at least some of the supposed fingerprint experts involved. The whole 'Scotch botch' mess continued floating around the fingerprint community like a bad smell for years.

Eventually, a full inquiry into the case by the Scottish government found that the fingermark found at the scene was not McKie's. Not only that, they also noted that the fingermark found on the tin box in Asbury's home, which was identified as belonging to the victim, Marion Ross, wasn't made by her either. The Fingerprint Inquiry believed there had been no conspiracy on the part of the SCRO, yet you had two wrongful identifications in the same case made by the same supposed fingerprint experts. No wonder it cast a lasting shadow over the entire fingerprint community.

Many of us on the course were also worried about inadvertently revealing an accused's previous convictions in court. Many fingerprint identifications are made by matching a crime scene mark to a set of legally held fingerprints in the National Collection. Fingerprints are taken under various legal acts when investigating crime or when a person is sent to prison. The mention of such sets of prints may indicate that a person has previous convictions, and the defence will jump all over this, saying that such evidence is prejudicial to their client.

Again, the instructors' advice was simple. The judge, the prosecution and the defence know how fingerprint identifications are made. A 'hit' is made against a set already in the collection (unless a suspect's prints have been supplied specifically in relation to the charge before the court), the ident is verified, and the investigation team is informed. A new set of prints is then taken from the suspect, and it is this set that is used to demonstrate the identification in court.

To explain the process, you must be careful how you word things. Semantics are very important. The initial hit is regarded as confidential information communicated to the investigation team from a reliable source. If pressed by the defence on the matter and the jury is present, we were advised to indicate to the judge that there may be a problem with answering that question. The judge will know what's going on and will usually ask the jury to step out while the matter is clarified. In the District Court, where there is no jury, then it is a more straightforward matter. In any case, once again, the advice is to steer things back to your identification evidence and reiterate that the fingerprints before the court were taken in relation to that specific case.

The final area where we needed expert guidance was the issue of 'transplanted' marks and identifying when the fingermarks were made – their age. Sometimes, the defence will try to suggest that their client's fingermark was planted at the scene and will quiz you about the possibility of this having happened. Yes, it is possible to transplant a fingermark, but the steps and logistics involved are so convoluted that the chances of carrying it out successfully are practically zero.

Firstly, you would need access to an object with the person's latent (invisible or hidden) fingermark on it. Then, you would have to successfully lift that mark using lifting tape or another method like a gel lift, not knowing if you've captured the mark or if it contains enough detail to identify it. Then you would have to do one of two things: either travel to the crime scene and place the lifted mark on some surface, again, not knowing if there is sufficient detail in it or even if it will be found by the SOCO examining the scene; or you would have to transplant it onto some object and then place that object at the scene in the hope that it will be found and examined. Phew! Yes, transplanting can be done, but only in controlled laboratory conditions, and it is usually possible to detect if a mark has been transplanted by its poor quality and possible indications showing the use of a previous lifting method.

During the course, we got to have a go at transplanting fingermarks in the classroom, but the results were quite poor. It helped to build our confidence when tackling the subject during our courtroom exercises. Sure, you can agree in court that transplanting a fingermark is possible, although quite difficult. Again, we were advised to steer it back to our experience and expertise: 'In my opinion, the identified fingermark before the court was not transplanted in such a manner. The only transplantation that occurred was when the mark was developed at the scene or on the exhibit and lifted by means of fingerprint lifting tape and placed on the fingerprint lift card.'

We also sought some clarification regarding the ageing of fingermarks. Sometimes, you might get asked in court how long the fingermark could have been there. Well, the truth is that there is no way to determine the age of a mark. There are too many variables involved. For example, what sort of surface was it deposited on? Was it open to the elements? Was it made in sweat? Or blood? Or dirt? Also, people perspire differently. Some people may excrete a lot of sweat, while others leave barely any. All these factors combine to mean that a fingermark cannot be reliably aged. The only way to determine the rough timeframe of when a mark was made is by having other supportive evidence. In the murder of Declan Gavin, where Brian Rattigan's palm print was identified on the restaurant door, evidence was given that the glass had only recently been replaced. The glass was also cleaned regularly, so the palm mark could only have been left in the short timeframe since the last cleaning. Another example would be if a mark was found on a newspaper. The mark could only have been left on it since the date the newspaper was printed.

A few years later, I gave evidence in a District Court hearing concerning a burglary in which a DVD player had been stolen. The burglar had unplugged the player from an adaptor plugged into the wall, and the SOCO examining the scene developed a lovely thumbprint on it, which I subsequently identified. The hearing was in the District Court in the old Richmond Hospital in Grangegorman in Dublin, which was a much more pleasant environment than the old district courts beside the Bridewell garda station. This was before the construction of the new

Criminal Courts of Justice (CCJ) at the junction of Parkgate Street and Infirmary Road.

Being a District Court case, there was no jury. It also meant that the defence barrister had free reign to try to muddy the waters concerning my evidence. The District Court is where I've experienced the most challenges to my expert evidence as a fingerprint and, later, a handwriting expert. They can pretty much ask you anything.

So I gave my evidence of identification, detailing my findings in the usual way: 'In my opinion, the thumbmark found on the plug adaptor was made by the same person that made the right thumbprint impression on the set of fingerprints bearing the name *Joe Bloggs*.'

The defence accepted that it was indeed his client's thumbprint. He then asked me how long the mark was present on the exhibit. I answered that there is no definitive way to age such a mark. Still, it was my opinion – my qualified opinion – that the mark appeared quite fresh and contained a good deal of identifying characteristics, and I believed it hadn't been there for a long time.

The barrister then stated that the mark might have come to be on the adaptor because his client had been browsing in an electrical store and may have picked it up, inadvertently leaving his thumb mark on it. It was a plausible, if unlikely, theory. However, the prosecution had done their homework. The homeowner was called into the box and testified that the plug adaptor had been in the house for years. It was an old house, and the electrical fittings used old-style circular-pin plugs, which were scarce by then. On top of this, it was verified that *Mr Bloggs* was a foreign national who had only been in Ireland for a short period.

The judge had heard enough. The fingerprint identification evidence was sound, and it simply wasn't believable that the suspect happened to pick up an ancient adaptor while out browsing in electrical outlets. *Bloggs* was convicted and, as is quite typical, got off with a slap on the wrist. I didn't mind. I'd done my bit and, by that stage of my career, hadn't yet reached the point of full-on cynicism concerning court proceedings.

Before our final mock court examinations on the advanced course, members of the Crown Prosecution Service (CPS) arrived to put us to the test with tricky cross-examinations. I was first up against the CPS. Once again, going first worked in my favour as they went pretty easy on me, gradually upping the pressure on everyone else that followed.

Then came the day for the final mock court examination. We had already done the final searching assessment, which I was pretty confident about. I would be last to take the stand, so there was no need for me to turn up to class until the afternoon. After going over the notes of my mock case file, I donned my suit and headed down to the training centre to face the music.

External fingerprint experts were called in to assess us. I took the stand, took the oath, and got stuck in to my evidence. I explained to the court, as clearly as I could, the methodology of fingerprint identification using photographic enlargements and charts for reference. I fielded any awkward questions thrown at me and kept returning to my evidence. The whole thing didn't seem to last very long, but I was over half an hour on the stand, and when I finished and stepped outside, my shirt was stuck to me with sweat.

I didn't have to wait long before they started calling us individually into the instructors' office to be told whether we had passed. First up was Mr Darwin's knob. As expected, the examiners had led him on a wild goose chase. They had thrown out the crumbs, and he had gobbled them up, babbling and waffling and moving further and further away from his identification evidence. His prowess at searching marks and vast knowledge of all things fingerprint-related couldn't help him keep his mouth shut. He didn't pass.

Unfortunately, the chap from the Mediterranean was next and didn't pass either. He had given an excellent final courtroom presentation, but missed too many idents in the practical searching exam. Allen was called in before me. After about five minutes, he returned to the classroom with a big, goofy grin from ear to ear. He had passed. Of course he had passed. Allen was always cool under fire. Totally unflappable. Then it was my turn. I don't really remember what the instructors said, but I went into that office as a trainee and came out as a fingerprint expert!

I was deemed competent to produce my own fingerprint identification evidence in court. Up to this point, any idents that I made would be handed over to a fully qualified member of the section to prepare a fingerprint chart in court. Now, I would have to get the photographic enlargements of the identified mark and the corresponding print on the fingerprint form and do my own charts.

The chart is an important aid used to demonstrate the identification to the judge, the barristers and the jury. Irish courts still operate under the old numeric system, so a chart must be prepared to show a minimum of 12 ridge characteristics in coincident sequence in both the identified mark and the corresponding print. If required, the fingerprint expert can use the chart to demonstrate the matching ridge endings, bifurcations and so on to the court. It is also helpful to have some generic enlargements available to illustrate the different types of fingerprint patterns that are encountered.

Preparing comparison charts came naturally to me as it tapped into my artistic skills and eye for precision. All comparison charts had to be approved by the head of the section before they could be used in court.

Having been under fire from qualified fingerprint experts for three weeks on the advanced course, I felt equipped to tackle any future stints in the witness box. I was no longer terrified of court and even found that I enjoyed giving evidence now. When it came to fingerprint identification, I knew I would be the most qualified person in the courtroom. If I stuck to my guns about the veracity of my findings and kept circling back to the evidence no matter what the defence threw at me, then I'd get through it.

Of course, I couldn't afford to be complacent when it came to court. One always remains nervous before giving evidence, and it is important not to come across as nonchalant or arrogant. You could never be sure what might be hurled your way during cross-examination, so it was a case of being ready for anything, regardless of how straightforward your evidence seemed. I guess it comes back to that old saying: 'Fail to prepare, prepare to fail.' It was always disappointing if a conviction wasn't secured in the end, but at least I always left the courtroom knowing I did my best and put across my testimony in a professional and coherent manner.

As well as becoming a fingerprint expert, I was now regarded as an expert when examining crime scenes. I would no longer assist another fingerprint member at crime scenes; instead, the buck would stop with me. I didn't have to wait long before I was sent out on my first couple of jobs as a newly minted expert, and they both turned out to be interesting and memorable, for totally different reasons. By now, I also had the added responsibility of becoming a parent, as my son Orin was born in 2001.

15

OFF THE LEASH

Although nature commences with reason and ends in experience, it is necessary for us to do the opposite, that is to commence with experience and from this to proceed to investigate the reason.
Leonardo da Vinci

Fatal Fire – Drogheda

The body of a man was discovered after a fire in a run-down house on a quiet residential street in Drogheda during the winter of 2002. The deceased, who was in his thirties, was found in the front room on the ground floor.

I was among a team sent to the scene of the blaze the following day. As fire was involved in the death, Seamus and Geraldine from the Ballistics Section were part of the team, with the former acting as the crime scene manager. Martin from the Photography Section was also with us.

The fire was not extensive, so the house was still intact but full of smoke damage. As soon as Martin had taken his initial photographs of the scene, I approached the front door and was immediately assaulted by the odour. It was horrific, a mixture of the usual smell of death that I'd become somewhat accustomed to, coupled with the awful stench of cooked flesh.

Even with my face mask securely fastened over my nose and mouth, I could get the odour. I stepped through the front door and turned right into the front room. Behind the door, to my left, the deceased's body sat on a dilapidated old couch, fully clothed and sitting bolt upright. I could see that neither his body nor the couch were burnt or singed by flames. Instead, it appeared as if he had been ... cooked.

I noticed bunches of partially burnt papers strewn in the corner of the front room. More blackened papers were found in the kitchen leading off from the front room, and others were on the stairs. With the considerable smoke damage, finding fingerprints would be difficult, so I just bagged what I could for examination back at the chemical room.

Martin snapped away with his camera while Seamus and Geraldine went through the scene to ascertain how the fire had started. They deduced that there had been three 'seats' or origins of fire: in the sitting room, where the body was located, in the kitchen and at the foot of the stairs.

There was no sign of a break-in or that a struggle had taken place. All the windows had been shut, which meant less oxygen to feed the fire. Instead, the fire had burned slowly, generating smoke and fumes and building up an enormous amount of heat in the front room, turning it into an oven. The unfortunate man had been sitting in this oven and had likely died from smoke inhalation. Smoke restricts the flow of oxygen into the body and also contains lethal toxic substances. The immense heat in the room would have caused the soft tissue and muscles to contract, which also caused the joints to flex. As a result, the body had taken on what is referred to as a 'pugilist' pose, with the knees bent and the arms curled up at the elbows. This would make it more difficult to remove the body from the scene.

When the undertaker arrived, I noticed the two more seasoned Bureau members, Seamus and Martin, were suddenly engaged with investigating gardaí outside. They left it to Geraldine and me to bag the body. As soon as we went to move the deceased, a blast of noxious gas escaped from his mouth, followed by a small torrent of body fluids, which Ger took the brunt of. The smell was almost overpowering, but we continued with the grim task.

We knew taking a break outside would be pointless because we'd only have to return and face the stench again. We had a difficult time manoeuvring the limbs into a straighter position because the muscles and soft tissue were so contracted. However, we finally got it done, and the undertakers could remove the body to the mortuary in Our Lady of Lourdes Hospital, only a short journey away.

We finished our examination of the scene, with Seamus and Martin now miraculously back by our sides, and headed to the hospital for the post-mortem. It would be the last post-mortem I would attend with Professor John Harbison as the examining pathologist.

The mortuary at the Lourdes Hospital was small. It adjoined a tiny morticians' office, where I had to wait hours for the examination to finish so I could print the body. This meant that there was no escape from the stifling smell. I remember the walls of the morticians' office were covered with a collection of 'colourful' postcards showing different sorts of naked bodies from the ones that usually occupied the examination table next door.

A small chapel was located down the corridor for mourners to pay their respects to their dearly departed. As the post-mortem was going on, a group of bereaved people gathered for a relative lying in repose there. There was no way that these poor people would not have noticed the awful aromas wafting up from the post-mortem nearby. The smell was still infused into my clothes and hair (back when I had hair) when I got home late that night, and it took a lot of scrubbing to clear it.

When Professor Harbison finished with his examination, I went in to take a set of prints. This proved difficult because the heat of the fire around the body caused the fingers to clench into fists. I asked Professor Harbison if he would cut the tendons in the backs of the hands so that the digits would be easier to manipulate. He duly obliged.

A local SOCO, Tom, gave me some much-appreciated help in obtaining the prints. He held the hands and extended each finger while I took the inked impressions. Picture the scene: the deceased was lying on the table, still opened up after a thorough internal examination. Tom was closest to the corpse, holding a hand for me when he felt something touch him on the deceased's side. He leapt three feet in the air, thinking the body had moved. It took him a few seconds to realise the mobile phone in his pocket was vibrating. It was a welcome moment of levity during a grim task.

The results of the post-mortem showed that the man had died as a result of smoke inhalation. He also had a significant amount of alcohol in his system. It couldn't be ascertained whether he had deliberately set the fires to commit suicide or, with no central heating in the house, he had lit a few small fires to keep warm and had fallen asleep. I'd like to think that he felt nothing as those fumes overwhelmed him.

Hush, Hush

A few weeks after attending the Drogheda fire scene, I was working the late shift, beavering away on a few case files. My skipper, Brendan, received a phone call from the superintendent in Clondalkin, requesting a Bureau team for a top-secret mission. I was selected as the fingerprint representative. Brendan had no information for us besides instructions to meet with local gardaí and armed support units at a private dwelling in Clondalkin. What was going on?

Off a few of us went, without a clue as to what lay ahead. We were met at the scene by local gardaí, members from the National Bureau of Criminal Investigation (NBCI) and plain-clothes members from the Emergency Response Unit (ERU). Information had been received that stolen property was stowed in the attic of the house. The gardaí had already searched the address and had arrested the two occupants. The Bureau had been called to facilitate the removal of the stolen property and to gather any useful evidence.

Stolen property? What sort of property required armed support and such a degree of secrecy? We made our way inside and were shown the entrance to the attic. It didn't take a genius to figure out that we were dealing with something of significant value, hence all the cloak-and-dagger stuff. The photographer, Liam, climbed the ladder and took video footage and photographs of what he saw there. Then, the ballistics expert, Mick, and I had a gander. Near the attic trap door, I could see several rectangular shapes wrapped in sheets and secured with tape.

That's when the NBCI members told us they suspected the items in the attic were paintings stolen months earlier from Russborough House in Blessington, County Wicklow. Russborough House was home to the Beit Collection, which contained many priceless works of art. This was the most recent of several robberies in which criminal gangs had stolen paintings from the collection. Martin 'The General' Cahill had masterminded a previous heist in 1986.

Very carefully, we removed the wrapped items from the attic. There wasn't a lot for me to do from a fingerprint point of view, as the suspects who had been arrested lived at that address and would have legitimate access to all of its nooks and crannies. I still examined the entrance to the attic and removed the trap door so I could examine it properly back in the chemical room. My colleague also removed an imitation firearm tucked away in the attic.

Then, we headed back to the Bureau under armed escort and brought the five wrapped packages down into the secure ballistics lock-up in the basement. An art expert came to the Bureau to verify if what had been found were indeed the stolen paintings from the most recent Russborough heist. My colleague and I carefully removed the sheets covering each item, with me retaining the adhesive tape for further fingermarks analysis. Then the art boffin had a good look.

It only took him a few minutes to confirm that the five paintings were the ones that had been nicked in September of that year. They were as follows: *The Cornfield* by Jacob van Ruisdael, *The Adoration of the Shepherds* by Adriaen van Ostade, *A Calm Sea* by Willem van de Velde, *Venus Supplicating Jupiter* and *Portrait of a Dominican Monk* by Peter Paul Rubens.

They were all dated from the seventeenth century, and the art expert estimated their value to be €18.5 million. No wonder we'd had an armed escort! He described them as being both *priceless* and *valueless* at the same time, as whoever had stolen them would never be able to sell them legitimately.

The artist in me couldn't help but be impressed. I got to hold two works by the famous Flemish artist Rubens, painted almost 400 years previously. But if I could have nabbed one of those paintings for myself, it might have been *Venus Supplicating Jupiter*. It would have looked splendid hanging above the fireplace.

It was a surreal experience to see these works of art laid out on the floor of the armoury, surrounded by guns of every size and make. Needless to say, I didn't take out my fingerprint brush and look for marks. My examinations would be solely on the tape from the wrappings and the attic door.

The man who lived in the house where the paintings were found was charged with handling stolen property, and his wife was charged because of her knowledge that the stolen property was present. Both made full admissions. While no identifiable marks developed on the imitation firearm, I did manage to identify fingermarks from the attic door as the homeowner's, so at least I could fill in an entry in the ident book.

Our top-secret mission was a nice break from the usual scenes of death and destruction, but not long after my brush (sorry!) with fine art, I would be back examining scenes of violent crime and my first murder scene as a fingerprint expert.

16

THE GRUDGE

To punish someone for your own mistakes or the consequences of your own actions, to harm another by shifting blame that is rightly yours; this is a wretched and cowardly sin.
Richelle E. Goodrich

The Murder of Raymond Sallinger

Gardaí received a tip-off in 1986 that led to the detection of a drug-dealing enterprise in Fairview in north Dublin. Christy 'the Dapper Don' Kinahan was caught red-handed with a large quantity of heroin and received a relatively lenient sentence of six years in jail. Kinahan believed that an associate, Raymond Sallinger, had been the one who ratted him out, and he waited 17 years before he exacted his revenge.

Even though he wasn't the source of the confidential tip-off, Sallinger fled Ireland in fear of Kinahan's retribution and lived in

London until late 2002, only returning to Dublin because his wife was dying from cancer.

On the night of 28 January 2003, Raymond Sallinger was supping pints and watching football on the television in Farrell's pub on New Street in the south inner city. A few minutes before 10 p.m., a masked man walked into the pub and shot him a number of times before making his getaway. Paramedics rushed to the scene. They worked on Sallinger as he lay in a pool of blood before bringing him to hospital, where he succumbed to his wounds.

The following morning, I packed my fingerprint kit into an unmarked Bureau car and drove the short distance to Farrell's, meeting the rest of the team at the scene. You might think that a murder in such a public place is a risky undertaking for any would-be assassin. Still, if the trigger man has transportation to ferry him to the location and spirit him away, and he takes precautions not to be recognised, then it presents few problems for a determined killer.

The victim is caught off-guard, with no way to escape, and nobody is going to try any heroics with an armed man. In the immediate aftermath, there is shock and confusion, enabling the attacker to slip away. It only takes a matter of seconds to carry out the job. Of course, things can sometimes go terribly wrong for the gun man, as was the case on Christmas Eve 2023, when Tristan Sherry opened fire with a machine pistol in Browne's Steakhouse in Blanchardstown just after 8 p.m., hitting Jason Hennessy a number of times. Before he could make his escape, Sherry was overpowered by associates of Hennessy and was beaten and fatally stabbed. Jason Hennessy died in hospital 11 days later.

From a fingerprint point of view, the scene at Farrell's pub was likely to generate any number of fingermarks, but few, if any, would be of much use from an evidential point of view.

With the body waiting for us at the Dublin City Morgue in Marino, we went through the scene as best we could. The patrons had abandoned numerous unfinished drinks and I went through the motions, examining glasses left on the bar and the tables. Thankfully, it had been a relatively slow night in Farrell's. I later identified many of the marks from the various individuals drinking there, but it's not an offence to skull a pint.

I also examined the exterior windows in case a spotter had been peeking in prior to giving the signal that Sallinger was inside, but found nothing useful. A detective from Kevin Street garda station handed me two spent bullet casings retrieved from the floor near the body, and I passed these on to the ballistics expert at the post-mortem. We returned to the scene when the post-mortem was completed, but there wasn't much in the way of useful physical evidence.

Days later, it was my day off, and I had an NCT test for my car. Patches of ice made the roads hazardous, and I drove carefully to the NCT facility off the Ballymun exit on the M50. My phone rang as I was about to return home. It was work, and they needed me to come in. The getaway car used in the murder of Raymond Sallinger had been located, and they needed it to be examined.

I drove straight to garda headquarters and met up with Mark from Ballistics and Derek from the Photography Section – two top blokes. The car, a navy Audi A4 Quattro, had been brought to the garage at Kevin Street garda station, so the three of us headed there, where we met Detective Inspector Gabriel

O'Gara, overseeing the investigation. The detective inspector brought us out to the garage, where the recovered vehicle awaited us. He told us that an attempt had been made to burn the car, but the would-be arsonist had made a crucial mistake. He had left the windows and doors shut, and the fire quickly burnt itself out because of a lack of oxygen. This was a stroke of luck for us because the interior was largely intact, apart from some smoke damage.

While Mark went about taking fibre lifts from the seats, I examined the exterior and interior of the car and removed the false registration plates for examination back at the chemical room. I also removed the plastic container used for the petrol that the would-be arsonists splashed over the car seats. Most promising of all was a crumpled piece of a *Daily Star* newspaper lying on the driver's seat. It was partially burnt and had most likely been lit and thrown into the car in the hope of igniting the petrol and destroying the whole vehicle. But the culprit had slammed the door shut and walked away, and with the windows firmly closed, the fire had fizzled out. Newspapers are excellent for retaining latent fingermarks, so I bagged the *Daily Star*, hoping it might contain some good news for the investigation and me.

Back at the chemical room, I got to work examining the various items I retrieved from the car. The registration plates and the plastic container did not yield anything of use, but I was banking on the newspaper to give me something. Whoever had set the fire assumed the paper would be completely destroyed, so maybe they handled it without wearing gloves.

The friction skin surfaces of the hands and feet contain the body's highest density of eccrine sweat glands. While the function of sweat on the rest of the body is to remove waste and cool the skin through evaporation, the glands found on the volar surface of the hands and feet emit sweat to increase friction, thereby reducing slippage. These sweat glands are more active when a person is nervous or in a 'fight or flight' situation. Eccrine sweat is composed of approximately 99 per cent water and 1 per cent solids. These solids consist of inorganic salts like sodium chloride and organic compounds like urea, amino acids and peptides. When a person touches a surface, the pores of the friction skin may leave a residue of sweat, depositing a latent or 'hidden' mark.

The most commonly used method to develop latent finger marks on porous surfaces like newspaper is a chemical called ninhydrin. Ninhydrin reacts with the amino acids in sweat, producing a pinkish-purple stain. You draw the item to be examined through the ninhydrin solution and allow it to dry before placing it in a special oven where you heat it at around 80 degrees Celsius in a humid environment of around 70 per cent.

I treated the newspaper from the car and put it in the oven for around 15 minutes. As I'd hoped, some lovely clear marks popped up, including one I deduced as a left thumb. When you look at fingerprints long enough, you recognise the particular shapes of certain digits. Thumbprints are quite distinct, being wider than the rest of the fingers and possessing distinguishing ridge formations at their tops. The flow and direction of the ridges help indicate whether they came from the right or left hand. I was confident that the thumb mark that had developed was a left thumb. I labelled the mark with my initials and the case number and had Derek photograph it for me. Before long, I had a nice photograph of the mark to search on AFIS.

By this time, it was late in the evening, and the AFIS suite was relatively quiet. I grabbed a spare screen and used the small camera on the desk to capture an image of the mark. I now had a high-definition image of the scanned fingermark on the screen. Now, I had to plot in the ridge characteristics by clicking on them and dragging the cursor in the direction of the ridge flow. The more clearly the characteristics were plotted, the more information AFIS would have when running a search through the database.

As it was a clear and well-defined mark, I had no trouble plotting in plenty of ridge characteristics. I nominated the pattern and told AFIS to search for left thumbs only by inputting the digit as a number '6' (left thumb). Just to cover all the bases, I also fired off a search without a nominated digit, but I knew that if AFIS was going to 'hit', it would be a left thumb.

Within five minutes, the unique search number appeared in the queue of returned searches. I clicked on it, and up popped an image of the developed mark and an image of the left thumbprint from the top of the list of the 30 respondents that AFIS had selected. I knew straight away that it was a hit. The score was through the roof, but I still scrutinised the images to ensure that the ridge characteristics were in agreement. I didn't click the 'ident' tab on the screen just yet.

First, I went down to the other end of the section to retrieve the inked set of prints from the collection. I couldn't help but be excited as I waited for the carousel to trundle around to the shelf I wanted. Each set of prints carries a unique number, identifying which batch it is in and what number it is in that batch. There are one hundred sets of prints for each batch, and if a person has been printed more than once, then any subsequent sets of fingerprints are given a check digit and filed together with the earliest set.

I selected the box containing the batch I was looking for and leafed through the sets of prints until I came to the one I needed. There it was. Now, I had a name to go with the thumb. But first, I had to make it official. I brought the set of fingerprints back to my desk in AFIS and did a one-to-one comparison with the mark from the newspaper. There was no doubt. It was an ident. I then nabbed two other experts from the late unit, and they took their time making their own comparisons. They were both in agreement with me; the mark on the newspaper was made by the left thumb of a man called Martin Cervi.

Martin Cervi was a close associate of the Kinahans and served as a facilitator, sourcing drugs and firearms for the cartel. He was also a friend of Gerry 'the Monk' Hutch, who had put in a good word for him with the Kinahans. Cervi would later assist Hutch with property deals in Portugal when Hutch was trying to raise extra cash to fund his impending feud with the Kinahans. This feud spiralled out of control after the murder of David Byrne in the Regency Hotel in 2016.

I informed Detective Inspector O'Gara about the identification, and one of the fingerprints sergeants said I should call to the chief super's office and give him the good news too, which I did.

Exactly one month later, I was asked to come down to Kevin Street garda station, where Martin Cervi was being interviewed following his arrest as part of the Raymond Sallinger murder inquiry. The investigation team wanted me to put the fingerprint identification evidence to Cervi to see if he had any explanation for how his thumbprint had come to be on the newspaper found in the getaway car. It took all of three minutes. I placed the evidence bag containing the newspaper on the desk before him and informed him of my findings. I told him I was satisfied beyond doubt that he had made the mark and asked him if he had anything to say. Cervi replied in the same manner as he had to many of the previous questions put to him by the interviewing gardaí: 'I've nothing to say.' That was it. I'd done my part. All that was left was to prepare my identification evidence for production in court – if, that is, Cervi was charged.

As it turns out, he wasn't. Although the investigation team was satisfied that because of the fingerprint evidence, coupled with other enquiries and confidential information received, Martin Cervi and his associates were involved in the murder of Raymond Sallinger, the Director of Public Prosecutions disagreed, and no charges were brought against Cervi for the crime. With links to both the Kinahans and Gerry Hutch, Cervi could have sided with either when the feud erupted some years later, but he didn't live long enough to make the choice. Martin Cervi died in the Netherlands in 2016 from a suspected heart attack.

I was still pleased. My first murder investigation as a fingerprint expert had resulted in an ident, which only raised my confidence and further cemented my conviction that I was doing the job I was meant to do. I was now ten years into my career, and finally felt that I was an important cog in the machinery of An Garda Síochána.

The murder of Raymond Sallinger remains unsolved, but his violent end was one of the earliest deaths attributed to the Kinahan cartel. It helped solidify the gang's reputation for ruthless violence and their long memory for vengeance upon anyone whom they perceived had wronged them.

17

SHANNONSIDE

Urbs Antiqua Fuit Studiisque Asperrima Belli – There was an ancient city very fierce in the skills of war.
From the Limerick Coat of Arms

Who would have guessed that a schoolyard fight between two girls would result in up to 20 murders, as well as many more stabbings, beatings, arson and pipe bomb attacks? One of my first cases in my role as a fingerprint expert was a fatal stabbing in February 2003. A vicious feud was in full swing in Limerick city during this period, sparked by a schoolyard fight between the daughters of Christy Keane and his associate Eddie Ryan, which ended in one girl being slashed in the face.

Both men were involved in the drug trade in the city, and the row between their daughters escalated into a bitter falling-out. An attempt was made on Christy Keane's life as he sat in his car while waiting for his kids to finish school. The assassin's gun jammed, and Keane took swift revenge. Two nights later, as Eddie Ryan sat in the Moose Bar, two men entered and shot him dead.

The Ryan family joined forces with the McCarthy-Dundon gang in an attempt to wrestle the drug trade away from Keane, who had partnered up with the Collopy gang. The Keane-Collopy gang operated out of St Mary's Park in the north of Limerick city, and the McCarthy-Dundon faction was based less than 4 kilometres away in Ballinacurra Weston, south of the city. The ruthless and bitter feud would turn both areas and many other parts of Limerick into a battlefield.

Outside of Dublin, I travelled to Limerick city more than any other place during my years in the Bureau. While I spent countless hours cooling my heels in the courts of our capital city, I also clocked up many miles attending court hearings and trials in the Treaty City. It reached the point where the state car I drove could have made the journey on autopilot, such was the regularity of my visits to Limerick's District and Circuit Courts. I headed into this melting pot on two jobs in the spring of 2003. Neither of them was actually connected with the feud, but I remember them well for different reasons.

The Killing of Edward Cully

Edward Cully's body was still in situ when I arrived at the scene of a fatal stabbing at Merval Crescent, Clareview, in Limerick city. The young man, just 18 years old, had been stabbed to death at a house party at the address on 9 February 2003. I arrived hours later to see the teenager's body lying on the floor in the kitchen.

Nineteen-year-old Keith McMahon had been arrested for the crime a matter of hours after the teenager's death. He had been among a group of youths, including Cully, drinking and taking drugs in the house. McMahon told the gardaí that a slagging match had got out of hand and that he hadn't intended to stab Cully, just to frighten him. Yet, two other youths present who gave evidence at the ensuing trial said a row had broken out, and McMahon had jumped up from the table, grabbed a knife from the kitchen worktop and stabbed Edward Cully several times.

We waited at the scene for the assistant state pathologist, Dr Margot Bolster, to arrive so she could carry out a preliminary examination of the body. This typically involves taking the body temperature with a rectal thermometer, measuring the atmospheric temperature, and examining the body for rigor mortis.

I remember very little blood at the scene, but this is not unusual with stabbings, as often the bleeding can be mostly internal. After the body was removed to a Limerick hospital, we attended the post-mortem, returning to the scene around 6 p.m. I bagged numerous bottles and cans as well as some blister packs of various tablets from the kitchen table. Those who had been present in the house had legitimate access, which meant that any fingermarks I discovered wouldn't make or break the case. The blood-stained knife with which McMahon had carried out the attack had been thrown into the sink, with the handle submerged in water. I knew this would lessen my chances of getting any identifiable fingermarks. Sure enough, when the Forensic Laboratory returned the knife a few days later, none were found.

The job was straightforward and didn't require an overnight stay in Limerick. The team, who included Eadaoin the photographer and Mick from Ballistics, headed back to Dublin, stopping off at Treacy's bar outside Portlaoise for a slap-up steak dinner, along with a couple of pints for those not driving, to celebrate my thirty-first birthday that day.

Mules are often quick to resort to derogatory terms when talking about people involved in criminal activity. It's a fact that many homicide victims may have a connection to crime. The unfortunate victim in this case, however, Edward Cully, was only regarded as a talented footballer who had even played for Ireland at under-14 level.

As Eadaoin and I sat supping pints at the bar, Mick, an absolute gentleman, said something that stuck with me for the rest of my time in the Bureau. He said that the victim in a murder investigation can never tell us what happened. Not verbally, anyway. But as crime scene investigators, it is our duty to glean as much information as possible from the scene and the body. Then, in essence, we are there to speak on behalf of the deceased, regardless of who they were while alive. It is an immense and important responsibility, no matter what the ultimate outcome of the investigation might be.

Sometimes, as with the scene at Merval Crescent, there just isn't much in the way of useful fingerprint evidence to be gleaned. The murder weapon had been flung in water, and everyone present had legitimate access to the house, yet it was still my duty to carry out a thorough examination. It can be frustrating when you feel like you have nothing constructive to give to the investigation team, but I always remember what one of my old sergeants used to say about it: 'You never *expect* to find anything. All you can do is *hope*. If something is there, you'll find it. If there is nothing, then at least you'll know you still did your job to the best of your ability.'

The Murder of Katelyn Ryan

Robert and Jacqueline Ryan awoke to find their terraced family home in Limerick full of smoke on 6 April 2003. They scrambled to get seven children – five of their own and two other kids staying over for a slumber party – out of the house on Lenihan Avenue in the Prospect area of the city.

Five children escaped through a rear window. Jacqueline could hear her infant daughter crying in the front bedroom but couldn't see anything because of the thick smoke. She groped around, found the 1-year-old and, clutching her in her arms, she jumped from the upstairs window, injuring her back. Her husband escaped through the same window. However, in the smoke, chaos and confusion, 4-year-old Katelyn Ryan was left behind.

When the fire brigade arrived and entered the house, they found Katelyn in her parents' bedroom. She had crawled into the bed, but when the flames and smoke overwhelmed her, she had fallen to the floor. She was found lying between the bed and the wardrobe. They took her to hospital with third-degree burns over 75 per cent of her body. The child was still in critical condition when I arrived as part of the investigation into the arson attack at the house. The investigation took place two months after the killing of Edward Cully.

The Bureau team also consisted of Liam from Photography and Geraldine from Ballistics. Tensions were high in the Prospect area, one of many flashpoints in the city in the feud between the Keane-Collopy and McCarthy-Dundon gangs. As a result, disconcertingly, we had armed protection at the scene. The local super and the detective inspector filled us in on the background of the incident.

The fire broke out at approximately 7 a.m. We could see extensive fire and smoke damage throughout the house, and the firefighters had thrown a lot of household furniture and other items out the windows as they fought to bring the blaze under control. There was practically nothing left for me to examine for fingermarks, so I assisted Ger as she carried out her examination to determine the seat of the fire. She found traces of accelerant inside the front door, so she was satisfied that this was where the conflagration had started. The fire had spread from here, with the stairs acting like a funnel for the smoke and flames.

This tallied with the information that the gardaí were getting from 22-year-old Patrick Slattery, who was already in custody. Slattery told gardaí that he was getting harassed by Katelyn's 14-year-old brother. After being slagged by his friends over his trouble with the teenager, Slattery said he 'just snapped'. Taking a can of petrol from the garden shed behind his house, he went to Lenihan Avenue, poured the petrol through the letterbox and set it alight before running away. He said that he had not intended for anyone to get hurt and just wanted to scare the 14-year-old Ryan boy.

While sifting through the debris in the front garden, we came across the mattress from the bedroom above, where Katelyn was found. We could see one small area on top of the mattress that the fire hadn't scorched. We surmised that this was where little Katelyn had been cowering until the fumes or flames got to her. It was a harrowing thing to picture in your mind.

Two days after the fire at Lenihan Avenue, Katelyn Ryan died, having never regained consciousness. Patrick Slattery was subsequently charged with her murder.

In February of the following year, I returned to Limerick for the Edward Cully murder trial, accompanied by Eadaoin from

Photography. I hadn't much in the way of evidence, but the defence counsel still gave me a grilling. He tried to make a big deal out of numerous little tablets left behind on the kitchen table at the scene of the stabbing.

I calmly informed the court that my role was to find or develop fingermarks at the scene, and, in my expert opinion, no such evidence could have been gleaned from tiny little pills. After I said this, he let silence hang in the air, waiting for me to add more. I said nothing. He gave the jury a flamboyant swish of his robes and an exasperated 'harrumph!', before adding, 'I have no further questions.'

Keith McMahon was later convicted of the manslaughter of Edward Cully and was sentenced to 12 years, which was later reduced to eight by the Court of Criminal Appeal.

By coincidence, that was also the same day that Patrick Slattery was given life for the murder of Katelyn Ryan. Two unlawful deaths. A stabbing and a death caused by arson, yet the ultimate findings of the court and the sentences doled out were different. It was just another example of the fickle nature of the justice system. I was present in court when Mr Justice Paul Carney handed down Slattery's sentence and witnessed angry scenes in court with Katelyn's family shouting at Slattery as he was led away. I couldn't help but think about that mattress we saw in the garden on Lenihan Avenue. The image of the unburnt section in the shape of a little girl has stayed with me over the years.

18

THE SWITCH

There will be nightmares. And every day when you wake up, it will be the first thing you think about. Until one day, it will be the second thing.
Raymond Reddington, The Blacklist

As a member of the Technical Bureau, I was exposed to a lot of gruesome stuff, although far less than many of my colleagues. The bloodier aspects of the job never really bothered me. It didn't affect my work, and I never brought it home with me. There were times, however, when I'd take a step back and say to myself, 'Just what the fuck am I doing?'

One March morning in 2003, Niall from Fingerprints and I had to go to Dublin City Morgue in Marino. The facility had moved there after the old City Morgue was demolished in 1999 and was then housed at the O'Brien Institute off Malahide Road, on the same campus where fire brigade members were trained.

A badly decomposed body had been found in undergrowth in the Phoenix Park. Foul play wasn't suspected, and it appeared that the deceased had been living rough. No identifying material was found on the corpse, and dental records had drawn a blank. We were tasked with obtaining a set of fingerprints in the hope that the body could be identified.

The morgue was quieter than usual that morning. Typically, any time I had to go there, it would be for a post-mortem pertaining to a murder or suspicious death, so you'd have the pathologist, morticians, Bureau members and investigating gardaí all hovering around. That morning, the mortician brought us to the otherwise empty examination area, opened one of the large drawers and slid out the black body bag. Then he wished us luck and left us to it.

Bodies kept in a morgue are stored in positive-temperature refrigerators at around 2 degrees Celsius. This does not stop decomposition but slows it, meaning the body can be stored for a few weeks. Negative-temperature refrigerators are used in forensic institutes and freeze the body completely – a process that allows them to keep the corpse for much longer.

When the body had been found, it was already in an advanced state of decomposition. So, when we opened the bag, we were greeted by remains comprising little more than black mush in a roughly human shape. Partial mummification had occurred too. This can happen if a body has lain for a considerable time in a cold environment that remains relatively dry. As you can imagine, the smell was powerful, so I tried taking shallow breaths only. The body remained clothed, as any attempt to remove clothing would have caused the whole corpse to come apart. There was also a smattering of little white maggots and a whole smorgasbord of fleas and mites. Thankfully, most of the critters were dead.

There was no way we were going to obtain an inked set of prints because the skin was too moist, and the outer layer of friction skin had come away from the body. I decided to use Mikrosil in the hope I could glean at least some identifiable marks. Mikrosil is a forensic casting material and is excellent at capturing fine detail. As well as taking fingerprint casts, it can be used for tool mark impressions and impressions from the firing pins in guns. It only takes a short time to set as well.

Niall assisted me as I mixed the Mikrosil putty with the catalyst using a spatula and then applied the mixture to the tips of the fingers I judged to be in the best condition. We managed to obtain two fingerprint casts that I reckoned were identifiable, then we zipped up the bag and, task completed, stepped out for some much-needed fresh air. By now, it was nearly lunchtime, so we stopped off at a nearby filling station for a couple of hefty all-day breakfast rolls.

As we sat in the car, munching on rolls as big as your forearm, it struck me how easily we could deal with something so harrowing and still head off afterwards for grub. I had been in the Bureau less than five years and was already used to dealing with blood and guts and gloop. It wasn't that I was becoming blasé about such things, or even trying to be 'a hard man'. No, it's always more of a case of being able to compartmentalise this stuff. To do the job, you need to be able to flick a 'switch' in your head from *normal mode* to *prepared for fucking anything and plough on mode*.

Sometimes, the switch might not work, or you have to flick it a few times before it clicks. I've seen it with everybody I've worked with on crime scenes; the job needs to be done, and once you get over the initial shock of the nastiness in store, the investigator instinct kicks in and you zero in on the collection of whatever type of evidence you are looking for.

I remember having to go to the lock-up in Santry in connection with a murder investigation in Tallaght, where the victim was shot through the glass patio front door of his house. When I got to the lock-up, another Bureau team was examining a car at the centre of another investigation. The interior of this car was completely covered with clotted blood and brain matter.

A man called Victor Murphy had been the front-seat passenger in the car and had been clutching a sawn-off shotgun in his hands. Murphy and the other occupants of the vehicle were possibly heading for a confrontation with another group they were feuding with. As they sped through a Finglas halting site, the car hit a speed bump, and Murphy, whose thumb was resting on the trigger, discharged the shotgun, hitting himself in the face and decorating the inside of the car. His 'mates' then dumped him at Dunsink Lane and abandoned the vehicle.

I was taken aback when I saw the state of the car interior, but my old mate Allen was the fingerprint expert on the job, and he and the rest of the team were already in full-on investigation mode. They were attempting to work out the angle of discharge of the shotgun based on where Murphy had been sitting and the pattern and distribution of the blood and tissue. They were in the zone; switches firmly clicked to work mode despite the gore around them.

Different people have different ways of dealing with the assault to the senses that comes with crime scene investigation. I think it's important to talk about it with the rest of the team and, if necessary, with professional counsellors. Gallows humour and toughing it out will only take you so far. There is also the danger of seeking solace in alcohol, which was prevalent in my early years in the Bureau, considering the widespread drinking culture in the job back then.

Of course, when I started in the Bureau, there were no dedicated counselling services, and if you spoke about how some of the grisly stuff was affecting you, some of the dinosaurs would consider it a weakness. Thankfully, all that has changed, and professional counselling is offered to all garda members who deal with shocking or disturbing events.

Many people find an outlet for relaxation by playing sports, walking, hiking, reading or gardening – anything that focuses the mind or distracts from experiences that can test the limits of mental endurance. I love reading, drawing and painting, or I de-stress by firing up a game console. I always tried to come home with my switch flicked back into *normal mode*.

I guess that's what happened as Niall and I chowed down on our rolls after our trip to the morgue. While obtaining partial prints from the body, we were totally invested in the task. The sights and smells were partially filtered out because we had flicked that switch. Now, as we sat having our lunch, the normal world came back into focus. The switch was on 'normal mode' until we needed to be in 'work mode' again.

Men and women in An Garda Síochána are typically employed in their positions for decades. Many of them, including Bureau members and SOCOs all over the country, are constantly exposed to stuff outside the experiences of most members of the public. In police forces in other countries, people can often only stay in these roles for limited periods, reducing the risk of issues caused by the stressful situations they handle. While this is a laudable policy in some cases, it also means regularly training new staff. The cumulative years of experience in An Garda Síochána's crime scene investigations is worth its weight in gold. In my opinion, as long as proper supports are in place, it should be up to each individual to decide when it's time for them to move on.

For many years, one of my colleagues in the Bureau fulfilled his duties professionally and meticulously. He had many investigations under his belt and experienced some truly awful scenes without a problem. Then, one particular job got to him. The switch malfunctioned, and he needed to step back from the frontline and get the proper help.

He was intelligent enough to know when he needed to look after himself, and everybody was supportive. The way he told it made a whole lot of sense to me. He said he tucked away the horrible things he witnessed at crime scenes in a little matchbox in his head until there was no more room in the box. He was fully transparent about seeking help for himself, which has to be applauded. He also made a full recovery and returned to full duties afterwards.

When I left the morgue, and after Niall and I had polished off the breakfast rolls, I brought the Mikrosil casts from the unidentified body back to the Bureau, where I used them to make inked impressions. I had these photographed, and the images were reversed left to right before running searches of them through AFIS.

This proved challenging. In normal friction skin, the ridge details are part of the top or outer layer of skin, the *epidermis*. However, the body's decomposition meant most of the epidermis was gone. So, the prints came from the inner layer of the friction skin, the *dermis*. The epidermis is attached to the dermis by a series of peg-like formations called *dermal papillae*. These pegs fit into pockets on the underside of the epidermis, forming parallel rows underneath the friction ridges. The dermal surface takes on the negative shape of the bottom of the epidermis.

So, I had to plot the ridge characteristics on AFIS, bearing in mind that what would have been an individual ridge on the epidermis was now represented by *two* parallel rows of dermal papillae. I also had to plot around the inked impressions of a few unfortunate fleas encased in the Mikrosil. It took some time, but I was finally satisfied that I had the points plotted correctly and ran numerous searches through AFIS. There was no match. I left the prints for a few days, returned to them with a fresh pair of eyes, and replotted the detail again, but I still had no luck. A short time later, I attended the Coroner's Court to give evidence that no fingerprint identification had been made. As far as I know, the body was interred without a name.

Almost a year later, I was sorting through some stuff at work and came across the inked impressions I had made from the casts. I decided to give it one more shot. To my surprise, I got a hit. I retrieved the set of prints from the collection to verify the ident, and it turned out that they belonged to an English man. It was quite an old set of prints, and they had been in the collection for years, but AFIS hadn't hit on them in my earlier searches. It was a good reminder, particularly with difficult fingermarks, that it's always advisable to run multiple searches and perhaps to let other experts search them too, as even very slight variations in the plotting of the ridge characteristics can mean the difference between a hit or a miss.

Once I had verified the ident, I passed the information through the relevant channels. I can only assume that the deceased was finally given his rightful name and that any family or relatives were informed.

19

THE TIGER

If there is any human tragedy, there is only one, it occurs when we forget who we are and remain silent while a stranger takes up residence inside our skin.
James Lee Burke

An old acquaintance of mine came calling in 2004. After I left Howth garda station and joined the Bureau, I had been too busy with fingerprint training and crime scene examination to make time for this old companion. However, now I had settled into my stride as an expert, I once again felt the hand of depression resting on my shoulder.

A favourite author of mine, James Lee Burke, often referred to the evil in the world using William Blake's tiger, from the poem 'The Tyger', 1794, as an allegory. That tiger was out there, padding around in the jungle, waiting to pounce on the unsuspecting. I've heard depression being referred to as a black dog that follows you around, but for me, I prefer that image of the tiger. You can't see it because of the thick canopy of life, but you know it's there. Sometimes you can hear it breathing or the undergrowth crackling under its huge paws, and on really bad days you can smell its musk and feel its hot breath on your neck.

Depression is different for everyone who suffers from it. You could say that it's as unique to each individual as your fingerprints are, and like fingerprints, it persists throughout your life.

I'd like to think that there is much less of a stigma attached to depression these days because, after all, it's no different than suffering from asthma or diabetes or any other long-term condition. However, it can be much more difficult to diagnose. Everybody gets down. We all can feel shitty from time to time, but depression is different. It can be crushing and debilitating, sucking the joy out of everything. It can also be incredibly infuriating because you can't understand *why* you feel so crap.

For me, it comes in waves. You're riding the crest one moment, then sliding down the other side into the doldrums. I get tired and lethargic. I lose interest in doing what I love, and everything seems grey. I feel like I'm carrying a lead weight around in my stomach. I get angry at myself and become irritable around other people, and all I want to do is crawl into bed and pull the covers over my head until the next wave lifts me back up, hoping that when it does, my time in the sunshine will last a bit longer.

I guess I've suffered on and off with depression since my late teens. I remember noticing something wasn't quite right on an absolutely beautiful day while walking in St Stephen's Green during my lunch break from the Murakami-Wolf animation studio. All around me, people were enjoying the sunshine and lazing on the grass, chatting with friends, but I felt like a bag of damp shite. I had to bite my lip to prevent myself from bursting out crying, and I was both furious and scared because I just didn't know why this was happening. The wave passed, the tiger wandered off, and I was my usual self again before long, but it was the first time that I realised it was possible to be depressed while being a perfectly normal 18-year-old lad with a good job, great family and no worries.

When I joined An Garda Síochána, I was usually too busy with training or pints excursions to drop my guard long enough and let the low mood seep in. Still, it would grip me from time to time. In the following years, when things were slow in Command and Control, or I was alone on nights as station orderly in Howth, I'd look up and see the tiger's breath on window glass. *Hey boy, don't forget me.*

By 2004, I had been an expert for two years with most of my courses and studies behind me when the old depression started coming back with more regularity. These black moods usually happened when my brain and hands weren't busy or engaged in productive work – like when I didn't have a heap of exhibits to examine or I had long periods searching files without getting a hit. I would feel tired all the time. Often, I'd come home from work and go to bed for a few hours, even in the summer, when I'd hear the sounds of my son Orin and his little cousin Gemma playing in the garden.

I finally went to my GP for the official diagnosis and started taking the first of many different antidepressants that would be prescribed over the years. These medications did take the edge off, but it can take a long time to find the right one, and I had a few blips along the way.

I had a bad reaction to one in particular. It started with this feeling of dread creeping up on me as I drove to work. It sounds bizarre, but I could *hear* my eyes moving in my head. When I arrived into work, I headed for the quiet of the small room in the chemical section where we kept the Quaser. Try as I might, I just couldn't shake the anxiety and trembling. I realised I was having a breakdown at work.

I telephoned the office upstairs and asked my good friend Glenn to come down to me. I couldn't even find the words to explain what was wrong, and broke down crying. Glenn fetched my skipper, Brendan and another good mate, Jimmy, and they rallied around me. Jimmy drove me home, with Glenn following in my car. It was over a month before I was fit to return to work, but I was immensely grateful for the kindness and understanding that my work colleagues afforded me.

I eventually found a concoction to suit me, but antidepressants aren't a cure. They don't stop depression. It still drops on me from time to time, but for me, antidepressants cushion the fall.

Around this time, the unthinkable popped into my mind – *was I happy in my job?* I loved working in Fingerprints, and even the more gruesome aspects of the work didn't bother me, but I wasn't feeling challenged anymore. I had been in the Bureau for nearly seven years and had become an expert when I was thirty. I still had a minimum of 20 years' service left. Could I see myself doing the same job for the next two decades?

This uncertainty was also coloured by other factors coming to the fore in the Bureau. It was a transitory time in the Fingerprints Section. The section had many senior staff who, unlike me, had gone through a different training regime from the intermediate and advanced courses in Durham. Many old-timers had been there for 20 years or more, and the rest of us 'new bloods' were still considered junior. The old and the new were completely different breeds and clashed from time to time.

Promotions within the section led to one or other factions having their feathers ruffled. This was compounded when the statutory retirement age for members was extended from 57 to 60 years. This meant the next generation would have to wait longer for promotion, as some 'dinosaurs' held on until the last minute. It didn't bother me as I had no intention of going for promotion, but it did cause tensions with younger members who were ambitious for a supervisory role.

It was also around this time that the first tendrils of a tenacious creeping vine started to wrap themselves around the foundations of the Technical Bureau. The International Organisation for Standardisation (ISO) is a Swiss-based, independent, non-governmental organisation established in 1946, which has around 170 countries as members. The ISO is everywhere, with over 25,000 'standards' across every conceivable industry – transport, environment, health, manufacturing, energy, aircraft, food, clothing and agriculture. From prosthetic limbs to the threads on screws, if it exists as a product, then ISO has a 'standard' for its production.

To quote from their website, ISO 'brings together experts to share knowledge and develop voluntary, consensus-based, market-relevant international standards that support innovation and provide solutions to global challenges'. Very noble. Having ISO accreditation looks very impressive on any company's resume. Of course, such certification isn't free and can cost anywhere between a couple of thousand euros and tens of thousands.

After three years of crossing t's and dotting i's in the prescribed manner, the Bureau was awarded ISO 9001:2000 accreditation in 2004. The accreditation was for a Quality Management System, which I won't try to explain. Let me refer to the blurb from the website: 'ISO 9001 is a globally recognised standard of Quality Management that helps organisations of all sizes and sectors to implement their performance to meet customer expectations and demonstrate their commitment to quality. Implementation of ISO 9001 means your organisation has put in place effective procedures and trained staff to deliver flawless products or services time after time.' Again, very nice, but don't piss down my back and tell me it's raining.

Call me a Luddite. Call me a cynic. But it's my opinion that what initially started as a nice accolade for the Bureau quickly turned into a monster. Every year, in the run-up to the annual ISO audit, multiple Bureau members were tied up organising the reams of paperwork pertaining to the running of each section so that when the assessors descended from the clouds with their beatific smiles, they would grant us a stay of execution and outline 'suggestions' for how we could do better the following year before departing on their golden chariots.

While I agreed with the principle of setting standards to ensure a proper service was provided to gardaí investigating crime, I could see that slavish adherence to ISO dictates was only generating more paperwork – much more paperwork – and that only negatively affected our role as a national support service.

But ISO was here to stay, and like a teenager trying a joint of hash for the first time, the 9001 accreditation was the gateway drug for even more labour-intensive pencil-pushing. In my opinion, getting this accreditation was slowly becoming more important to some management sections than the Technical Bureau's actual duties.

As I was only a detective garda with no lofty ambitions about going for promotion, any complaints I had about the whole ISO saga would have fallen on deaf ears. So I just carried on doing my job as best I could and tried not to let it annoy me too much, but it was sometimes very difficult to keep my mouth shut. I was taking medication that helped with my depression, and I'd also gone for some counselling, which was helpful. The tiger would circle from time to time, sometimes venturing close to my campfire, but I could usually scare him back into the jungle. I just had to make sure that I didn't run out of flaming torches.

I needed to keep busy, to stay focused. As Captain Willard says in *Apocalypse Now*: 'Everyone gets everything he wants. I wanted a mission. And for my sins, they gave me one.' Or two.

20

THE DEEPEST CUT

It's a hell of a thing, killing a man. You take away all
he's got and all he's ever gonna have.
Clint Eastwood, Unforgiven

Entering the white scenes-of-crime tent, I was shocked to see the
levels of violence that had been inflicted on the body. The scene
was horrendous, even for a crime scene expert. The man was lying
face down, his head brutally caved in. His blood and bits of brain
matter were matted in the grass around him. I could see many
injuries and what appeared to be deep defensive wounds on the
hands. We would soon learn the victim had been attacked with
at least two different weapons, most likely a knife and a heavier
object like a hatchet or an axe. His body bore 17 different cuts,
stabs and chops. He also had multiple fractures to the skull as a
result of blunt force trauma, and his throat had been slit from ear

to ear. It had been a ferocious and sustained attack. A literal case of *overkill*.

In my 10 years working in the Fingerprints Section, I was involved in numerous murder investigations and suspicious deaths. Some of these involved the use of firearms, but far more prevalent were crimes in which the victim suffered sharp force injuries. Crimes of this nature involve injuries produced by pointed objects or objects with sharp edges, resulting in the traumatic separation of tissues and the underlying organs.

Sharp force injuries can be split into three categories: stab wounds, incised wounds and chop wounds. A stab wound is made in a direction that is perpendicular to the skin surface, and the wound is deep rather than long. Implements such as knives, forks, scissors, screwdrivers or any cylindrical object with a pointed tip can inflict these wounds. The elasticity of the skin and flexibility of body tissues and organs make it possible to have a five-inch-deep wound made by a three-inch blade. Stabbings are not always bloody. The entry wound or wounds are usually quite small, and quite often death is caused by massive internal bleeding.

Incised wounds are made tangential or parallel to the skin surface, producing wounds that are long as opposed to deep and are typically made by knives, razors, box-cutters or broken glass.

Finally, chop wounds are a combination of sharp wounds and blunt force trauma and are inflicted by bulky or fast-moving objects with sharp edges, like hammers, axes and hatchets.

In 2005, I went on three jobs in which the victims died from sharp force injuries, and remarkably, all three tragic cases shared another bizarre feature in common.

The Murder of Liam Moloney

I arrived at work on Saturday, 12 February 2005 at 5 p.m. just as a request came in for a Technical Bureau team to travel to Ennis, County Clare. There had been a murder. I was nominated as the fingerprint expert, so I hit the road, sharing a car with Aidan, who was to be the crime scene manager.

It was dark when we arrived, and as the scene was outdoors, we wouldn't get to it until the next morning. Instead, we went to Ennis garda station, where we spoke with Superintendent John Kerin, who was in charge of the investigation. The body of a man had been found on the grounds of Port House, a vacant property near the village of Ruan, about six miles from Ennis. The man's identity hadn't been established, but the super wasn't ruling out the possibility of the death being linked to the Limerick feud that was still in full swing. He said there were extensive injuries to the body, and it looked as though the man had been tortured before he was killed.

We headed to our digs in the Two Mile Inn, a popular spot for gardaí on the road until it closed in 2010. We went to the bar and met up with members from the National Bureau of Criminal Investigation (NBCI), who had also been called out for the murder investigation.

I remember quizzing the detective superintendent from NBCI about the investigation into the murder of young mother Rachel O'Reilly, which had happened the previous October and was still very much in the media spotlight. He wouldn't say much on the subject but indicated the investigation team were awaiting the mobile phone *pinging* information. That information ended up playing a vital role in Joe O'Reilly's conviction for the murder of his wife Rachel O'Reilly two years later.

The next morning was bitterly cold. The team met with the super at Ennis garda station, and he updated us on new information gathered overnight. The dead man was believed to be a local hackney driver called Liam Moloney, a separated father of four who had recently retired from Aer Lingus and had lived in a flat in Barrack Close in Ennis.

His maroon Mazda 626 had been found parked up near Considine's bar in Barefield, just outside Ennis. An attempt had been made to burn it, but like with the car from the Raymond Sallinger murder, the windows had been shut, so the fire hadn't taken hold. It seemed whoever killed Mr Moloney and dumped his body out at Port House had then driven back to Considine's and tried to destroy the car. Considine's was on the way to where the body was located, so that was going to be our first stop.

We arrived at the location and approached the abandoned car. We couldn't see inside because of the smoke damage, and we didn't touch the exterior or try to open the doors. Aidan knew we would have a lot of work ahead of us, so he arranged to have the car transported back to Dublin to be examined by a separate team.

We headed out the Cragaweelcross road in the direction where the body had been found. The scene was pretty much in the middle of nowhere, with nothing but fields and the odd farmyard. We arrived at the stone-walled entrance leading to Port House and saw the white scenes-of-crime tent that had been erected over the body several yards beyond. We suited up, and even though we'd been forewarned that the victim suffered extensive injuries, I was still shocked when I got my first good look at Liam Moloney's body. During an examination of the victim, we saw his trouser pockets had been turned inside out.

Deputy state pathologist Dr Michael Curtis then arrived at the scene, and he examined the body in situ before it was removed to the Mid-Western Regional Hospital in Dooradoyle, Limerick for the post-mortem.

During the lengthy examination of Mr Moloney's body, Dr Curtis noted all the different cuts and chops and deduced he was killed by at least two different weapons, one of which must have been a hatchet or axe. He observed that the man's throat was cut and that there were multiple fractures to the skull.

Back in Dublin, the victim's Mazda was being examined by the second team, and it had been noted that the radio Liam Moloney had used for calls in his work as a hackney was missing from the car. A knife had been found in the vehicle and was being examined to determine if it had been one of the weapons used by the murderer.

By this time, the Divisional Search Team had been deployed and were fanning out around the main scene, looking for the radio. The ballistics expert and I also searched a cattle yard with a slurry pit close to the scene. We were considering having it drained before we had a stroke of luck. Superintendent Kerin had called out to the scene to see how the search team was getting on, and while he was walking along the road, he spotted the missing radio caught in the branches of a roadside ditch. It was retrieved for examination back at the Bureau.

By speaking with Mr Moloney's last customers, it had been ascertained that he had been killed sometime between 7.30 p.m. and 8.30 p.m. on the Friday night.

Later that evening, we were called to Mr Moloney's flat in Barrack Close. His keys had not been found, and it looked like his attacker might have returned to the address to look for money or valuables. Some members from NBCI spoke with the security man at Barrack Close, a gated development with a CCTV camera covering the entrance. The security footage from the camera showed a man entering the complex about an hour after the presumed time of the murder. He was obviously aware of the camera and carried an umbrella to shield his face. He had entered Mr Moloney's flat and was seen leaving eight minutes later.

We searched the flat but found little sign of any disturbance apart from a wardrobe that appeared to have been rifled through. By this time, I had a set of fingerprints taken from the body during the post-mortem, and any identifiable marks that I developed all belonged to the deceased.

By early the next day, information began to trickle in regarding a possible suspect. Several witnesses reported seeing a man in Ennis who was known to Liam Moloney. Some witnesses also reported that this man supposedly owed the deceased money. His description matched that of witnesses who had seen a man acting suspiciously outside Barrack Close in the hours prior to the murder. He was also seen making a call from a payphone in the town on the day of the murder, which I also had to examine. Another witness came forward who said that they had seen this man burning clothes in the back garden of his rented house near Ballinskelligs in Kerry. The suspect's name was Anthony Kelly.

Gardaí from both the Clare and Kerry divisions, backed up by members from NBCI, descended on Kelly's house on 24 February. He was arrested following the discovery of a stolen sawn-off shotgun in the house. Before long, he admitted his involvement in the murder of Liam Moloney.

He said that he had arranged to meet Moloney at Considine's bar on the night of the murder. Kelly asked Moloney to drive him to Ruan, saying he was meeting his girlfriend there. They set off for Ruan, with Kelly sitting in the back seat behind the driver. When they approached the entrance to Port House, he asked Liam to pull over into the gateway, and that was when he viciously attacked him from behind, slashing and stabbing with the knife and bringing the axe head down on his skull repeatedly. As a final coup de grâce, he slit the poor man's throat. He also told gardaí that he had enlisted the help of a 15-year-old youth to help him clean the axe head and meat cleaver used in the attack. He instructed the boy to get rid of the weapons. After gardaí conducted searches in and around Caragh Lake and Rossbeigh Beach, the weapons were recovered. They arrested the boy for withholding information.

Kelly admitted to the killing but denied murdering Liam Moloney. As a result, fingerprint evidence did not come into play. The case hinged on whether the accused was insane at the time of the murder.

At Kelly's trial for murder in 2007, Dr Michael Curtis told the court that the injuries inflicted on Mr Moloney were likely caused by implements produced by the prosecution: the axe head, the meat cleaver and the knife that had been found in the car. It had an eight-inch blade.

Anthony Kelly said that he had felt possessed and heard voices telling him to kill the hackney driver. It was true, at least, that Kelly was a fantasist. While he had been living in America, he had faked his own kidnapping in a bid to extort money from his uncle, and on the night of the murder he told Liam Moloney that they were going to meet a Swedish girlfriend, who didn't exist.

However, the jury didn't buy the insanity story, and Anthony Kelly was convicted and received the mandatory life sentence. The motive for the savage murder of Liam Moloney was plain old greed. Kelly believed that the murdered man had a significant amount of cash in his flat, perhaps from when he received a lump sum upon his retirement from Aer Lingus. All that Kelly found was €600 and the few quid he had pilfered from the dead man's pockets after he had dumped him in an isolated laneway on a cold winter night.

The killing of Liam Moloney was the most brutal murder scene investigation that I was ever involved in. To kill a person with a knife is an up-close-and-personal assault. The victim's personal space is violated in the most heinous way, with the perpetrator close enough to get their unfortunate target's blood on their hands and even to feel the brush of their final breath as life leaves them.

The Murder of Raymond Browne

In the early hours of 2 April 2005, paramedics were called out to a house on Clonshaugh Drive in Coolock on the north side of Dublin. An altercation between several people in the front garden of the house resulted in the stabbing of 33-year-old Raymond Browne. Browne was taken to hospital but died from his injuries. Another man, Emmet Taaffe, was also injured, receiving a slash wound to his arm. I was part of the Bureau team who assembled to examine the scene.

It was outdoors – a small front garden and the immediate area outside the driveway. Mr Browne died in hospital, so there was no scenes-of-crime tent and no body to be removed. Instead, we found the usual assortment of cans and bottles and a baseball bat, which had been used in the melee. Our goal was to locate the knife used in the stabbing, but there was no sign of it. We found a block of knives in the kitchen of the house, with one missing from the set. This block of knives was exactly the same type as the one I had seen in the kitchen at the Edward Cully crime scene in 2003.

The investigating gardaí from Coolock conducted door-to-door enquiries, and it was established that the knife had been spirited away from the scene and dumped in a wheelie bin outside a house that backed onto Clonshaugh Drive. We managed to retrieve it, but it had been cleaned, so I could not develop any fingermarks on it.

Dr Michael Curtis was once again the pathologist assigned to the case. I travelled to Marino for the post-mortem and to obtain a set of prints from Raymond Browne's body. As I waited, I spent time watching Dr Curtis examining the wounds.

In cases of sharp force injuries, it is important to examine the clothing of the deceased as well, as this can assist investigators in establishing the characteristics of the weapon used. As with most cases of fatal stabbings, the exterior wounds on the skin were relatively small. The edges of these types of wounds are called the *margins*, and the width of the wound is the distance between the margins. The depth of the wound is ascertained by measuring from the margins to the deepest point of the wound. This is called the *long axis* of the wound. Occasionally, depending on the degree of force used during the stabbing, marks or contusions may be found around the entrance wounds, for example an imprint of the edge of the handle or hilt of the knife, but this wasn't the case with the wounds on Mr Browne.

Dr Curtis asked me to assist him in determining the track of the stab wounds. I held the edges of the chest cavity open while he inserted long metal probes into the wounds. Raymond Browne had been stabbed three times in the side, just below his armpit. Dr Curtis pointed out that two of the wounds had been largely superficial and hadn't pierced the chest cavity. The third wound had. It had caused internal bleeding, which had resulted in his death.

By this time, the gardaí had a suspect in custody. Raymond Browne and Emmet Taaffe had attacked a group of teenagers in retaliation for an assault on Taaffe's brother earlier that night. Two locals, Peter Dolan and Noel Courtney, had been walking past the junction of Clonshaugh Drive and Moatview Avenue when they saw a fight among a group of people in a front garden. Noel Courtney saw that his son was one of the teenagers under attack, so he stepped into the row. Peter Dolan also joined the affray before running into the house and grabbing the knife from the kitchen. He used this knife to slash Taaffe's arm and stab Browne.

It seemed to be an open and shut case. Peter Dolan was charged with the murder of Raymond Browne, and the case went to trial three years later.

The offence of murder occurs if a person intended to kill or cause serious injury to another person, who dies as a result. Murder convictions can include situations where a killing was planned or where the accused is aware that the natural consequences of their actions would lead to the death of another. The most important thing to prove is *intent*.

Manslaughter is the unlawful killing of a person. This is when there are extenuating circumstances such as *provocation* or *self-*

defence, or the accused was reckless or negligent, but the act of causing bodily harm was unintentional.

In February 2008, after less than two hours of deliberation, the jury in the trial of Peter Dolan for the murder of Raymond Browne returned a unanimous verdict of *not guilty*. They also found him not guilty of the assault on Emmet Taaffe. Before they had begun their deliberations, Mr Justice Paul Carney said that they had to consider the acts of *provocation* and *self-defence* in deciding their verdict.

The courtroom can be a singularly peculiar place. Nothing can be taken for granted, and in jury trials, nobody can ever be sure of the outcome until the foreman of the jury announces the verdict. Prosecution and defence barristers are intelligent people who earn their crust by looking at the evidence in a case from every angle. Arguments and counterarguments are adjudicated by the learned judge, who advises the jury on points of law. At the end of the trial, the jury must decide if the prosecution has proved their case based on the evidence presented. In the case of Peter Dolan, they decided that the prosecution had not proved that the killing of Raymond Browne was an act of murder.

The Murder of Mindaugas Janavicius

When a young Lithuanian man, Mindaugas Janavicius, was fatally stabbed on Sunday, 24 July 2005, after a house party in County Monaghan, I was back on the road again. This time, I was part of a Bureau team who, except for myself, was all-female – Eadaoin the photographer, Ger from Ballistics and Laura from the Mapping Section.

The Mapping Section was based in Harcourt Square, and its members' core duties are the surveying of crime scenes and preparing maps and plans to scale for use as exhibits in court. They also provide maps for display in incident rooms set up during large-scale investigations and regularly provide plans in relation to fatal road accidents. The modern Mapping Section uses state-of-the-art digital surveying instruments and computer-aided design software to produce these exhibits, and the mapping expert is usually the first witness to present evidence during a trial.

When we got to the primary scene, a house on Roslea Road in Clones, the body was still in situ in an upstairs box bedroom. One of the three parked cars outside had smashed windows, and the driver's door had been wrenched outwards. I arranged for these vehicles to be towed to Santry for examination later.

Once Eadaoin finished with her initial photographing of the scene, the rest of us could enter. The 21-year-old Mr Janavicius was lying on his back on the floor of the bedroom with what appeared to be a single stab wound to the chest. There wasn't much blood in the bedroom, but we noted a sporadic trail of blood that led outside and away from the scene. Ger took blood samples for testing back at the Forensic Science Laboratory and numbered and marked the trail with little orange cones. It appeared the attacker had cut himself, perhaps with the knife used in the stabbing.

Dr Marie Cassidy arrived to conduct her preliminary examination of the body, which was then removed to Cavan General Hospital. It was late by the time we were finished at the post-mortem, so after a night in Cavan town, we returned to the scene the following morning.

The knife had been discarded in the bedroom, and I could see what appeared to be blood stains on the blade. I bagged this vital exhibit to treat it for fingermarks back at HQ. Around this time, members from NBCI arrived at the scene. I knew the detective inspector, Gerry Harrington – a former detective sergeant in Malahide when I was stationed there.

Gerry wanted the crime scene manager to attend a case conference that was being held at Clones garda station. I had to tell him the Bureau hadn't sent a crime scene manager because, for some reason, it hadn't 'suited' anyone. It was the weekend, so I guess my more learned colleagues all had plans. Procedures were more lenient in those days. I hadn't been sent on the crime scene manager's course, so I declined the suggestion that I take on the role for this investigation. As a result, we all headed to the conference when we finished at the primary scene.

From there, we were asked to go to another house in a townland called Corcummins, about three miles outside of Clones. It was a fairly isolated location. On the night of the murder, a birthday party had been held at the house and attended by a large crowd of people, including the deceased and the main suspect in the stabbing. The majority of them were Lithuanian nationals. A row had broken out among several of the revellers, and that was when the damage was done to the car we saw at Roslea Road. The suspect had allegedly followed Mr Janavicius back to Clones, and the gardaí had a witness who had been sitting in the living room in the house at Roslea Road when he arrived. This witness stated that the man had gone into the kitchen and grabbed a knife before disappearing up the stairs, presumably to carry out his attack.

I was a bit pissed off going to this second location. The house party altercation had happened before the stabbing, and in my opinion, we shouldn't have been sent to search around the address and the adjoining fields. We went through the motions, and I gathered plenty of cans and bottles and tried my best to look interested for the benefit of the few television cameras set up nearby.

I was also royally pissed off a few days later when an irate inspector turned up at the Bureau with yet more bottles from Corcummins. He complained that we should have bagged them at the scene. I made it quite clear we weren't rubbish collectors. Picking up and examining a multitude of discarded cans and bottles would not solve the murder. It would only serve to identify who had been drinking what, as long as everybody present had provided their fingerprints. This was unlikely, as many people at the party lived across the border in Fermanagh. Besides, if he was that concerned about a few bottles, he should have gotten the local SOCOs to powder them for marks.

Back in Dublin, I brought the blood-stained knife up to the lab so it could be swabbed for blood and DNA. I also managed to examine the cars that had been towed back to Santry. Between the cars and the various exhibits from the two scenes, I generated a tonne of fingermarks and managed to identify six people. But these idents were really just for elimination purposes, as none of the individuals was the man whom the witness had seen taking the knife from the kitchen at Roslea Road. I was hoping the knife would be my ace in the hole.

From closely examining the knife, I knew there was a partial mark on the blade near where it was attached to the handle. The position of the mark indicated that a thumb or forefinger was likely to have made it. So, when I received the knife back from the lab, I decided that the best way to proceed for fingerprints would be to treat it with amido black. It doesn't develop marks as such, but it reacts with the proteins present in blood. It can intensify marks left in blood by staining them a blue-black colour, rendering the marks easier to see and photograph.

Treatment of an exhibit with amido black is a wetting process mainly used on non-porous surfaces. Firstly, the blood stain has to be stabilised or fixed by immersing the exhibit in methanol. Then, the exhibit is stained using the working solution, which consists of a chemical called naphthalene black, along with methanol and glacial acetic acid. The exhibit must then go through a series of washes with glacial acetic acid, methanol and distilled water before it is allowed to air dry, and any marks present can then be photographed.

As I'd hoped, following my treatment of the knife with amido black, a reasonably clear partial fingermark could be seen on the blade. The Forensic Laboratory had also determined that the blood was indeed that of the deceased, Mindaugas Janavicius. Now, all I had to do was identify the mark. I had Eadaoin photograph it, and then I got down to business.

My first port of call was to compare the mark against the set of prints that I'd taken from the deceased. Perhaps he'd grabbed the blade as he was being attacked? But I quickly eliminated him as the person who had left the print. By this stage in the investigation, I had several dozen sets of fingerprints taken from many of the people who had been at the party in Corcummins and from the few people who had been in the house at Roslea Road. I went through each one, initially checking the questioned mark against thumbs and forefingers and then all the other fingers. I did this several times, giving my eyes a good rest between each round of comparisons. I was satisfied that the mark on the knife hadn't been made by any of them.

The one set of fingerprints that I was lacking were those belonging to the main suspect. That man's name was Laimonas Mackevicius. The witness at Roslea Road saw him taking the knife from the kitchen before heading upstairs. Following the stabbing, we learnt that some acquaintances drove him over the border to Belfast, and from there, he fled to Spain. I needed to get my hands on Laimonas Mackevicius' fingerprints.

Like many people who had been at the party in Corcummins, Mackevicius was a Lithuanian national. Military service is compulsory in Lithuania for all males aged between 18 and 23, with each conscript expected to serve a minimum of nine months in the armed forces. This policy was abolished in 2008 but reinstated in 2015. A copy of all conscripts' fingerprints is kept on record.

The investigation team contacted the Lithuanian authorities and arranged to have a copy of the suspect's fingerprints forwarded so I could compare them with the mark on the knife. The prints were waiting for me when I arrived at work early on 12 August.

The fingermark had been seared into my retinas for the previous two weeks. I knew it inside out. I nervously slipped the copy of Laimonas Mackevicius' fingerprints out of the brown envelope they arrived in and zeroed in on the right forefinger. It looked promising. The pattern was correct. I grabbed my hand magnifier and sat at my desk to compare the new set of fingerprints with the mark from the knife. I tuned out the background office chatter. A bomb could have gone off on the roof and I wouldn't have heard it. My eye flicked back and forth between the clear rolled forefinger impression and the blurrier mark made in blood. As is usually the case with chemically developed marks, the photographs were in black and white to provide better contrast.

I compared each visible ridge characteristic with the corresponding ones on the set of prints. I allowed for possible slippage in the mark and was aware that some of the ridges were reversed, meaning they appeared white while the furrows between them were dark. This *shift* isn't unusual in marks made in a wet medium such as blood. All the visible characteristics were in agreement, and none were in disagreement. But I knew that I still had to keep my powder dry.

I handed over the photograph of the mark on the knife and Mackevicius' prints to another lad on the unit, who in turn passed them on again after he was finished with his comparison. A strict methodology called *ACE-V* (Analysis, Comparison, Evaluation and Verification) must be adhered to. My two colleagues agreed with my findings. I could now contact the investigation team and tell them the news. I was satisfied beyond doubt that the bloody mark on the knife was made by the right forefinger of the person whose fingerprints form bore the name Laimonas Mackevicius.

Following this, things proceeded both swiftly and slowly. Swiftly in the sense that I moved straight onto another case file, and slowly in that it would take another two years before the case would come to court. When gardaí tracked down Mackevicius in Spain, he agreed to return to Ireland voluntarily. He was arrested for the murder of Mindaugas Janavicius as soon as he arrived at Dublin Airport.

In February 2007, Mackevicius went on trial for murder in Cavan, the first time that the Central Criminal Court had sat in the town. He admitted to manslaughter but pleaded not guilty to the more serious charge of murder. I attended to give evidence along with the rest of the Bureau team. By this time, I had prepared my comparison chart, demonstrating my identification with the required number of ridge characteristics in coincident sequence. Witness by witness, the trial trundled along, with Laura from Mapping and Eadaoin from Photography being among the first to give evidence.

Before the prosecution could call me, the witness who had identified Mackevicius in the house at Roslea Road took to the box. As soon as he was sworn in with the help of an interpreter, the investigation team knew that something was up. He appeared nervous and reluctant to answer the questions being put to him by the prosecution. When it came to the statements he had made to gardaí regarding what he had seen in the house, he bottled up.

Again and again, the prosecution asked him what he had seen, but he refused to point out Mackevicius to the court. The prosecution barrister asked the judge for permission to treat him as a hostile witness, but the young man just wouldn't play ball. Without his evidence, the case couldn't be proved that Mackevicius had entered the house and retrieved the knife with the intent to kill or cause serious injury to Mindaugas Janavicius.

Following the witness's refusal to answer questions, the judge sent the jury out. The prosecution had no choice but to withdraw the charge of murder. The trial went ahead, and the court accepted

Mackevicius' admission of manslaughter. He was sentenced to five years in prison.

A year later, after the Peter Dolan trial, I couldn't help thinking about the similarities between the two fatal stabbings. Both had involved the perpetrator obtaining a knife from the scene and using it to inflict sharp force injuries on their victims and yet neither of them had resulted in a murder conviction. It could be argued that the Clones murder involved a more definite *intent* on behalf of the accused, yet the outcome was the same. Two young men had died, and only five years (if that) of prison time would be served. I make a point of not taking court proceedings personally, but sometimes the system leaves a bad taste in the mouth.

Each of the three knifed victims, Mindaugas Janavicius, Raymond Browne and Edward Cully, also bizarrely share another detail in common: in each case, the weapon was snatched from a kitchen and was the same kind of blade from the same type of knife set. I wonder if some shopping outlet out there was advertising 'slashed prices for our premium, no-nonsense wonder weapons'.

21

LAST IMPRESSIONS

> A person needs new experiences. They jar something deep inside, allowing them to grow. Without change, something sleeps inside us and seldom awakens. The sleeper must awaken.
> *Duke Leto Atreides,* Dune

As murders go, the Gary Douch case was one of the most memorable. It wasn't particularly gruesome or bloody, and the small and confined scene presented no problems from an evidence collection point of view. It was the location that made a lasting impression on me – Mountjoy Prison. It was also to be one of the last murder investigations that I was involved in as a fingerprint expert.

That occasional niggling feeling that I needed to move on became a persistent itch throughout 2005. I wasn't happy. It was becoming increasingly difficult to escape the tiger as it prowled through the jungle. I had good and bad days, and sometimes, when I was alone in the chemical room, I had to fight the urge to punch my fist through the wall.

It wasn't just me, though. There was a general malaise among the members in the Fingerprints Section. Nobody could quite put their finger on the reason, but there seemed to be a bad atmosphere in the place. Management's insistence that we follow the dictates of the ISO auditors played a part in it, as 'process papers' and procedures seemed to push the actual meat and potatoes of our true function further and further into the background.

Some good friends transferred out of the section, and others pursued new opportunities. The Western Australia Police Force began a recruitment drive, looking for gardaí willing to join. Successful applicants and their families would be given full Australian citizenship, and the pay was reasonable too. It was a tempting proposition, and three members of the Fingerprints Section applied for it. Two of the applicants were my good friends Glenn and Rodney, and by the end of 2006, they had upped sticks and headed off to Perth.

Of course, I was happy for them, but I was also gutted that they were gone. The three of us had always been close and looked out for one another during tough times, but I no longer had them to bounce off. Although I still had plenty of great mates in the Bureau, I couldn't help feeling somewhat lonely and lost. The Fingerprints Section had, up to that point, always been on an even keel, but now the deck had taken on a pronounced list.

Around this time, I began making tentative enquiries about a move within the Bureau. Going back out into uniform was definitely off the books for me, and I wanted to continue using the skills I'd learnt during my eight years in Fingerprints. I was aware that Detective Inspector Sean Lynch had recently retired as head of the Documents and Handwriting Examination Section. He was replaced by Mick Moore, who was promoted to inspector, leaving a vacancy in the section. I had a few informal chats with Mick, in which I expressed my interest in joining the Section. Mick was open to the possibility, but the position had not yet been advertised. In An Garda Síochána, vacancies must be advertised in a HQ circular, and then a competition is held between the applicants, who also must interview for the position.

I informed my supervisors in the Fingerprints Section of my desire to move, most of whom advised against it. They pointed out I'd lose money moving to the Documents and Handwriting Section (D&HW), as they only worked Monday to Friday, with no weekends or nights. This would mean no big pay cheque every four weeks. I didn't care about the money. I had never been hungry for overtime, unlike many of the old-timers who clocked up obscene amounts every roster. I wanted a change, a new challenge that would still allow me to employ and improve many of the skills I had already learnt. I spoke to my super about it, who hummed and hawed and basically danced around the subject. I also talked to my chief super, Nóirín O'Sullivan, who would become garda commissioner nine years later. The chief was more open to the idea. I remember her acknowledging that there was indeed 'a *lacuna*' in D&HW, but she added I would have to wait until a position was advertised. A *lacuna*? I had to look it up. I thought she was talking about a make of car. A *lacuna* means 'a gap' or 'a missing piece'. I felt I would fit that gap nicely.

After all, it should have been relatively straightforward. The Fingerprints Section and D&HW were both part of the Bureau, and the Bureau was considered to be like a garda *district* or *division*. Chiefs and supers regularly shifted personnel around their districts and divisions without the need for competitions to be held. It would have only taken the stroke of a pen, and I could have transferred from the second floor of the Bureau building down to the first floor. But it wasn't to be. I had to wait for that HQ circular. Mick assured me he would keep me in the loop and let me know when the competition was advertised. He knew I was a good worker with a keen eye for detail. With Sean Lynch gone, D&HW was down to one handwriting expert. I knew I had what it took to take on that role.

In the meantime, there were plenty of fingerprint case files to work through. Every day, there was an influx of new cases from SOCOs all over the country, each with fingermarks from burglaries, stolen cars, recovered property and many other investigations. Crime scene exhibits had to be examined too, so there was no shortage of work to get stuck into. Statements and charts needed to be prepared for court, and, of course, there were call-outs. It was the luck of the draw which ones you were sent to. Some were serious investigations taking up a lot of time, and others were more straightforward and did not lead to full investigations. It all depended on whether you were working when a job came in and if you were available or tied up with a court case.

The Murder of Gary Douch

Gary Douch, a 20 year old from Coolock, was serving a three-year sentence in Mountjoy for assault in the summer of 2006. He had made it known to the prison authorities that his life was in danger due to ill feelings between himself and some other inmates in the area of the prison in which he was housed.

The prison transferred him to the basement of B Wing, where prisoners who had been threatened were segregated from the main prison population. On the night of 31 July, Douch was placed in a holding cell in the wing, along with six other inmates. One of those was a man called Stephen Egan.

Egan was on remand in Mountjoy on theft and robbery charges. He was 23 years old and, like Gary Douch, had spent most of his adult life in prison. He had a reputation for being disruptive and potentially violent and had spent time in Cloverhill, St Patrick's Institution, Wheatfield and the Limerick, Cork and Midlands prisons. Egan had been moved around *seven* different jails and institutions in the years leading up to 2006. He had also been transferred from the Central Mental Hospital in Dundrum one month before being placed in the holding cell in Mountjoy.

In the early hours of 1 August 2006, Stephen Egan launched an unprovoked attack on Gary Douch. The other inmates present said that Egan went 'mad' and proceeded to beat, kick and strangle Douch until the young man stopped moving. The other prisoners didn't call out to the prison guards because they were afraid of being attacked too. They poured water under the small gap at the bottom of the cell door in an unsuccessful attempt to get the guards' attention. When Egan went to the other end of the cell to relieve himself, they covered Douch's prone body with blankets and a duvet.

At 6.30 a.m., when prison officers opened the cell, the prisoners quietly filed out and told one guard that Gary Douch was still inside. The alarm was raised, and he was removed to the hospital but was pronounced dead within the hour.

I was among the Bureau team who arrived at Mountjoy later that morning. Several prison officers met us to escort us through many locked doors and barred gates to B Wing. Constant noise surrounded us as the several hundred inmates talked and shouted incessantly. Even though we were separated from the prisoners at all times, it was still a very intimidating experience.

When we got to the basement, they showed us the holding cell where the assault had taken place. It was at one end of the wing, separated from the main cell block by floor-to-ceiling iron bars. The prisoners were out of their cells, chatting with each other. I was expecting to be heckled by some of them, but they largely ignored us as we slipped on our white suits. Most of them were smoking, as were a few of the prison officers. It was one luxury that wasn't denied.

I stepped inside once the photographer completed his preliminary cataloguing of the cell interior. I didn't know what to expect. I knew it wouldn't be overly clean or modern as that part of the prison was old, but I was still shocked by what I saw.

The cell was about the size of an average-sized living room, with a concrete bench running along one side. There were a few small windows high up on the walls. The walls were covered in graffiti and crude drawings and stained with stuff I didn't want to think about. There was one toilet in a little alcove, but it was completely blocked with paper.

The floor was littered with newspaper, a few blankets, plastic cups and empty crisp packets. With no working toilet, the prisoners had relieved themselves on the floor, so the place was reeking with urine and excrement. I could see where some prisoners had pushed wadded newspaper up against the edge of the door and tried to funnel water out into the hall beyond to alert the guards when Stephen Egan attacked Gary Douch. I didn't want to think about how seven men had to endure such conditions. Animals in the zoo have better sleeping quarters.

I gathered up bits of newspaper and little plastic bags which had held the toothbrush and toothpaste the prisoners were given. There was no point in powdering the walls for fingermarks. I was bound to get a tonne of idents, but what would that prove? These men were already in prison. There was no murder weapon to examine either. I was really only going through the motions.

Out in the main cell area, the prisoners were now lining up for their grub. If they needed to interact with the prison staff, they always addressed them in terms like 'Mister Murphy' or 'Jones'. No first names were used, even among the guards themselves. I supposed it was a security measure. You wouldn't want the inmates to know your full name. When lunch was over, everything was tidied away, floors were mopped clean, and then the prisoners were locked back in their cells.

It didn't take us long to finish with the holding cell, and I was relieved when we got back outside to the fresh air. There had been such an oppressive atmosphere in the place. I don't know how the prison officers could stick it. Whatever they get paid, they certainly earn it.

As expected, I got plenty of idents from the bits and pieces that I took from the holding cell, including all the inmates that had been there during the assault, as well as other previous occupants, but none of these idents were going to be in dispute. Stephen Egan was charged with the murder of Gary Douch, but on the first day of the trial, the court accepted a guilty plea to manslaughter. Egan was convicted of manslaughter due to diminished responsibility and received a life sentence. He was transferred to Portlaoise Prison, where his mental health continued to deteriorate. He would spend long stretches of time in a padded cell and needed to be escorted at all times by prison staff in full riot gear.

A Commission of Investigation into the death of Gary Douch was eventually set up, and they published their findings in 2014, seven and a half years after his killing. It ran to nearly 800 pages and outlined the failings of the prison system concerning both Douch and Egan. It criticised the handling of prisoners requesting protection and the way Egan was treated without regard to his ongoing need for psychiatric care. It was also highly critical of the conditions in Mountjoy and Irish prisons in general.

Since the death of Gary Douch, there have been extensive refurbishments and many improvements to living conditions in Mountjoy. 'Slopping out' has become a thing of the past, in Mountjoy at least, since 2014. Before that, inmates had to use pots or buckets as toilets, and these remained in the cells overnight, only being emptied by the prisoners once a day. Now, every cell has a fully plumbed toilet. Overcrowding is still a problem, so maybe alternatives to custody could be looked into for more minor offences. Imprisonment is rightly regarded as a deterrent to crime, but even those convicted of the most awful wrongdoing deserve an acceptable quality of life while serving their sentences.

I never set foot inside Mountjoy or any other prison again. Still, I think all gardaí, as part of their training, should see the inside of a jail and gain an insight into the life experience of many of the people they will arrest over the course of their careers.

When Drinking Turns to Destruction

Many crimes involving violence share a common catalyst: alcohol. When individuals prone to aggressive behaviour consume excessive amounts of alcohol, it becomes more likely that they will commit impulsive violent crimes. Drinking to excess affects self-control, decision-making and emotional processing. Normal brain functioning gets disrupted, and minor disagreements quickly escalate into physical confrontations because the drunk person feels unnecessarily threatened. I encountered remarkably similar circumstances in two crime scenes during my final year in the Fingerprints Section.

On the afternoon of 23 September 2005, James Burke was dropped off at The Square shopping centre in Tallaght by his uncle. James was 20 years old and had grown up in England. He had only moved to Ireland with his family a few weeks before, so he had no friends in Dublin. His uncle had given him some money for cigarettes and the arcade machines in The Square.

As the evening wore on, James struck up a conversation with a lad called Kevin Walsh, who was 16 then and already had 34 previous convictions. The two bought cans of beer and went drinking near the Liffey Valley Shopping Centre, where Walsh met up with his girlfriend, Lisa Brady.

The three sat drinking in an overgrown area between the Marks & Spencer car park and the boundary wall that separated the shopping complex from the N4 motorway. Before long, a row broke out between James and Kevin. Walsh later said that it had started over spilt beer, but Lisa Brady told gardaí that Walsh had taken a disliking to Burke because of his English accent.

Burke allegedly threw the first punch but was quickly knocked to the ground, where he tried to grab onto Walsh's leg. Walsh rained blow after blow down on him, and when Burke let go and stopped moving, Walsh continued to hit him and repeatedly banged Burke's head off the ground until blood poured from his nose and mouth.

Lisa Brady finally dragged Walsh away from Burke's prone body, and the two of them fled the scene. They managed to get a lift home from a friend, but neither told anyone about what had happened because they feared they would get into trouble. The following day, the two of them again met at Liffey Valley. When Walsh left to get the bus home, Lisa headed back to the spot where they had been drinking the previous evening and saw James Burke was still lying where they'd left him. She phoned Walsh and told him, but it wasn't until the next day that she told her father what had happened, and he contacted the gardaí.

I arrived at the scene on the evening of 25 September, two days after the assault. The Bureau team had to descend a steep embankment to access the scene. We must have looked comical as we slipped and slid down the damp grass, all decked out in our white suits and clutching our kit bags.

The local gardaí had erected a crime scene tent over James Burke's body, but there was precious little else in the way of useful exhibits for me, except for the few empty cans scattered about. When Dr Curtis arrived, I helped him to navigate the tricky descent, and after he conducted his preliminary examination, the body was removed for the post-mortem. The cause of death was blunt force trauma to the head caused by repeated punches and kicks.

The few exhibits I retrieved from the scene yielded several fingermarks belonging to the deceased and Kevin Walsh. When seeking identifiable fingermarks on non-porous surfaces such as beer cans, the most common method used is super glue or *cyanoacrylate vapour*. To develop fingerprints, the item to be treated is placed into a special cabinet with a small plate where a few drops of glue are heated in a foil dish. The vapour from the glue polymerises and adheres to the latent marks, leaving a white deposit. The operator needs to keep an eye on the process because if the exhibit is left in the cabinet too long, too much polymerised glue may stick to the marks, blurring the detail. Fingermarks developed using this method can then be photographed. As the ridge detail will appear as white, negative images are made to make it easier to carry out comparisons or plot points for searching on AFIS.

The fingermarks I developed on the cans helped to corroborate Kevin Walsh and Lisa Brady's story that they had been drinking with James Burke, but I was not called to give evidence at the subsequent trial because fingermarks on mobile items like cans carried no evidential weight regarding the actual attack.

Kevin Walsh was charged with the murder of James Burke, to which he pleaded not guilty. He was eventually found guilty of manslaughter and was sentenced to eight years but with the final five years suspended. However, he was subsequently jailed for the violent hijacking of a taxi in 2013.

At around 3 a.m. on Sunday, 7 January 2024, an ambulance was called to a property in Lucan and Kevin Walsh was treated for a stab wound. He had taken a taxi from his family home in Allenton Green, Tallaght, to the apartment in Shackleton Hall where he was living. When emergency services tried to find out what had happened, Walsh refused to tell them. His life of crime ended at age 34 when he died in the early hours of that morning and an investigation into his murder began.

I couldn't help but feel sorry for James Burke. He had left his old life and friends behind when his family moved to Dublin. I've no doubt he would have been eager to make new acquaintances, but the first young person he met that day ended up beating him to death and leaving his body undiscovered for two days, lying only yards away from one of the busiest roads in Dublin city.

My last excursion to Limerick as part of a Technical Bureau team involved a tragically similar case to that of James Burke. On 25 May 2006, the eve of his 25th birthday, Keith Ryan went out drinking with friends in an area known as the Wetlands in the Westfields area of the city. The group split up when it began to rain, and Keith Ryan headed off on foot towards the Shannon Bridge. However, he was viciously attacked along a walkway running under the bridge. He received extensive head injuries from an individual or individuals stamping on his forehead and face.

Following her post-mortem examination of Keith Ryan's body, Dr Marie Cassidy concluded that he had died as a result of inhaling his own blood, compounded by the injuries he had received and the high level of alcohol in his system.

The scene provided nothing in the way of useful fingerprint evidence. Any rubbish and debris in the area where Keith Ryan had died had been severely soaked by rainfall, and in any case, it appeared that he had just stopped under the bridge to go to the toilet. There was no murder weapon, no freshly discarded cans. Practically nothing to help tell the story of what had happened.

It meant we finished at the scene relatively quickly. I thought I was in for a long night, and instead I got to head off for a bit of grub and a few pints before bedding down at the good ol' Two Mile Inn.

With little of value gleaned from the scene, evidence had to come from elsewhere, but gardaí were already zeroing in on two local men, Thomas Ryan and Tony O'Brien. Aided by CCTV cameras in the area, they were able to track the two men's movements in the vicinity of the scene at the time of the assault. The men were arrested. They had been drinking in several pubs and were on their way to a party in the Pennywell area when they met Keith Ryan. A row broke out, and the two men brutally assaulted him. They were eventually found guilty of manslaughter, receiving 17 years' imprisonment between them.

I still pondered the similarity between Keith Ryan and James Burke's fates. Both had been young men who had simply gone out and passed a little time sinking a few cans outdoors before running afoul of alcohol-fuelled aggressors who savagely beat them to death.

Alcohol is classified as a *depressant*. It slows down the activity of the central nervous system, which can result in impaired judgement, slurred speech, drowsiness and lack of coordination. I also think that it can act as a stimulant for individuals with a propensity for aggression and violence. I like a drink, but whenever

I consume too much, I either become funny and boisterous or quiet and melancholy and usually wind up on my knees talking to God on the big white telephone. Alcohol exacerbates my natural traits – being witty and sarcastic or depressive and pessimistic. I'm not an expert on mental health, nor do I pretend to know what makes people tick, but I believe alcohol is like petrol to fire when mixed with the psychological makeup of certain individuals, especially when consumed to excess.

We can only ever truly know ourselves. We can usually approximate the behaviours of close friends and family, but when you throw alcohol and strangers into the mix, the results can be disastrous and sometimes deadly.

My final two jobs as a fingerprint expert were initially categorised as *suspicious deaths* and also involved the consumption of excessive alcohol, but for different reasons.

The first scene was on the outskirts of Galway city, where an elderly gentleman was found dead in the upstairs bedroom of his house. The gardaí noted that the back door of the house was open. Could it have been a burglary that went wrong? After examining the scene, the Bureau team concluded that there was no sign of a forced entry or evidence of any struggle. The deceased had lain undiscovered for several days, so decomposition had set in, but there were no obvious signs of any injuries. He was quite a large man, and we had great difficulty getting his body down the narrow staircase after placing him in the coffin. We headed off to the post-mortem, where it was deduced he died from natural causes.

As it happened, there was a second Bureau team in Galway that day, who had also been at a job that turned out to be non-suspicious. That night, we all met up, skipping a late dinner in favour of copious pints. I was going through a low patch, weighed down with depression as well as frustration over the lengthy wait to transfer to D&HW, so I drank more than I normally would. A lot more.

Needless to say, I spent the whole night being as sick as a small hospital, curled up beside the loo in the hotel room I was sharing with the Bureau mapper. The poor chap had to go to the fire escape to relieve himself because I couldn't stray two feet from the toilet. To make matters worse, we had to go back to the scene the following day to finish up a few things. I don't think I've ever felt so crap as I did that day, powdering and trying to lift marks with a disgusting taste in my mouth and the still-present aroma of the days-old dead body hanging in the air.

My final scene as a fingerprint expert was at a flat near the Guinness Brewery in Dublin. We were met at the door by that familiar wall of dead-body smell. The flat was small but neat and well-kept. The dead man was lying face-down in the living room area. There was no sign of a break-in or disturbance except for a small table that had been knocked over near the body. We noted a large amount of blood around the body, which was also all over the sheets and pillow of the single bed in the cramped bedroom.

The deceased had been lying there for several days, and the body was already in quite an advanced state of decay. I remember we had a difficult time trying to 'detach' him from the floor and keep him in one piece. The smell was overpowering, but we succeeded in getting the body wrapped up so it could be transported to the City Morgue.

Dr Marie Cassidy performed the post-mortem, where she ascertained that the man had died due to blood loss from a laceration to the back of the head. There was also a high level of alcohol in his system.

Back at the scene, we thoroughly searched the flat, and the photographer found a heavy overcoat hanging up in the wardrobe. The rear of the coat collar was saturated with blood.

The gardaí canvassed the area for witnesses who might have seen the deceased recently. They learnt the man regularly frequented pubs in the locality and was often seen in an intoxicated state, sometimes so drunk that he would stumble about. The pieces of the puzzle slotted into place.

He was believed to have taken a tumble while inebriated, probably when he was on the way home from a night out. Upon returning to the flat, he hung his coat in the wardrobe, probably not noticing the blood on the collar, and went to bed fully clothed. The high level of alcohol in his system would likely have impeded his blood from clotting properly, so the laceration on his scalp continued to bleed.

Later, he must have arisen, most likely very weak and light-headed from the blood loss, and made it only a few feet into the living room before falling, face first, knocking over the small table. And there he lay until the people in the adjoining flats noticed the smell several days later.

It was a lonely death, a stark reminder of how easily life can be snuffed out and how a night on the town, sinking pints, can have dire consequences. For me, it was reminiscent of one of the first jobs I had ever gone on – the death of the man on the South Circular Road in 1999, who had sat drinking while bleeding profusely from a small wound on his forehead.

The flat near the Guinness Brewery was the last time I would don the white suit. The post-mortem was the last one I would attend and the last time I would have to take fingerprints from a dead body. I wouldn't have to subject my senses to the sometimes horrific sights and smells that come as part and parcel of scenes-of-crime work.

I don't miss that aspect of the job, but I miss the camaraderie that comes from being part of a Bureau team, the intensity of the work, and that curiously addictive feeling of being 'in the zone' when the switch would click and I was totally focused on the job at hand. I would continue working in tandem with many of the fantastic people I came to know during my time in Fingerprints, but I would no longer be on the front line of crime scene investigation. My career in crime, however, was far from over.

22

THE BEST-KEPT SECRET

The last page turned is a perfect excuse to write a whole new book.

Toni Sorenson

I was bitterly disappointed when I didn't get the job in Documents and Handwriting after it was finally advertised early in 2006. However, I was told I was runner-up and a new vacancy in the section would arise shortly.

So I soldiered on in Fingerprints, but these days I just seemed to be spinning my wheels. The rush I used to get from making idents wasn't enough to keep me content, and the bad atmosphere wasn't abating either. The tiger was prowling ever closer and hardly a roster would go by without me throwing a few sickies due to my low mood.

In May 2007, I contacted the Garda Welfare Service and met one of their members for a coffee one evening in Cumiskey's pub near garda headquarters. I outlined my frustrations, my on–off struggle with depression and how I really needed a change. This meeting was on a Wednesday. On the Friday, I was on the road early as I had to travel to Limerick for court. As is often the case, the hearing was put back to another date, so I was back at HQ in the afternoon.

When I arrived in the office, I was told the chief wanted to see me. I went to Nóirín's office to learn I would start in D&HW on Monday morning. Wow! That was fast. It turned out the welfare officer I had spoken with was on good terms with the chief and told her she believed a move would be in my best interests and beneficial for the Documents and Handwriting Section. My final weekend working in Fingerprints went by in a haze. I said my farewells to my colleagues and finished that chapter in my career on the Sunday night. I arrived on the floor below bright-eyed and bushy-tailed on Monday morning, ready for whatever new challenges awaited me.

The D&HW Section was small and self-contained. I'd often liaised with its members while I was in the Fingerprints Section, and it always struck me how independent they were, tucked away in a few small offices on the first floor. The section had one detective inspector, a sergeant, a clerical officer and five mules (including myself). In many ways, D&HW was the best-kept secret in the Bureau.

For a time, I had to remain something of a 'secret' myself. I hadn't been officially transferred from the Fingerprints Section; I was merely 'accommodated' in D&HW. I would be there for nearly six months before a staff member transferred out on promotion, and an official vacancy was advertised. Then, I had to apply for the position and go through the interview process all over again. It made no sense to me, and I felt it was unfair to the other applicants, as the position was already earmarked for me. I remember sitting outside the office where the interviews were being conducted, and one of the other applicants said to me that she'd heard that 'some fucker from Fingerprints already had the position sewn up'. I kept schtum.

As soon as this 'fucker from Fingerprints' parachuted into D&HW, I was shown the filing cabinet containing all the pending case files. These were sorted into cases requiring handwriting and signature comparison, those containing questioned documents such as passports, currency and identity documents, and finally, 'ESDA' cases.

Despite living in a technologically advanced age, the 'hard-copy' document remains widely used in business, financial, social and personal affairs and, therefore, is used to perpetrate many crimes.

As its name suggests, the Documents and Handwriting Section has two core purposes – document examination, which deals with secure documents including passports, driving licences and currency, and handwriting examination to establish authorship. There are many ways to examine documents for signs that they are forged or altered.

The D&HW Section can detect impressions and indentations on paper with tools such as the Electrostatic Development Apparatus (ESDA). This can, for example, help trace the origin of an anonymous letter and indicate who authored it.

The section also uses a state-of-the-art video spectral comparator (VSC) with filters and light sources, including ultraviolet and infrared, that allow an examiner to visualise hidden security features or faded handwriting. The machine can also differentiate inks and reveal alterations on a document. D&HW experts use bitmap analysis to examine documents produced by certain colour printers and identify the model of the machine used and its possible location. They can establish if documents originate from the same machine and compare specimens from a suspect copier or printer through photocopy and print comparison techniques. The D&HW Section can also reassemble torn or shredded documents.

The D&HW Section also has an extensive hard-copy specimen library containing hundreds of specimen passports, driving licences and currencies from all over the world. They can also access secure websites like *DocumentChecker* by Keesing Technologies.

The members regularly work with the Forensic Laboratory and Fingerprints Section. For example, a threatening letter may need to be swabbed for DNA, so it's brought to the lab first, then to D&HW for examination, and finally, it may be sent to Fingerprints.

I 'officially' started work in D&HW in the winter of 2007 and would spend the next 15 years attached to the section. It was a real breath of fresh air. We were self-sufficient and were very much our own entity, insulated from any of the crap going on in the much larger sections of the Bureau. I loved it and looked forward to going to work every day. As anticipated, my wages took a hit because I lost out on any unsocial hours and weekend payments, but I didn't mind. I'd kept my expert allowance as I was still required to go to court for any fingerprint work that I'd done.

My daughter, Aleisha, was born in July 2006, so spending more time with her by working civilised hours, Monday to Friday, was great. The new job also did not require days away from home at crime scenes. And I loved that our small crew was confined to a single open-plan office, and we could engage in banter as we carried out our duties. I could still zone out the chatter and concentrate on my work when I needed to, and my eye for detail and experience in comparison disciplines meant I took to my new role like a duck to water. Every day was a school day. Once again, I'd landed on my feet and was exactly where I wanted to be.

23

HIDDEN IN PLAIN SIGHT: ESDA

There is always a pleasure in unravelling a mystery, in catching at the gossamer clue which will guide to certainty.
Elizabeth Gaskell

The Murder of Bobby Ryan

When it concluded in 2019, the trial of Patrick Quirke for the murder of Bobby Ryan was the longest in the history of the state, lasting 13 weeks. Part-time DJ Bobby Ryan (aka 'Mr Moonlight') was 52 years old when he went missing after leaving his girlfriend's house in the early hours of 3 June 2011.

Mr Moonlight had been seeing Mary Lowry, a widow who lived in a farmhouse at Fawnagowan in County Tipperary. Mrs Lowry had leased the farm to a man called Patrick Quirke, with whom she had had an on–off relationship. Bobby Ryan's car was found by his daughter on the afternoon of his disappearance in a car park at the nearby Kilshane Woods.

Twenty-two months later, in April 2013, Patrick Quirke reported to gardaí that he had found a decomposed body in an underground run-off tank at the farmyard in Fawnagowan. The tank was built in the 1970s to take wastewater from the nearby milking parlour, and Quirke said that he had opened it to retrieve water to mix with slurry. The body was identified as Bobby Ryan. The assistant state pathologist, who carried out the post-mortem, noted several head injuries and fractures to his ribs and thigh bone and suggested that death had been due to blunt force trauma, either from an assault or being hit by a vehicle. Bobby Ryan's body was naked when found, save for his watch, which was still on his wrist.

A full-scale murder investigation was launched, and before long, the gardaí began to unravel the web of jealousy and infatuation that 'Mr Moonlight' had unwittingly become entangled in. Patrick Quirke had wanted to rekindle his affair with Mary Lowry, but this wouldn't happen as long as Bobby Ryan was on the scene. Quirke would call to Mary Lowry's house, peek through the windows, interfere with Mary's post and steal items of clothing from her washing line. It was also established that Mary Lowry had told Quirke that she wouldn't be renewing his lease on her farm, leading gardaí to speculate that his 'discovery' of the body was staged, as he feared whoever took over the running of the farm would stumble across it.

The gardaí continued to gather evidence, including search history from Quirke's computer, which showed that he'd been looking up information on body decomposition, skin slippage, 'human remains' and DNA analysis. Documents were also seized from Quirke's house, showing written entries including 'Mary last one to see him' and 'Body naked, either murdered and clothes taken off or never left the house'. These handwritten notes were forwarded to D&HW and examined on the ESDA by my good friend and colleague, Detective Garda Jeremiah Moloney.

Before the introduction of the ESDA in 1977, indentations had to be examined using oblique or sideways lighting, but this was only useful with indentations already visible on the page. With the advent of the ESDA, hitherto completely invisible indentations could be developed. The value of the evidence that the ESDA can retrieve was highlighted by this highly publicised investigation into the murder of Bobby Ryan.

When a person writes on a page in a copybook or with other pages underneath, latent indentations of that writing will be deposited on the following pages. Depending on the writing pressure applied, indentations may be left on several subsequent pages. Providing the conditions are right, it is possible to use the ESDA machine to develop them, even many decades later.

Developed indentations act as a snapshot of the moment they were made. Once they have been deposited, they do not change. The ESDA process can reveal clear indentations and is almost as effective as carbon paper in reproducing handwritten information. It can also develop footwear impressions and fresh fingermarks.

A page for examination is laid on the ESDA's brass plate and covered by a transparent Mylar® polyester film, which is highly insulating. An electric charge is then applied to the surface by passing a sort of 'wand' over the surface several times. Next, a developing agent is poured, sprayed or brushed across the surface. This agent is made from millions of tiny glass beads mixed with a black toner powder. The toner adheres to the areas where indentations are present. Finally, the Mylar® film is lifted and placed on a white backing card. Any developed indentations can then be examined or photographed. For best results, the humidity needs to be controlled, so the ESDA at D&HW was kept in a little box room on the landing outside the main office.

No one can tell with 100 per cent certainty how the ESDA machine develops indented writing, but it's believed areas of indentation are less negatively charged than surrounding areas. This difference causes the toner to be attracted to the areas of indentation.

The quality of indentations depends on several factors, including the pressure used when writing, the thickness of the paper, the sharpness of the writing implement, and the number of stacked pages. The ESDA also has its limitations and cannot be used on previously wet paper. Newspaper, thick card and cardboard are also unsuitable for ESDA treatment.

It goes without saying that any type of exhibit should only be handled if you are wearing gloves. Extra care must be taken with exhibits to be examined with the ESDA. The best practice is to keep such items between thick cardboard sheets to prevent further indentations from being deposited.

I've lost count of the number of times I developed indented writing and discovered the SOCO or exhibits officer had placed the exhibit in the evidence bag first and then filled out the chain of custody details on the front. I'd work away with the ESDA and see some lovely clear indentations developing, only for them to read, 'Garda Joe Bloggs, 12345G, Dublin Garda Station'. Occasionally, you might even find the member's shopping list or the order for the chipper for the late unit!

When a person is writing, the depositing of indentations is not a planned act but an act of chance. Developed indentations can link a document to its author. For example, an anonymous letter may be linked to a copybook found in a suspect's home.

Very often, there is no suspect – only the questioned document is received for examination. Sometimes, it might be a threatening letter or a slip of paper passed to a cashier, ordering them to empty the till – 'or else'! When examining these for indentations, you are looking for indentations that point to the author's identity. I've had many instances of developing indentations where the actual name and address of the writer are discernible on an exhibit because they had written a normal letter on the page preceding the threatening piece of writing.

When indentations are developed using the ESDA, only clear and unambiguous writing is noted and forwarded to the investigating gardaí. Detective Garda Jer Moloney, who examined pages seized by gardaí investigating the murder of Bobby Ryan, was able to develop several clear handwritten entries that served to stoke the fire of suspicion that was building around Patrick Quirke. The developed indentations read as follows: 'What will the gardaí know?', 'Murdered poss ... in house', 'Location?', 'Dispose of clothes ... phone', 'Any other evidence', 'Mary had to see him, be with him', 'Needle in haystack', 'Bobby stayed in yard, ie two mins ten mins', 'Agitate need water'.

It made for compelling reading. Patrick Quirke was eventually charged with the murder of Bobby Ryan. The lengthy trial was comprised of mainly circumstantial evidence, including the indented writing that Jer found on the handwritten notes. No murder weapon was found, nor was there any evidence of where the actual killing had taken place.

Nevertheless, in May 2019, having deliberated for over 20 hours, the jury found Patrick Quirke guilty by a majority verdict of 10–2. He received the mandatory life sentence.

The evidence procured by the ESDA was a vital part of the prosecution's case. When available, this type of evidence can be invaluable in a criminal investigation. It is unambiguous: a literal snapshot of what the writer has committed to the page as hitherto invisible indented writing. It can be produced to a court or a jury without having to explain the content, as it's there for all to see.

I spent my first few months in D&HW processing ESDA cases daily. While many exhibits didn't yield any valuable indentations, a good deal did.

I remember one case where I examined a short letter of a threatening nature and developed indentations that revealed the address of a house. When gardaí went to the house, they were surprised to find that it was a 'grow house' being used for the cultivation of marijuana plants. Thanks to the ESDA, they secured a successful conviction for the sale or supply of drugs.

I was in my element, as I was pretty much left to my own devices. Every day, I would grab a few pending ESDA files and whittle away at them in the little examination room, often with the radio blaring music as I went about my task. Within three months, I had significantly reduced the backlog of ESDA cases, and I started to hone in on the next challenge in my new environs: security document examination.

24

PROTECT AND DEFEND

The Printing Press is either the greatest blessing or the greatest curse of modern times, sometimes one forgets which it is.

E.F. Schumacher

While becoming increasingly familiar with document fraud and forgeries, I nursed a dark secret about my own criminal behaviour – the day I successfully counterfeited Irish money. It was back when I was working in the Murakami-Wolf animation studio. I found myself at a loose end and had little work to do in the office one day. As they say, the devil finds work for idle hands, and I found a crumpled Irish £10 note in my pocket and photocopied it. It was a black and white photocopy, capturing just one side of the note, but then I filled it in with coloured pencils. The results were okay, but I didn't think my 'tenner' would fool anyone.

Later that evening, I met up with my mate Sean, and we went for a few pints in a pub in Skerries. I slipped Sean my counterfeit note as he headed to the bar to order some drinks, fully expecting him to be rumbled by the barman and get a good slagging. However, he returned to our table minutes later with two creamy pints and change! He wasn't too pleased when I told him he'd just bought the drinks with a coloured-in photocopy! In hindsight, it was a stupid thing to do, but this was a few years before I joined An Garda Síochána, and I never thought about the possible consequences.

The next morning, I was on the train to work when I overheard two lads talking in the seats behind me. One of them had been working behind the bar the previous night and was telling his friend that the boss had done his nut when he found my crude fabrication in the till. That was my one and only foray into the world of counterfeiting.

With the backlog of ESDA cases now under control, I started exposing myself to the examination of security documents. When D&HW was set up as part of the Technical Bureau, questioned handwriting and signature cases comprised most of the work. Over the years, however, there was an explosion in the number of questioned travel and identity documents. By the time I started in the D&HW Section, these documents made up the bulk of the workload.

Passports, identity documents, currency, cheques, and tax, insurance and NCT discs can all be classified as *secure documents*. This means they are produced with specific printing methods and contain special security features. These features serve two purposes: to assure anyone examining the document that it's genuine, and to

John Sweetman

act as safeguards or deterrents against anyone trying to create a counterfeit document.

There's some confusion with terms such as *counterfeit* and *forgery*, particularly when giving evidence about such documents in court. Forensic document examiners all over the world have their own take on these terms, but I always tried to keep it simple.

A counterfeit is the actual physical *object*, a passport, a €50 note, etc., made to imitate a genuine document with the intention to deceive or defraud. Meanwhile, forgery is the physical *act* of making a fraudulent or counterfeit document or alterations to a genuine document, thus rendering it false or invalid. The term *forgery* is frequently used with regard to questioned signatures.

People produce counterfeit or fraudulent documents for several reasons. It's often for financial gain or to avoid expenditure, such as using fake motor tax discs. Some seek greater opportunities to travel with counterfeit passports. Others want to conceal their identity to carry out illegal activities, hide a criminal record or avoid restrictions on travel.

I figured there was no point in blindly jumping into the questioned documents drawer and getting tied up in knots with all the myriad documents we received for examination. I decided to hone in on one particular type of secure document that was regularly received by the section – the Irish driving licence.

The D&HW Section had any amount of them waiting to be looked at, so I pulled out several cases at a time. I'd retrieve a genuine specimen and study the specific security features that should be present, and then I would examine the questioned licences with the VSC and the stereo microscope. Every member of D&HW had one of these microscopes on their desks. The stereo microscope has two viewing lenses, one for each eye, so when you look through it, your brain integrates what you see through the two lenses into a three-dimensional image of the object being scrutinised.

I spent several days looking at just Irish driving licences, the old type. They were made from paper but still contained several security safeguards such as a watermark, micro-print and ultraviolet features. It was a good way to get familiar with that document and determine if the item being examined was genuine. I wasn't a document expert yet, so I couldn't send out reports or statements on examined documents to the investigating gardaí, but I left notes in the file for whichever expert member would do the actual casework.

After I became familiar with the Irish driving licence, I moved on to other regularly received questioned documents such as euro banknotes, motor tax discs, credit card-style driving licences and identity cards. Just like when I started in the Fingerprints Section, I soaked up every detail of the documents I examined and every exhibit I scrutinised and gradually adjusted to the new role.

Schiphol Airport in the Netherlands is one of the busiest airports in the world, with almost 72 million passengers passing through it in 2019. It's a vast place, covering an area of over 10 square miles. Not long after I joined the D&HW Section, another colleague and I were sent to Schiphol for a week. We were guests of the Royal Netherlands Marechaussee, the military police in charge of security at the airport. The military police man the booths at passport control and examine the travel documents of the passengers arriving and departing. I spent some time shadowing a few of our hosts and was very impressed with their vast knowledge of all the different passports. If something didn't seem right with a passenger's documents, the member in the booth would pick up the phone and straight away that passenger would be taken to a separate office for further investigation so as not to cause any undue delay in the lines. It was a very slick operation.

I would return to the Netherlands a few years later for an intensive two-week course on printing techniques used to produce security documents. It's important for a document examiner to be knowledgeable about this stuff, but even more helpful to see the actual processes in action.

Many types of security features are present in travel and identity documents. They protect the document from alteration and would-be counterfeiters. Banknotes, cheques and vehicle documents also contain numerous safeguards, including micro-print, watermarks and tactile features like raised print. Some documents even contain deliberate errors or variations, such as intentional spelling mistakes, which often go unnoticed by counterfeiters.

As printing technology continues to improve and innovate, so too do the efforts of the forgers. The printing companies always strive to remain one step ahead, continually revising and updating their products. Sometimes, the forgers can achieve results that are difficult to differentiate from the genuine article. However, when such items are thoroughly scrutinised, there will always be at least one element that gives the game away.

High-end security features are too expensive to reproduce illegitimately and are among the most reliable deterrents. These include *scrambled indicia*, a hidden code often contained within the photograph of a passport holder that can only be seen with a special viewing lens. Another expensive security feature is *thermochromic ink*, which changes colour when heat is applied, usually by rubbing it with your finger.

No modern security document relies on a single safeguard. The combination of several safeguards is needed to deter fabrications from being produced.

There is no such thing as a perfect counterfeit or fabrication. By definition, it would be impossible to detect. Some counterfeits do come close, though, so, just like the printing companies, forensic document examiners have to stay frosty, keeping up with new and improved safeguards and emerging trends and improvements to combat the counterfeiters.

I needed to learn fast and be prepared for what a defence barrister could throw my way, particularly in the District Court. My experience as a fingerprint expert told me that 'anything goes'.

I didn't think I had enough room in my brain to absorb the new D&HW information after 10 years in the Fingerprints Section. But the new information sank in, and soon I was examining and reporting on all sorts of questioned documents cases and presenting evidence in court. Often, these cases were on the lesser end of criminal offending and heard in the District Court at Chancery Street in Dublin.

This is the lowest tier of court in Ireland, where minor offences are dealt with. With more serious offences, a book of evidence is prepared and served on the accused. If the judge believes there is a sufficient case to answer, it is sent to the Circuit Court or Central Criminal Court, and a trial is conducted by jury.

I remember giving evidence in a cheque fraud case in the District Court. By now, in my career as a garda, I was well used to giving evidence, and this was a simple and straightforward matter. The accused had tried to pass a bogus cheque in a financial institution. I was giving evidence to confirm that the cheque was a counterfeit, as it lacked the security features and printing techniques that should be present in that document.

The exhibit was submitted to D&HW along with a blank white envelope. The accused said that a 'friend' had given him the envelope containing the cheque, asking him to cash it. The questioned cheque was flagged, seized and eventually found its way to my desk for examination.

At court, I was called to the witness box, took the oath, introduced myself and addressed the prosecution's questions about the questioned cheque.

'Yes, Judge,' I said, 'the questioned cheque lacks the correct security features that should be present in a genuine cheque of this type, namely, ultraviolet features, a watermark and certain printing techniques. In my expert opinion, exhibit JS1 is a counterfeit document.'

The prosecution asked me to answer questions from his 'learned friend', so I turned my attention to the defence barrister. The defence barrister asked me if I was sure the cheque was a counterfeit. I was sure. How sure? Beyond doubt. His black robes swung from his shoulders like a tyrannical old schoolmaster, and he posed with one foot resting on his chair, huffing, puffing and pontificating about my testimony. As he fired questions at me, he twirled an impressive, walrus-like moustache. He must have watched too many episodes of *Rumpole of the Bailey*.

Could the defendant have known that it was a counterfeit?

I don't know.

This continued for a while before the barrister tried a different approach.

'What about the envelope?' he said.

'The envelope?' I replied.

'Did you examine the envelope?'

'No. The cheque was the questioned item to be examined.'

I didn't know where he was going with this.

'So, guard, you didn't examine the envelope?'

'No.'

'Therefore, you can't tell the court whether or not the envelope was a counterfeit?'

He let the question hang in the air for a moment, looking all pleased with himself.

'Well, Judge,' I said, directing my answer to the judge as you are supposed to, 'an envelope is an envelope. It's not purporting to be anything else.'

'But what if this envelope was fabricated by the person or persons who fabricated the cheque?'

I wanted to say these 'persons' could have bought one rather than conjuring one up, but I kept quiet, save for a sigh, as I looked at the judge, who was smirking.

'Well, guard?' said the barrister.

I understand it is the defence's job to represent the accused and to explore every avenue of the evidence, but this was pure horseshit. No amount of stern and severe questioning would add sugar to it, regardless of the 'learned man's' impressive demeanour and Hogwarts-esque billowing cloak and natty wig.

Thankfully, the judge had heard enough and asked the defence where he was going with this. Chastised but still supremely 'learned', the barrister ended with a flourish of 'no further questions'. The case was proven, and the defendant was convicted and received a token fine. Feckin' District Court. Anything goes. When the new Criminal Courts of Justice (CCJ courts) complex opened in later years, it's little wonder I rechristened it, tongue in cheek, the Criminal Court of Jesters.

25

SEEKING ILLUMINATION

Where the light is brightest, the shadows are deepest.
Johann Wolfgang von Goethe

The Murder of Jastine Valdez

Twenty-four-year-old Jastine Valdez boarded a bus in Bray for the quick journey to Enniskerry, where she lived with her Filipino parents, on Saturday, 19 May 2018. Jastine had moved to Ireland to join her parents only three years earlier. The young accountancy student had attended an appointment at the garda station in Bray that day concerning the renewal of her residency permit.

As she prepared to alight from the bus in Enniskerry that Saturday evening at around 6 p.m., she was unaware of the black Nissan Qashqai following close behind. Jastine was in regular contact with her parents, and the journey from the bus to her home took 15 minutes. When she didn't arrive and they couldn't contact her, her parents reported her missing.

Gardaí had already received reports of other concerning incidents near Enniskerry that evening. A woman reported seeing a female being bundled into the back of a black Qashqai on the R760 south of Enniskerry. A man driving in the same area said he had passed a black jeep and saw an Asian woman in the back, screaming and banging on the windows. A major garda operation was put in place to locate the black Qashqai and the movements of similar cars in the Dublin and Wicklow areas.

In the early hours of the following morning, gardaí narrowed down the search. They called to the home of a man who owned such a vehicle, but his wife told them he hadn't been home since the previous night.

Mark Hennessy was a 40-year-old father of two who worked on building sites as a 'banksman' or safety officer overseeing crane operations. Hennessy had come to the attention of the gardaí before for public order and drug offences. He was due in court later that month on drink-driving charges. Family members would later say that his life was spiralling out of control due to drinking and addiction to cocaine.

Gardaí learnt that around 5.40 p.m. that Saturday, Hennessy had popped into the Ramblers Rest pub in Ballybrack. He didn't stay long, and CCTV captured him getting into his car and driving towards Enniskerry. Shortly afterwards, the black Qashqai was captured by CCTV on the bus that Jastine was travelling on. Hennessy's SUV was following the bus and was seen overtaking it just before the stop where Jastine alighted near the entrance to Powerscourt Estate. Hennessy abducted her shortly after she got off the bus as gardaí found her discarded mobile phone near the location.

Mark Hennessy needed to be found, and fast. A huge manhunt began. Every moment that passed would lessen the chances of finding Jastine Valdez alive.

The following day, on Sunday afternoon, family members saw him in a Killiney car park, apparently alone, but he had driven off. Later that night, around 8 p.m., the black Qashqai was spotted in Cherrywood Business Park in Loughlinstown, with Hennessy sitting behind the wheel. Gardaí approached the vehicle and ordered him to get out, but he refused. He started to slash himself with a Stanley knife. Fearing that Jastine was still in the car with him and that her life was in danger, a garda fired his weapon at Hennessy, wounding him in the shoulder and chest. The bullet ricocheted off his collarbone and severed an artery. He bled out and was dead within minutes, his body slumped across the passenger seat.

It was later learnt that Hennessy had phoned his wife only moments before being confronted by the gardaí at Cherrywood Business Park, telling her, 'I'm not coming back.'

When gardaí searched the car, they found no sign of Jastine, but they saw a note heavily stained with Hennessy's blood. They could not read most of it but made out a few scrawled words, 'Puck's Castle' and 'sorry', before the blood congealed.

Puck's Castle is a ruin in a wooded area near a golf course in Rathmichael, close to Shankill. A major search operation was put in motion, with members of the gardaí and army combing the area. At 3.45 p.m. the following afternoon, Jastine Valdez's body was located in thick gorse bushes. She had been strangled.

It was later ascertained that Hennessy had killed her within an hour of having abducted her. He had callously dumped her body and gone on a drink- and cocaine-fuelled binge. Videos emerged of him laughing and drinking in a Dublin pub on Saturday night, apparently without a care in the world, only hours after he had murdered the young woman.

In the aftermath of Jastine's death, attention turned to the blood-soaked note found in Hennessy's car. When the note arrived on my desk, the hope was that it could help explain why Hennessy brutally murdered the innocent student.

Writing inks are mass-produced, but there are variations in different brands of pens. By viewing the questioned handwritten details under infrared illumination, it is sometimes possible to observe stark differences in how individual inks fluoresce.

After Mark Hennessy's death, his final note was brought to the Technical Bureau in the hope that its contents could be recovered. Little was legible on the page because it had been soaked in Hennessy's blood. No one knew why Jastine Valdez had been abducted and murdered by Hennessy, and investigators wanted to read his note in case it left any clues.

The decision was made to chemically treat the note so as to wash away the blood. However, there was also the chance that this could destroy the writing. So, first, the letter was brought for examination to the D&HW Section, where I took possession of it. It had been preserved in a shallow black box to prevent the surface from adhering to anything unnecessarily.

Upon opening the box, I was met with the coppery smell of blood. The page was almost completely saturated with it, and parts of it had torn when the blood had dried. I could make out some faint handwriting, but most of it was illegible.

I donned a face mask and protective gloves, carefully removed the note from the box and placed it on a transparent sheet of low-tack plastic. I did my best to flatten out any creases and began to take notes of the small amount of visible writing, but most of the written content had been obliterated by the heavy blood-staining.

I knew the best chance to make out the writing would be to examine the note with the VSC. Blood does not fluoresce, so if I could fluoresce the ink or even the paper surface, I might be able to decipher the written content. Using a combination of ultraviolet and infrared wavelengths, I was gradually able to 'filter out' the blood, enabling me to see what lay beneath. It took some time, but I could eventually make out what Mark Hennessy had written.

The note contained the aforementioned reference to Puck's Castle, along with his admission of having killed Jastine Valdez and dumping her body at that location. He then went on to apologise, both to his own family and the family of the victim, and stated that he intended to die by suicide. What was missing, however, was any motive for the killing. He gave no reason for doing what he'd done.

I took multiple images of my findings for the information of the investigation team and then brought the note down to the chemical room in Fingerprints. One of my former colleagues was able to disperse the blood-staining by immersing the note in a series of washes. The handwritten content was then clearly legible and able to be photographed, and tallied with what I had deciphered.

I was pleased that I could help the investigation, if only in a small way. It was also comforting to know that I could still flick that 'switch' and get into a down-to-business mode when required.

It wasn't the first time that I had to examine handwritten notes left by killers or their victims, but it was the first time that I had used the ever-reliable VSC to penetrate a blanket of blood and reveal the last words written by a murderer.

Mark Hennessy was a complete stranger to Jastine Valdez. It couldn't be determined if he had seen her previously in the area and become infatuated with her and followed her or if it had just been a completely random abduction. Whatever his reasons had been, they died with him.

A man who had known Mark Hennessy described him as a 'happy-go-lucky guy. He never caused trouble. You'd never hear any complaints about him. He would be the last guy you would suspect'. Unfortunately, more often than not, 'the last guys you would suspect' end up carrying out the most horrific crimes.

As is the custom in the Philippines, Jastine Valdez lay in repose for two days, and hundreds of people filed in and out of the funeral home in Bray to pay their respects. Many of them were members of the Filipino community, but many more were total strangers who felt compelled to stand in solidarity with her devastated family. Her hardworking parents, Teresita and Danilo, said that Jastine planned to settle in Ireland, buy a house here and make a new life. They described her as 'a fun-loving, wonderful, caring daughter and friend' before adding, 'She is always in our hearts and in the hearts of the people of Ireland.'

The video spectral comparator VSC is an invaluable piece of equipment where writing has been obscured or obliterated, and so it proved in the investigation into the murder of Jastine Valdez.

As all examinations carried out in D&HW are non-destructive – the exhibit must remain in the same condition as when it was received. The VSC is vital as it enables an examiner to 'see through' materials that obliterate writing. It also helps see through attempts at deliberate deception or alteration by differentiating between inks through the use of various wavelengths of light, typically in the infrared end of the spectrum.

Writing inks are mass-produced, but there are variations in different brands of pens. By viewing the questioned handwritten details under infrared illumination, it is sometimes possible to observe stark differences in how individual inks fluoresce.

Writing obliterated by correction fluid

Revealed with infrared light

Scribbled-over writing

Revealed with infrared

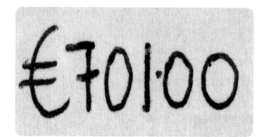

Questioned amount on cheque

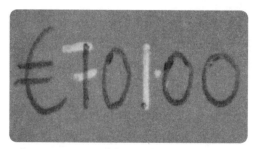

Alterations visible under infrared

I remember many cases where the VSC uncovered irrefutable evidence of document alterations. For two in particular, I was able to perfectly illustrate that the exhibits under scrutiny had been deliberately altered for financial gain.

Both cases involved several questioned cheques. The first concerned a company, let's call it Naturo, which had lost a lot of money as the victim of cheque fraud. Several cheques, made out as payable to the company, had gone missing. Suspicion soon fell on one of the female employees. Her husband had set up another company called Natura and cashed the missing cheques. Some of the 'Natura' cheques were seized and forwarded to D&HW for examination.

To the naked eye, the cheques appeared legit, with the company name clearly written in blue pen. Using the VSC, I zoomed in on the payee details and cycled through the different settings of infrared light. I quickly saw that a second ink had been used to add a small stroke to the last letter, altering it from its original 'o' so that it now read as 'a'. It had been an ingenious little amendment, with no need for erasures, obliterations or damage to the background ultraviolet safeguards.

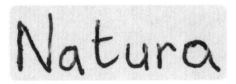

Questioned payee name

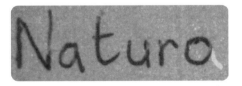

Alteration visible under infrared

The second cheque fraud case was quite similar but less well-executed. It again concerned misappropriated cheques, this time in a legal firm. These cheques had been made out to be payable as VAT (Value Added Tax). A member of the firm called Natalie Flynn (not a real name) had tried to cash several cheques made out in her name, and I was tasked with examining some of them. Once again, using the good old VSC, I was able to determine that alterations were made to the payee details. Flynn had altered 'VAT' by incorporating it into her own name so that it now read as 'NATALIE FLYNN'. An additional pen stroke to the 'V' was added, so it looked like an 'N', and then she added 'ATALIE' after the 'T'. It was clever but somewhat odd looking because the VAT had included periods or full stops after each letter, so she did the same with the additional letters of her forename.

Questioned payee name

Alterations visible under infrared

These cases exemplify the simple but highly effective results of using the VSC. Like with the ESDA, the results can be clear and unambiguous and are easily illustrated to investigating gardaí and the courts by using printed enlargements.

26

HURRY UP AND WAIT – COURT TALES

Boredom ought to be one of the seven deadly sins. It
deserves the honour.
Frederick Buechner

I spent nearly 30 years of my life as a sworn member of An
Garda Síochána. I dread to think how much of that time was
spent numbing my arse on hard benches in courtrooms and their
environs. It is a necessary evil of the job when you're an expert
witness. I didn't even have the time-consuming distractions of
a frontline garda who juggles charge sheets, books of evidence,
custody records, exhibits and witness lists.

Attending court usually meant hours of sitting around, waiting
to be called to give evidence and frequently being told that the
case wasn't going ahead or that I was no longer needed. I've never
resented having to attend, especially if it was for a hearing in
some far-flung part of the country, which meant that I could claim

overtime and subsistence allowance. But I also saw it as my duty as a member of the National Support Services to be at the beck and call of the gardaí investigating crime, even when the Bureau was no longer a designated part of 'Support Services'. Even after retiring, I would always make myself available to give evidence in cases I had been involved in while still serving.

In my early years as a mule, court scared the shit out of me. It all seemed so confusing, even with simple summary offences. It wasn't helped by the lack of courtroom preparation exercises during training, where learning to march seemed to take precedence. Nor was it helpful that my brief time in uniform was spent behind a desk in Command and Control or in relatively quiet stations where court appearances were scarce. When I'd have a hearing in court on a Monday morning, I'd spend the entire weekend in a state of panic, worrying over the impending case. It felt like an enormous blade swinging like a pendulum above me, and with each swoosh, it got closer and closer to my head. I hardly slept a wink those weekends.

The whole court experience could sometimes be mercifully brief, and your case could be called, heard and dealt with in one sitting. More frequently, however, it's an extremely long-drawn-out affair, taking months or even years to reach a conclusion. One such instance concerned an incident when I was stationed in Howth. Two drunken thugs had cut loose in a pub in the village, smashing up furniture and causing other damage to the bar. We arrested them a short distance away and conveyed them to the station, where they had to be carried, kicking and screaming, into the cells. They were transferred to cells in the Bridewell garda station overnight, and the next morning, with barely any sleep, I had to retrieve them from the holding cells and bring them before a sitting of the District Court. As they both pleaded not guilty, they were bailed, with the case sent forward to be heard in the Circuit Court in a couple of months. One of these beauties did a runner, but the other one duly turned up for court, as I did, on the allotted date. What followed was a pantomime with the case constantly being put back to another date because the jury hadn't been chosen, or the judge wasn't available, or the courtroom wasn't free, or the defendant was sick, or a defence barrister was busy, or a defence witness wasn't available. This shite went on for *three years*, by which time I had long since left Howth and was on my way to becoming a fingerprint expert.

During this time, after assisting in the examination of firearms smuggled into Ireland, I was requested to attend as a witness in a Miami trial. I was all set to go, along with other members from the Bureau, but discovered I had a conflicting court date – the umpteenth time that a hearing in the Howth case was due to go ahead.

I contacted the authorities in Miami and explained my difficulty. They said it wasn't a problem and arranged for me to fly out the following week. Needless to say, the Howth case didn't go ahead, but one of the other Bureau members who travelled to America was allowed to present my evidence in court in my absence. I was no longer required. Shit. I had missed out on a trip to sunny Miami, all because of a bloody court case that never went anywhere. To add insult to injury, when the lads flew back from the States, I was sent to the airport to collect them.

Finally, it looked as if the case was going to go ahead, but on the morning of the hearing, one of my witnesses, the barman at the pub in Howth, telephoned to say that his girlfriend had gone into labour and he wouldn't be able to make it. This was the only time in this whole farce someone from the prosecution side wasn't available, so I thought the hearing would just be put back again. But no. The judge didn't take kindly to another delay and struck out the case. Three feckin' years. To tell the truth, I was just relieved that the whole mess was finished, but it really shone a light on the often haphazard workings of the courts.

With the advanced fingerprint course under my belt, I no longer felt nervous about attending court. I was fully prepared for whatever scuds might be thrown my way in the witness box. I was never complacent about giving expert testimony, but once the fear and trepidation were gone, boredom was never very far away.

Like countless other mules, I would spend hours upon hours hanging around in the old Four Courts complex, waiting to give evidence in whatever trial I was involved in. The Four Courts was, and is, very impressive, especially under the vaulted dome of the Round Hall. However, there was one vital flaw in its design – there were damn all seats in a hall filled with countless gardaí, members of the judiciary and witnesses while the court was in session. Members of the public usually occupied the few benches in the place, so I spent hours, sometimes days, leaning against a pillar or nipping out for a smoke. Otherwise, I'd attempt to rest my ample arse on one of the decorative metal railings around the hall pillars, which rose about six inches off the ground. The Four Courts didn't do much for my dodgy back. Even when one did manage to get into the actual courtroom, it was usually crammed and standing room only. And if one was lucky enough to grab a seat, those hard wooden benches soon had your butt demanding that you stand again. The esteemed judge was the only person with a nice, comfy leather chair. I didn't begrudge it to them, as he or she would have to sit in court all day, five days a week, listening to and adjudicating on countless cases, from the mundane to the monstrous.

Back then, I turned up for court in a nice suit. However, with a shaved head and non-regulation goatee, I wasn't always recognised as a detective garda. On one occasion, as I stood at the back of a crowded courtroom, someone approached to ask if I was the Bulgarian translator! As the years wore on, my goatee turned into an impressive beard, still totally non-regulation, and my tattoos extended all the way to my hands. The suit gave way to dark jeans, a shirt, no tie, and occasionally a smart jacket. On more than one occasion, the court guard, or even the judges themselves, asked who I was while I sat reviewing my case file in court.

From time to time, depending on the outcome of a criminal investigation, a civil action might follow. I might be called to give evidence again in the civil proceedings, usually in cases concerning questioned signatures.

I was called to give evidence in a civil case where an elderly gentleman, 'Stephen', was involved in a property dispute with his son and daughter. The case was heard in one of the old Circuit Courts on Chancery Street with only six of us in attendance: Stephen, his two adult children, the judge, a retired mule who had been involved in the criminal investigation, and me.

It should have been a reasonably brief affair, perhaps taking half a day. Instead, Stephen, a prize tulip, decided to represent himself, and it went on for three days. The old guy fancied himself as a thespian, so he treated the hearing as an opportunity for theatrics. When questioning a witness, he liked to leap from his pew, spewing all sorts of nonsense while wildly gesticulating with his arms and brandishing bunches of paper as 'evidence'.

When it was my turn in the box, he began questioning me about the history of handwriting, asking me about ancient cave paintings and hieroglyphics – complete bullshit. I did my best to steer him back to the relevant evidence, but when he didn't want to hear it or when the judge admonished him for wasting time, Stephen feigned some malady: he needed to rest or take his medication. Finally, after three days of letting Stephen tie himself in knots, the judge dismissed the case. It didn't faze Stephen one bit. He strode out of court with his head held high, probably off to preach more of his 'wisdom' from another soapbox. I pitied his poor children.

Around the time of Stephen's one-man show, I had what I refer to as my *epiphany* regarding the court system. I was all set to 'affirm' one morning before giving evidence in Blanchardstown District Court.

I switched from swearing on the Bible and reciting the traditional oath, *I swear by Almighty God*, as I didn't have a religious bone in my body. The affirmation is no less serious and binding: 'I do solemnly, sincerely and truly declare and affirm that the evidence that I shall give shall be the truth, the whole truth and nothing but the truth.'

In my experience, it's easier for a witness, who may not have any religious beliefs, to make more of an impression on a judge when they affirm instead of taking the oath. It shows they are taking the whole thing more seriously instead of just rhyming off the old standard.

As usual, the courtroom was packed with gardaí, solicitors, members of the public, and a particular throng of 'habitual offenders'. These were committed and enthusiastic career criminals upon whom many guards would apply the crude but shorthand description, 'scrotes'.

As I sat at the back of the court, awaiting the judge's arrival, I couldn't help but notice a solicitor decked out in a shiny and, no doubt, expensive suit. He was quite a tall man, with a head even shinier than my own, and he was surrounded by potential clients, all clamouring for his attention. He smiled down at them, shook their hands and passed out business cards like the loaves and the fishes. A truly messianic figure. He was in hog-heaven. At the top of the food chain, with an endless supply of these repeat offenders to keep him busy and his suit shiny.

It was then that I looked beyond him to the front of the courtroom, where there was floor-to-ceiling wooden panelling on the wall behind the judge's raised bench. It was like bright neon letters appeared, covering the entire wall from left to right with this message: 'None of this bullshit matters in the slightest.' As epiphanies go, this was a bleak one. The scene of the sharp-suited solicitor amid his clientele was a stark manifestation of what I'd always known: this whole courtroom set-up was just a sham – a game. The only winners were the legal eagles, and the krill for their gullets – habitual criminals. The victims of crime, hardworking gardaí and ordinary members of the public were all just thrown into the mix. Occasionally, true justice prevails, but down at the lower end of criminal offending, it's just swings and roundabouts. A carousel. It just goes round and round, making you dizzy. Or sick. And I was sick.

If I looked to the seat beside me, I knew the tiger would be sitting there, yawning at the whole sorry spectacle. I felt deflated. The neon letters flickered and disappeared, and the judge arrived. Then, the game got going again. You haven't really experienced that peculiar mix of weariness and bewilderment until you've spent a day in one of the many District Courts of the land and listened to barristers and solicitors pleading their client's case. 'Yes, Judge, he has 110 previous convictions, but he has reached a turning point in his life.' Very well. Back on the streets to offend again. Same time next week.

I was tired of the whole rigmarole, but instead of letting it grind me down, I let it go. It was disheartening, but I continued on the merry-go-round. I would continue going to court and would continue to present myself as a professional and competent witness, but save for any serious trials where there was at least some chance of a just outcome for the victims of crime, I would just show up, do my bit, and then get back to processing case files.

I was lucky that there was always plenty of work to do. It was tangible, productive work that wasn't wrapped up in a ball of legalese, and it was work that I loved. For much of my last 15 years of service, I was supremely thankful to be immersed in the intricate and fascinating realm of Forensic Handwriting Examination.

27

THE WRITE STUFF

Humankind is defined by language, but civilisation is
defined by writing.
P.T. Daniels and W. Bright, The World's Writing
Systems

The Lindbergh Baby Kidnapping

On the evening of 1 March 1932, a baby was abducted from his
crib on the upper floor of the family's home near the town of
Hopewell in New Jersey. The kidnapping was about to make so
many headlines around the world that it would soon be referred to
as *the crime of the century*.

The child, 20-month-old Charles Augustus Jnr, was the son of
Anne Morrow Lindbergh and her husband, the celebrated aviator
Charles Lindbergh. American pilot and military officer Lindbergh
became a household name in 1927 when he completed the first

non-stop trans-Atlantic flight from New York to Paris in his plane, *The Spirit of St Louis*.

A ransom note left in the child's bedroom, demanding $50,000, which was paid by the Lindberghs. However, their baby was not returned. Instead, several more letters were received, with the ransom demand rising to $70,000. One of these letters instructed the Lindberghs to enlist a man called John Condon to act as an intermediary between the family and the kidnappers. Condon was a well-known Bronx personality and a retired school teacher.

Dear Sir! Have 50,000$ redy 2500$ in 20$ bills 15000$ in 10$ bills and 10,000$ in 5$ bills. After 2-4 days we will inform you were to deliver the Mony. We warn you for making anyding public or for the polise the child is in gut care. Indication for all letters are signature and 3 holes.

Following the instructions of the letter-writer, Condon placed a classified ad in the *New York American* newspaper, informing the kidnappers that the money was ready. A meeting was scheduled for late one evening in Woodlawn Cemetery in the Bronx. Condon met with a man who called himself 'John'. The man stayed in the shadows so Condon couldn't see his face, but he sounded 'foreign' and told Condon that he was a Scandinavian sailor, part of a gang of three men and two women.

Condon demanded proof that they had the baby, so John promised to return the child's sleeping suit. He also asked Condon: 'Would I burn if the package were dead?' but then quickly assured Condon that Charles Jnr was still alive.

On 16 March, more than two weeks after the baby's abduction, the Lindberghs were sent his sleeping suit along with yet another ransom letter. In response, they authorised Condon to place another ad reading, 'Money is ready. No cops. No Secret Service. I come alone.' He received a reply on 1 April telling him to deliver the money. Condon again met with John, telling him that only $50,000 had been raised. John took the money and said the baby was in the care of two women.

Nothing more was heard from the kidnappers. On 12 May, a truck driver, who stopped to relieve himself in some roadside bushes four and a half miles from the Lindbergh home, found the decomposing remains of an infant boy. The body was identified as Charles Lindbergh Jnr. An examination indicated that the cause of death was a severe blow to the head, which was believed to have occurred shortly after the kidnapping.

The tragedy of the Lindbergh baby kidnapping had a profound impact on American society. It led to increased public awareness and protective measures for the safety of children. The Lindbergh family was subjected to relentless media attention, which added to their pain and led to changes in the way such cases were subsequently covered and managed in the public eye.

The case also led to the enactment of the Federal Kidnapping Act of 1932, or *Lindbergh Law*, which made kidnapping a crime under the jurisdiction of the FBI, allowing for greater federal resources to be deployed in similar cases.

A massive investigation ensued, but it took two years for a breakthrough. By tracing ransom banknotes and gold certificates, a man called Richard Hauptmann was arrested in the Bronx in September 1934. He was an immigrant with several criminal convictions in Germany. The police also found $14,000 of the ransom money in his garage.

At his trial in 1935, eight fledgling handwriting experts, including an early pioneer in the field called Albert Osborn, gave evidence. Osborn is credited with launching handwriting identification as a distinct discipline. He also broadened his scope of study into the broader umbrella of *document examination*, including typewriting and ink. During the Lindbergh baby murder case, he and the other hand-writing specialists compared the similarities in specimens of Hauptmann's handwriting and the writing contained in the ransom notes.

Their testimony, along with other corroborating evidence, helped to secure a conviction. Richard Hauptmann was executed in the electric chair in Trenton State Prison, New Jersey, on 3 April 1936.

The roots of handwriting stretch back to neolithic man, some 20,000 years ago, painting crude drawings on cave walls. These early images, called *iconographs*, gradually developed into more complex depictions of actual events called *picture symbols* or *ideographs*.

The Phoenicians and Ancient Egyptians developed the first alphabets and schools of writing from 1700 BC onwards, followed by the development of the Greek alphabet around 350 BC. When the Romans conquered Greece, they borrowed from this alphabet, and by the first century BC, the 26-letter Roman or Latin alphabet was in use. Since then, this alphabet has remained largely unaltered and forms the script used to write many modern European languages, including English.

While handwriting and signatures have been used to personalise and ratify documents for thousands of years, it wasn't until the turn of the twentieth century that the potential of using handwriting as a means of individualisation was realised.

And it wasn't until the Lindbergh baby case in 1935 that a court of law accepted the first testimony of handwriting experts.

After successfully completing an intensive course on printing techniques in the Netherlands, I was deemed competent to examine and report on cases involving suspect document analysis. That's when I turned my attention to my ultimate goal – to become a forensic handwriting expert.

Anybody can learn to be a document examiner, but it takes a certain mindset to become a handwriting expert. Examining handwriting is a discipline that requires complete immersion and concentration. In some ways, handwriting identification is like fingerprint analysis. Everyone's handwriting is also different, so every case is different, but there are many more variables involved with handwriting. Handwriting analysis is more reliant on the expert opinion of the examiner and doesn't rely on security features or observations acquired with a magnifier or the VSC. Handwriting identification is also more challenging because a good expert has to know how to really sell their evidence while also keeping it digestible for a layperson to understand. I wanted to move to the next level and was confident that the skills I had learnt as a fingerprint expert would greatly benefit me.

One of the experts in the Handwriting Section had left, so there was a need to get someone else trained in handwriting and signature examination. I was sent to Document Evidence Ltd in Birmingham, which was staffed by several of the top UK handwriting experts. Most had formerly worked in the Home Office Forensic Science Service but left to set up in private business carrying out examinations for the police and defence work.

I was to undergo six weeks of intensive training at their offices in central Birmingham. Although I had tentatively examined some handwriting cases in the D&HW Section, I started from scratch under the expert tutelage of two of Document Evidence's members, Kim Hughes and Mike Allen.

It was quite intensive, 9 a.m. to 5 p.m., Monday to Friday, with my days immersed in handwriting comparison exercises and lectures. I also got to accompany Kim to a court sitting in Leicester to see him give evidence.

With my training now complete, I was eager to tackle real handwriting casework. I returned to the UK one last time a few years later as part of a postgraduate diploma in handwriting examination. I had to sit a written exam, submit three case studies, and attend an oral examination held at the Chartered Society of Forensic Sciences (CSFS) offices in Harrogate, Yorkshire. One of the adjudicators was Mike Allen from Document Evidence Ltd.

I passed with distinction and was awarded a postgraduate diploma from the University of Strathclyde, Glasgow – the first member of the D&HW Section to achieve such a qualification.

I was now a bona fide handwriting expert and could add an extra post-nominal after my name when providing statements and reports: Detective Garda John Sweetman 25926H CSFSDip.

I was exactly where I wanted to be and doing a job that I relished and for now, at least, the tiger was nowhere to be seen.

Stuff and Nonsense

Before I explain what handwriting and signature examination entails, it is important to state what it is not.

When I was still a serving member in An Garda Síochána, I was sometimes asked what I did for a living. When I replied I was a handwriting expert, it was invariably met with 'Ooohs' and 'Aahhs', frequently coupled with 'Oh! I wonder what you could tell about me if you saw my handwriting.'

They are confusing handwriting examination with *graphology*, which is, in my opinion, complete horseshit. Graphology is the supposed analysis of a person's handwriting to determine someone's personality. It is a pseudoscience with no scientific evidence to support its claims.

It is not recognised in Irish courts, nor in many other courts around the world, but it has remained popular in the private sector, particularly in France and the United States, where it is sometimes used for predicting personality traits and employee performance in people applying for jobs. Many studies have been carried out to test the validity of graphology, with the results being consistently dismissive.

Graphology also fails to meet the 'Daubert Standard' regarding the admissibility of expert witness testimony in America. This standard arose from a United States Supreme Court hearing in the '90s to determine the reliability of *expertise*. Several criteria have to be met to reach the Daubert Standard. The expertise has to be generally accepted in the scientific community and is subject to regular peer review. There must also be a way of testing and controlling standards and a known or potential error rate. Graphology does not meet any of these requirements, unlike other disciplines like fingerprints, DNA analysis and handwriting and signature examination.

Despite this, graphology is still big business, and Irish and UK courts do not mandate a Daubert-style threshold reliability test. So, some graphologists still appear in court by referring to themselves as handwriting experts. These so-called 'experts' are employed by defence lawyers to refute the findings of qualified handwriting examiners and 'handwriting experts'. Many of these people have achieved their supposed expert status by registering with online graphology 'schools' where, for a fee, you can get a nice certificate proclaiming your expertise. If faced with a real handwriting case, these individuals wouldn't know whether to scratch their watch or wind their ass.

In recent years, however, thanks to greater awareness about handwriting examination, the defence is more likely to employ fully qualified handwriting experts. Thankfully, a few bona fide independent handwriting experts are out there, including my old DI, Mick Moore, who set up his own practice after retiring in 2016. They also often hire witnesses from the UK. On several occasions, experts I met while in Document Evidence in Birmingham have travelled to Ireland to review exhibits I've examined.

So, when people ask me if I can determine a person's personality by looking at their handwriting, I tell them it's complete hokum. How someone dots their 'i's or crosses their 't's will not reveal whether they're a psychopath, or an introvert, or that they weren't loved as a child. There are, however, many interesting variables at play in the physical act of writing – and the next phase of my career would bring me into intimate contact with them.

28

BRAINWRITING

There are a thousand thoughts lying within a man that
he does not know till he takes up a pen to write.
William Makepeace Thackeray

Handwriting is an acquired skill. It is a complex neuromuscular
task, one of the most advanced achievements of the human hand.
The hand itself contains 27 bones controlled by more than 40
muscles, mostly in the lower arm, and these are connected to the
fingers by an intricate set of tendons. The act of handwriting
involves the smooth execution of a structured sequence of
coordinated movements in which each movement occurs at its
proper time and place in the sequence. The particular pattern
of these movements constitutes a writing style peculiar to each
individual.

DNA and fingerprint forensic analyses are inanimate and
invariable because blood is always blood, fingerprints are

immutable, and DNA doesn't change. However, the evidence being examined in handwriting cases is seldom consistent. Handwriting is the conscious and deliberate act of an *animate* person, and since human beings are not machines, there will always be variations in our handwriting every time we put pen to paper. Handwriting identification is the analysis of these variations or writing habits. It's also about evaluating the significance of similarities and differences in two pieces of writing.

When a questioned piece of handwriting is received for examination, such as an anonymous letter, it is necessary to have suitable specimen writing available for comparison. As *like* can only be compared with *like*, the questioned writing and the specimen writing must be in the same handwriting *style*. There are three types of handwriting styles: script, cursive and block.

Script is generally lowercase, un-joined writing. *Cursive* is joined, and *block* is block capitals. Of course, many writers will incorporate elements of all three styles in their writing, but, as a rule, like styles can only be compared with like. A proper handwriting comparison can't be carried out with, for example, a questioned letter in a cursive style and specimens in block.

A handwriting expert, when carrying out a comparison between questioned and specimen writing, looks at the variations in the constructions of each letter but also takes into account many other factors, such as the constructions of letters depending on their positions within words, the relationships between different letters, their relative proportions, the alignment of the writing, the spacing between words, and, if the writing is on ruled paper, the height of the writing above or below the lines. Punctuation marks, such as full stops or exclamation marks, or diacritics – marks above or below letters, such as a fada in Irish – are also taken into consideration.

When there is sufficient comparable writing, an examiner sketches examples of each letter, encompassing all the variations in its construction throughout the writing. This is done for both the questioned writing and the specimen. Then, these sketched notes are compared to evaluate any significant similarities and differences.

I often received material from investigating gardaí who say that 'oh, the "a"s are very similar', or 'the "p"s look the same', to which I'd reply, 'What about the other twenty-five letters?'

Some letters are quite simplistic in construction and may not lend themselves to much variation, whereas others can be made from several pen strokes, entailing much more scope for variation. The *evaluative weight* of all the observed similarities and differences leads to an opinion of shared authorship. When carrying out handwriting examinations, experts look at a combination of *class characteristics*, which stem from how a person was taught to write, and *individual characteristics*, displaying the idiosyncrasies and habits unique to each writer.

As with other comparative disciplines like fingerprint comparison, we used the ACE-V methodology: analysis, comparison, evaluation and verification. We also used a *scale of opinion* when arriving at a conclusion in D&HW. This ranged from *Conclusive* to *Strong*, *Limited* and *Inconclusive*. Sometimes, certain limiting factors could prevent me from giving a reliable opinion. This might be because there was only a small amount of writing available, or there was distortion in the writing because of the writing implement used or the surface being written on, or there was an element of disguise, or maybe because the writing was quite simplistic.

The fact is that every single handwriting case is different, as every single person writes differently. Handwriting identification is, therefore, governed by two basic principles. Firstly, no two people write exactly alike. Based on the collective experience of all handwriting experts, there have never been two *graphically mature* writers who write in precisely the same way.

Graphic maturity is when a person settles into a particular writing style that remains roughly the same for the rest of their life. This style then becomes their *master pattern*. *Natural variation* refers to the variations and idiosyncrasies a writer displays within their master pattern.

The second basic principle of handwriting identification is that no single person writes exactly the same way twice. *Natural variation* is seen in a writer's *master pattern*, and humans are not machines; therefore, they can't replicate all aspects of their writing twice.

When we first learn to write, we concentrate on constructing each individual letter. Then we learn to string letters together into words, then words into sentences, until writing becomes an almost subconscious activity. Our brains form whatever written communication we want to impart, and then, using the muscles and tendons in our arms, hands and fingers, we impart that information onto the page. In essence, handwriting is really *brainwriting*.

Everyone reaches graphic maturity at different stages in their lives, depending on the frequency with which they write. As kids, our writing varies until we settle into a style that is aesthetically pleasing and easy to construct. Sometimes, problems arise when a handwriting expert is given a questioned letter written by someone when they were young and specimen writing written more recently. The two pieces of writing are not comparable because the earlier writing comes from a time before they reached graphic maturity. Therefore, it is always desirable to have writing that is reasonably contemporaneous.

My own handwriting has changed over the years. When I sat my Leaving Certificate, I wrote in a largely cursive style. When I left school at 17 and began working at Murakami-Wolf, I no longer needed to write often. After that job, I worked with my dad on the farm for another two years, again not needing to write much. When I started training in Templemore and writing study notes and sitting exams, I found I could no longer write how I used to. I then began writing in a largely block style. So, if you had a sample of writing from my teens, you would see that it differed greatly from my writing when I was 21. I have no doubt that if I had gone straight to college after secondary school, my writing would have continued in the cursive style that I had become used to in school.

Some of us write beautifully, while others write terribly. This is called *graphic ability* and has little to do with a person's intelligence. Different people have different levels of skill when it comes to writing. We all know someone who is extremely intelligent yet has awful handwriting. Conversely, many people with below average intelligence can display beautiful, complex writing.

The golden rule when trying to determine common authorship between a questioned piece of writing and handwritten specimens is that you can never have too much material.

Handwriting examination is a quantitative/qualitative process. The more writing you have, the better overall idea you get of the natural variation to expect in an author's normal, undisguised handwriting. Also, if an element of deliberate disguise has been employed, the more writing that is available will increase the likelihood of the author slipping back into their normal hand. Maintaining a consistent level of disguise over a lengthy piece of writing is very difficult. So, whenever I was dealing with investigating gardaí who were trying to identify the author of some questioned writing, I would always ask them to provide as much specimen material as possible.

Sometimes, of course, there might only be a very small amount of questioned material, and no reliable opinion could be given. I recall one case where the volume of available writing wasn't a problem, but determining who wrote it took considerable time.

The Midlands Letters Investigation

The first letter that landed on my desk, which I described in the prologue to the book, was on 18 November 2015. Submitted by a detective garda from Athlone, the letter consisted of 23 pages of disturbing material with threats of sexual violence, rape and murder.

When I researched back through the files, I found another case from way back in 2004 where a 'hide' was found in a remote woodland area in the Meelaghans, near Tullamore. Written material found at the scene matched with the new letter and contained estimated times and distances from the hide to his 'hunting areas' and 'prey'.

I examined the pages for useful indentations but found nothing to shed further light on the letter-writer's identity. I made copies of the questioned material and forwarded the envelope and letter to the Fingerprints Section for further examination.

Within two weeks, two more cases were submitted – one from Birr and another from Tullamore. The handwriting from the 23-page letter was still fresh in my mind, and as soon as I opened the exhibits from the new files, I recognised the same author's hand.

These letters continued in the same vein as the other writings – more excruciating details about the writer's twisted fantasies. With no suspects, I had nothing to compare the questioned writing against. All I could do was inform the different investigating members about new cases and let everyone know they were looking for the same individual. They did their jobs, working together, trying to identify possible suspects.

The letters continued coming, with two more cases in 2016, both submitted from Athlone and a third in 2017 from Tullamore. Some letters had been sent to garda stations in the midlands; others to girls' schools. The longest letter – 56 pages – was sent to a school. This contained graphic information about how he planned to abduct, torture, rape and kill six named teenagers in the school who were aged between 15 and 16. His letters included details about stalking girls, parking near schools and masturbating outside. In another, he described himself as the 'beast of all sex beasts'. He described how he had followed teenage girls around a shopping centre. All of these cases were the work of one prolific writer. Less clear was whether they were the meanderings of a sick fantasist, or something even darker?

In total, I now had seven cases of anonymous letters, which I was satisfied were all the work of the same author. They had been submitted for investigation by different gardaí in various stations in the midlands, none of whom knew about the other cases until they submitted them to Documents and Handwriting.

I sent several of the letters to be examined by a DNA specialist in the Forensic Lab, Yvonne, who found the same DNA profile on all of them. Jim, a good friend of mine in the Fingerprints Section, chemically examined the letters and developed numerous fingermarks from them. However, an AFIS search of the marks came back negative.

I contacted some of the investigating members to inform them that, frustratingly, none of the letters had yielded any useful forensic information that might indicate the author's identity.

However, the net was narrowing. Now that the investigating gardaí were in contact with each other, they were working together to identify any possible suspects. An incident room was set up at Birr garda station, and they found more possible suspects and sent several specimens of handwriting to me. Still, none of the specimens matched the writings of our would-be rapist and murderer. But everyone remained committed to finding the letter-writer.

We surmised that the author was likely to be middle-aged as the art of letter writing is pretty much dying out with the younger generation. Also, the attached cuttings from pornographic magazines indicated it was someone who was either not very tech savvy or didn't have access to a computer or smartphone.

The first breakthrough was when a canny garda noted serial numbers on some stamps used to post the letters, and he managed to track these numbers down to a post office in Tullamore.

By painstakingly watching hours of CCTV footage from that post office, he identified another possible suspect and obtained specimen writing from him. Unfortunately, I had to give him bad news after examining it – I could not make a match.

Things went quiet for a while, but I kept all seven cases on my desk, hoping to eventually receive specimen material I could match. Sometime later, one of the investigating members reviewed the CCTV footage again. He whittled down potential suspects until only a handful remained. He asked the advice of a recently retired garda member who had served years in the Athlone–Tullamore area. The garda was familiar with many of the locals.

This was the dogged hard work and stroke of luck that the case needed because the ex-mule noticed a man in the footage, a part-time construction worker, who he described to his former colleague as a bit of an 'oddball'. He suggested that this man may be worth checking out. The single man lived with an elderly relative in a large farmhouse bordered by some woodland. Consistent with our earlier hunch, he was also middle-aged – in his late forties.

In a search of the suspect's home in June 2017, gardaí quickly uncovered four tins containing numerous letters similar to those submitted for examination. They also found what they described as a 'rape kit' containing ropes, cable ties, scissors, boxes of condoms, one wooden spade, Sudocrem and a syringe. The suspect also had accounts of the Graham Dwyer murder trial and two books on convicted rapist Larry Murphy.

Gardaí gave me the letters they found and further specimen handwriting from the individual. By this time, I was very familiar with the style and construction of the writing. As soon as I started looking at the new material, I knew I had a match. The writing style, letter constructions and relative proportions were all consistent with common authorship.

I brought my findings to my inspector, Mick, who agreed with my conclusions. Given the large amount of comparable material, I was satisfied that there was *conclusive* evidence this man had written all of the anonymous letters. His DNA and fingerprints also turned out to be a match with those found on the letters.

In another chilling discovery, investigating gardaí found another makeshift 'hide' in the woodlands near his house. The den was solid and well-made, measuring 8 feet by 16 feet. It was covered in plastic and was well concealed. The detectives had to crawl on their hands and knees to get there. They found a saw, a shovel, other implements and a collage of photographs of women. The earlier discovery of his smaller hide didn't seem to have dampened his resolve. If anything, he was even more prepared to, in his words, 'abduct, rape, torture and kill' schoolgirls.

He was immediately taken into custody and wasn't released. A year later, in June 2018, he pleaded guilty to charges relating to the possession and distribution of child pornography and sending packages containing obscene material. The judge ordered a psychiatrist's assessment of him. In March 2019, the case was adjourned as a second psychiatrist was recommended in order to deal with the treatment needed for the defendant.

The six named girls in the accused's letters submitted victim impact statements to the court. When they heard about the letters, they lived in fear that this stranger would abduct them. His letters had a huge negative impact on their well-being. The judge said the accused had destroyed the sense of safety which each of the girls had a right to feel.

One psychiatric report said that the accused presented a significant risk for further reoffending when returned to the community. The psychiatrist listed several factors for this, including his sexual deviation, homicidal ideation and the escalating severity of the letters and offences. She also listed the building of his latest den, approximately six weeks prior to his arrest, as a significant escalation in his sexual behaviour. The storage of a rape kit also indicated a heightened risk of reoffending, she said. She diagnosed him as suffering from sexual sadism disorder.

Judge Keenan Johnson described it as 'one of the most bizarre, extreme and disturbing cases' he ever dealt with and compared it to 'something from a Stephen King novel or a horror film'. The letters and the preparations the man made to bring his depraved plans to fruition convinced the court that he was a significant danger to society. In May 2019, after nearly two years in custody, 48-year-old Liam Finlay was finally sentenced to 15 years in prison, with the final three years suspended. He was also placed on the sex offenders register. A further condition of his release is that he doesn't reside in the counties of Offaly, Westmeath or Laois for the duration of the suspended sentence.

This man was a real 'ticking time bomb', as one of the senior investigating gardaí described him.

The public rarely hears about crime prevention, even though it's often more important than crime investigation. This proved to be the case on this occasion. Very few people would have heard of this case. There was very little coverage apart from what appeared in a local newspaper, the *Tullamore Tribune*. Yet, the combined effort of the tenacious investigating gardaí and the evidence provided by the Handwriting Section, the Forensic Lab and the Fingerprints Section may just have prevented this ticking time bomb from going off.

29

THE NAME GAME

I signed and sealed the deed, and called in witnesses,
and weighed out the silver on the scales.
Jeremiah 32:10

The Soldier's Signature

A corporal in the Defence Forces, let's call him Sean Butterly,
allegedly sent a typed letter to a garda chief superintendent in
the district. The letter was merely a complaint from a disgruntled
corporal, nothing threatening or malicious, but was signed 'Sean
Butterly'. Such communication was against army protocol and
regulations, so the military police were tasked with investigating
the matter when Sean Butterly denied sending the letter.

Two members of the military police delivered the questioned
letter to me for examination, along with five specimens of the
corporal's signature on various army forms. The disputed 'Sean

Butterly' signature was a legible construction and appeared quite fluent and natural, but when I began comparing it to the specimens, I saw anomalies. While the questioned signature was similar to two specimens, it didn't match with the other three.

Handwriting identification includes the examination of *signatures*. A signature is a form of personal identification frequently used as authorisation when signing a cheque or an application form. A person's signature is often very different in style and construction to their normal handwriting, so the two cannot be reliably compared. As a result, signature examination is usually carried out separately from the examination of a body of handwriting; i.e. handwriting can only be compared with handwriting, and signatures can only be compared with signatures. Additionally, only signatures purporting to be the same name can be compared to each other, so 'John Smith' can't be compared to 'Barry Murphy'.

A signature is a very personal creation, and, as with handwriting, it develops and evolves over time. It settles into a writer's mark of identity when it reaches a desired level of aesthetic satisfaction and ease of execution. Signature writing is a mostly subconscious act in a graphically mature writer. It may be simple in construction and quite legible, or it may contain embellishments, flourishes or complex line constructions with little or no discernible letters.

For a reliable signature comparison, at least 10 to 12 genuine specimen signatures should be available, preferably more. As signatures are often executed rapidly, they lend themselves to a greater amount of natural variation. Therefore, having as many specimens as possible will give the examiner a more informed idea of the level of this variation. They can decide if the questioned or disputed signature falls within this range.

The Irish Army's internal investigation into the corporal illustrates the necessity of obtaining sufficient specimen material. I couldn't come to a reliable conclusion comparing the questioned letter and five specimens of the corporal's signature.

I contacted the Military Police (MPs) and asked if they were certain the specimens were all genuine 'Sean Butterly' signatures. They assured me they were. As five specimens weren't enough to carry out a fully informed comparison, I requested they send more material, preferably incidental or course-of-business signatures. Handwriting and signature specimens can be incidental, meaning they have been written during everyday communications. Alternatively, the signatures can be *request* specimens that are specifically provided for the matter under investigation. There are pros and cons for both types of specimens. Incidental writing will not be disguised but may not be in the style of the disputed writing. With request specimens, the writer may employ an element of deliberate disguise. Also, the specimen may not accurately represent their usual writing if they are nervous or aware of the possible ramifications of their actions. Ideally, the best specimen material is a mixture of incidental and request.

The MPs furnished me with six additional specimen 'Sean Butterly' signatures, meaning I now had 11 specimens to work with. I started my examination and comparisons again, and it soon became apparent why I had noted dissimilarities between the disputed signature and some of the purportedly genuine specimens.

Different factors can influence the construction of a person's handwriting or signature, including fatigue, the influence of alcohol or drugs, poor pen control, spatial limitations, etc., but one crucial element can sometimes be overlooked – the *writing purpose.*

The perceived importance of the document can influence a person's signature. For example, they might take more care signing for a mortgage than for a pizza delivery. People may execute a more legible and aesthetically pleasing signature on more significant papers.

The specimen signatures provided were all from work-related forms. However, some were purely procedural, such as timesheets or delivery dockets, while others were more formal, including applications and reports. It quickly became apparent that Sean Butterly had two distinct signature styles: one for routine, daily documents and another for more formal documents like reports to senior officers. The disputed signature on the letter to the garda chief superintendent fell into this latter category. Armed with more illuminating specimens, I arrived at an informed conclusion: the corporal had written his formal 'Sean Butterly' signature on the letter in question.

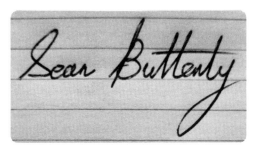

'*Formal' Sean Butterly signature*

'Informal' Sean Butterly signature

I prepared my report for the MPs, and several months later I was asked to attend a disciplinary inquiry held in Sean Butterly's barracks. I was well used to giving evidence in court, but this was an entirely different set-up. The hearing was held in the commandant's office, which was quite small. Sean Butterly and his army representative attended, as did the officer in charge of the investigation, two military police, the commandant and me. Instead of presenting my evidence from a witness box, I sat in the cramped room, leafing through my notes on my lap. It was a very formal affair with plenty of 'Yes, Commandant' and 'No, Commandant', but I got through it. Once I had presented my evidence, I was free to go, so I never heard the outcome. I can only assume that 'Sean Butterly' was disciplined.

This signature case wouldn't be the last time I had to examine the signatures or handwriting of people who could easily switch between different writing styles. Again, it served to show that you can never have too much material for comparison.

I've always liked signature comparison cases, even large ones with perhaps a hundred or more disputed signatures, such as big cheque fraud cases or social welfare investigations. I could disappear into the material, soaking up the intricate details and learning the patterns and flow of signatures under examination. You might think it's easier to compare simple, legible signatures, but in my experience, the opposite is often the case. Complex and elaborate signatures are more difficult for a forger to replicate, especially if no genuine signatures are available for reference. When attempting to forge these types of signatures, a writer has to consider *fluency* and *accuracy*. To achieve accuracy, they have to slow down the pen movement, which affects fluency, and if they speed up the writing to maintain fluency, then accuracy is affected.

Sometimes, a would-be forger may get their hands on documents containing the signature they wish to replicate. They might use this as a reference and attempt a free-hand simulation, or they might trace it and, using the paper, rewrite over the genuine signature using more pen pressure, leaving an indentation that they can then use as guidance. Such forgeries are usually detectable by their poor fluency. Oblique or sideways lighting might also reveal the indentation. More technologically savvy forgers might use editing software to copy and paste a genuine signature onto a document, leaving it difficult or impossible to determine the veracity of the signature.

Another factor to consider when dealing with disputed signatures is the act of autoforgery. This is when a person writes their signature on a document in a subtly different way than they usually do with the objective of later denying it's their genuine signature. In practice, this is quite difficult to achieve because the signature must be able to pass initial scrutiny yet contain some slight modification for the writer to deny it at a later date. With sufficient specimen material, a handwriting expert should be able to conclude the authorship of such signatures.

With handwriting comparisons, depending on the material available, an expert may identify an author *and* rule out another person from having written a body of writing. However, signatures can only be ascertained as either genuine *or* forgeries. If the latter is the case, it is usually impossible to link the forgery to a specific writer because any specimens they are asked to provide of the name in question will not be in the style of the disputed signature. Of course, linking them to the disputed signature may be possible through other means, such as someone witnessing them sign it.

As with handwriting examinations, I always found sketching out the signatures under scrutiny very helpful. I usually sketched the genuine specimens first, increasing my familiarity with their construction. I built a rhythm in my head, matching the ups and downs and flows of the pen movements, so when it came to a signature that didn't quite match this pattern, I took a closer look and tried to determine if the discrepancy pointed to it being a forgery.

Discrepancies or differences may also just be an aspect of natural variation or could be due to any number of influencing factors such as the surface being written on, the writing implement being used, illness, infirmity, medications or alcohol. Sometimes, as with our handwriting, 'accidentals' can occur. These are letter constructions or pen movements outside the normal level of natural variation and might occur because of a momentary interruption or lapse in concentration. As we are not machines, we can be prone to these little hiccups from time to time. I like to refer to these accidents as brain farts, and we're all guilty of squeezing one out now and again.

30

THE TIME MACHINE

*Evil is unspectacular and always human and shares our
bed and eats at our own table.*
W.H. Auden

The little girl's school copybook lay open on my desk. I picked up
my magnifying lens and began comparing it with the letter found
by her murdered mother's bed. I usually 'zoned out' everything and
immersed myself in the work, but the slightly lopsided penmanship
of a child distracted me. I wondered about her thoughts that night
as the contents of the letter were dictated to her.

The handwriting of young people rarely landed on my desk
for examination. The art of letter writing is dying, particularly
among the young, who are usually much more comfortable texting
or tweeting on social media. When carrying out a handwriting
examination, the actual content is usually not of paramount
importance to the expert, even though it would be for the

investigating *gardaí*. Instead, it's the construction of the individual letters and all of the other aspects of the writing that is scrutinised, and not necessarily the information imparted in the text.

However, I couldn't help but be struck by two letters I received in connection with two separate investigations. I pored over those letters for hours as I examined them. It wasn't just the tragic nature of the content that stood out. These letters were unusual because they were both penned by young females – one by an 11-year-old girl and the other by a young mother in her twenties. Both were murdered.

The Coward

Thirty-seven-year-old Seema Banu lived in an apartment in Llewellyn Court, Rathfarnham, with her 11-year-old daughter Asfira and son Faizan, who was six. She had travelled from India to live in Ireland with her children and husband, Sameer Syed, in 2018.

However, gardaí frequently called to their home in Llewellyn Court due to Syed's repeated assaults on his wife. Child protection services became involved because of concerns for the children's safety. In May 2020, after a particularly violent incident that left Seema unconscious, Syed was arrested. He was only released from custody under the provision that he stay away from the house.

On 28 October 2020, a member of the child protection unit in Tusla (the child and family welfare agency) called to Llewellyn Court. When they failed to get an answer at the door, gardaí were alerted. When they entered the house, they noticed ceiling damage because of a tap left running upstairs. Gardaí ascended the stairs to find Asfira and Faizan dead, lying face-down on a bed with scarves tied and knotted around their necks. In a separate room, they found Seema's body lying face-up with a ligature around her neck, knotted at the front. Placed neatly on her bedside table was a handwritten letter.

Suspicion quickly fell on Sameer Syed. It emerged that he had continued to call to the house after the earlier assault but, to disguise himself, he had dressed as a woman. Gardaí found CCTV footage showing a person boarding a bus in Rathmines at around 8 p.m. on 22 October, six days before the bodies of Seema and the children were found. This individual, who carried a bag, wore a dress, jacket, hat and dark glasses and took the number 14 bus towards Rathfarnham. They established that this was Syed and that the clothing wasn't a form of cultural dress or attire. He changed back into men's clothes before arriving at the house.

Gardaí retrieved a video recorded on Seema's mobile phone by her and her daughter Asfira at around 10 p.m. that night. Seema stated to the camera that the injuries she had previously claimed to have sustained in the May assault were, in fact, self-inflicted. Asfira also appeared on the video, saying, 'Dad loves us a lot. He loves us so much.' Seema then produced a written document, describing it as her final statement, denying that the assault took place. This document was the letter found on her bedside table.

As gardaí continued their investigation into the deaths, it became evident Seema was living in fear of her husband and wished to return to India with the children. Syed had beaten her on several occasions, even before arriving in Ireland. On Christmas Eve 2018, a security guard in Dunnes Stores in Sandyford noticed a woman and two children crying in the shop. He also saw them being forcibly grabbed and pulled by a man in their company. The security guard ejected the man from the store. The woman and children turned out to be Seema, Asfira and Faizan. They were given food, as they hadn't eaten since the previous evening, and Seema told the Hindi-speaking guard that her husband was beating and torturing her. She said, 'He is dangerous. He will kill me. I just want to go back to India.' She also said that she had money and passports ready for some time. She wanted to flee with the children but was terrified of what Sameer would do if he caught her.

The investigation continued, and Sameer Syed was arrested under suspicion of murdering his wife and children. At first, he denied everything and alleged that Seema had killed Asfira and Faizan before dying by suicide. He pointed out the handwritten letter, in which Seema stated that she was mentally unwell and feared she might do something terrible. Syed also denied being at the house on the night that Seema and the children were believed to have been murdered, but he made a crucial error. Although he had left his mobile phone in the flat where he was staying, he had brought a second 'burner' phone with him, and gardaí determined that this phone was at Llewellyn Court on the night of the killings.

The letter came to me to be examined. As Seema had little or no English, the letter had allegedly been dictated to and written by Asfira. The actual authorship of the letter wasn't in question, but the writing still had to be 'proven' before it could be produced as evidence in court. I was given schoolwork written by the young girl as the specimen writing.

As I carried out my comparisons, scrutinising the neat script, I couldn't help thinking about Asfira's confusion and fear, ordered to write about her mother's supposed mental problems, knowing that it was all lies. We knew it was Sameer who dictated the letter to his daughter to throw suspicion on Seema. The letter was like a sort of time machine, taking me back to the night she wrote it, perhaps only hours before she, her mother and her little brother would die.

The pathologist who examined the bodies stated that Asfira and Faizan died by ligature strangulation. Seema was also strangled, and the ligature was applied to her neck after death. The pathologist stated that self-strangulation was highly unlikely.

Sameer Syed eventually admitted to having murdered Seema but denied having killed his children. However, his fingerprints were found on plastic bags placed under Asfira's head. He had murdered them and then his wife, staging it to look like she had killed Asfira and Faizan before dying by suicide. It was thought that he intended to die by suicide after carrying out the slayings, but he chickened out.

Sameer Syed was charged with the murders of his wife and children, but on 9 June 2022, only days before his trial was due to start, he finally followed through with his original intention and hanged himself in his cell in the Midlands Prison in Portlaoise. It was the last act of a cowardly and cold-hearted killer.

The Murder of Jasmine McGonagle
Gardaí raced to a house in Forest Park in Killygordon, a small village in east Donegal, in the early hours of 4 January 2019.

They were responding to a 999 call made at 4.21 a.m. by a young woman living there. She was a 27-year-old mother of two, Jasmine McGonagle, an aspiring model and actress. She lived in Forest Park with 28-year-old Richard Burke and her two daughters, aged eight years and 18 months respectively. Jasmine said on the phone that she was in fear of her life.

When gardaí arrived at the address, Burke confronted them, brandishing a meat cleaver. He swung it at one of the members, narrowly missing him, and a stand-off ensued, with the gardaí not able to get inside. A guard got to the rear of the house, looked through a small gap in the kitchen curtains and saw a woman lying in a pool of blood.

A trained negotiator and the Garda Armed Support Unit were dispatched to the scene, and the stand-off continued. However, gardaí spotted Jasmine's 8-year-old daughter at the front bedroom window, and at 7.30 a.m. the decision was made for an immediate forced entry. When the gardaí gained access, they found Burke had barricaded himself in at the rear of the house. He confronted them with a hammer, so he was tasered and subdued. They found a large knife in a scabbard in his jacket. Jasmine's lifeless body was found in the kitchen. She had been viciously beaten and strangled. Her two daughters were unharmed.

Richard Burke had never held down a job in his life and had 23 previous convictions for criminal damage, assault and possession of knives. He had been in an on–off relationship with Jasmine for several years and was the father of her 18-month-old daughter. Burke had a history of violent and erratic behaviour, compounded by his years of drug abuse. He once bought a used Nissan Micra for Jasmine to woo her back during a break in their relationship.

One day, in a fit of rage, he took the car, crashed it and set fire to it. He had previously been detained in a psychiatric unit because of his violent outbursts.

While being interviewed, Burke told gardaí that on the night of Jasmine's death, they had been arguing, and when he found out that she had made a 999 call, he 'just blanked and went absolutely fucking ballistic', pummelling her and strangling her with a piece of rope. He was still clutching the rope when the gardaí arrived.

Forensic analysis of the scene indicated that the majority of the beating had taken place with Jasmine cowering on the kitchen floor. Death was caused by ligature strangulation, with concussion and blood loss from multiple blunt and sharp force injuries being contributing factors. Such was the ferocity of the attack that some of Jasmine's hair extensions were ripped out and found on the draining board and the kitchen floor.

During the investigation into Jasmine's murder, a handwritten letter was found. It made its way to D&HW and ended up on my desk. The content of the letter was important to the investigating gardaí as it gave an insight into the abusive relationship Jasmine was trapped in. As with the letter written by Asfira Syed, the authorship of the letter still had to be proven.

The undated letter, which was thought to have been written in the months leading up to the murder, was addressed to 'Richard'. It was four pages long, written in a fluent and confident script style. It spoke of the fear she felt, being trapped in a relationship with the volatile Burke:

'I'm sick of you thinking you can do whatever you want and get away with it.'

'Trying to smash my house up and saying I was lucky to be breathing.'

'You threatened to kill me and [my daughter]'

She wrote how Burke had 'beat up the puppy' and 'held me hostage in my own garden'. Jasmine said she was 'too scared to go into my back garden'.

'Do your family not know how much you hate them and how you say you're gonna shoot them all?'

I was struck by Jasmine's bravery and her determination to stay strong and protect her two girls.

'You can find someone else to threaten to kill.'

Richard Burke was charged with the murder of Jasmine McGonagle. At the subsequent trial in 2023, the prosecuting barrister described the crime as a 'senseless and horrific' act. Burke was ultimately convicted of manslaughter due to diminished responsibility, complicated by his years of drug abuse. He was sentenced to 14 years. I think he got off lightly.

In her impact statement, Jasmine's mother, Jacqueline, spoke of the day her daughter died: 'My world fell apart.' Jasmine's life and future had been 'horrifically taken from her'. Jasmine's eldest daughter, now 12, also gave a statement. She said, 'I wish Mammy had never ever met him. He has ruined our lives, and we can never get Mammy back.' She also described how Burke had been teaching Jasmine martial arts, but it was him she really needed defending from.

Jasmine's murder also split up the two half-sisters, as the eldest girl went to live with her father while the younger child went to live with Jasmine's sister. The older girl continued to have nightmares, afraid that Burke would escape and come to kill her. Even trips to the cinema or the hairdresser's were overwhelming for her.

Before the trial, I took out the file and reviewed what Jasmine had written. Jasmine's letter was ultimately accepted into evidence, so I wasn't called as a witness, but this was before I was notified that I wouldn't be needed.

It was then I was reminded that the specimen handwriting I received for comparison was an application form for social housing support written by Jasmine on 4 January 2017, exactly two years to the day before her murder.

Jasmine's letter and the specimen writing were another example of being able to step back through time to a moment in her life when she still had hopes and dreams of achieving her modelling and acting goals and providing the best possible upbringing for her two girls. Jasmine hadn't signed her name to the letter she had written to Richard Burke. Instead, she ended it with two words: 'Never Again.' She wouldn't have known it, but this signing-off was prophetic for all the wrong reasons. Never again would she be able to plan for her future. Never again would her two girls live together. Never again would they be able to hug their mother. Never again.

The final two words from Jasmine's letter

31

CONCEALMENT AND CONFESSION

Sooner or later, everyone sits down to a banquet of consequences.

Robert Louis Stevenson

A Killer's Confession

The cold-blooded murder of teenager Melanie McCarthy McNamara took place in Tallaght in Dublin on 8 February 2012. Melanie, who was 16 years old, was sitting in a car in Brookview Way, Tallaght, with two young men, including her boyfriend, Christopher Moran. A black Hyundai Santa Fe pulled alongside them with a sawn-off shotgun pointing out one of the windows. A shot was discharged, hitting Melanie in the head. She died a short time later in hospital.

Evil exists, as do evil people. However, for me, the commission of an 'evil' act suggests the person responsible possesses cunning.

They may have a twisted intelligence tied up with an arrogance or warped ideology that makes them believe their actions are justified. Sometimes, however, certain people carry out senseless acts for no reason other than being just plain *bad*. I believe Melanie McCarthy McNamara's murder is such an example.

The Santa Fe was found a short time later, abandoned in Citywest, having run out of petrol. The shotgun and cartridges were found nearby. Despite no fingerprints being found on the weapon or the car, two suspects were soon arrested by gardaí and charged in relation to the murder. One of these individuals was a young man called Keith Hall. He had 111 previous convictions, an impressive tally for someone who was only 22 years old. He represented another good repeat customer for the men in the shiny suits.

Hall pleaded not guilty to the charge of murdering Melanie McCarthy McNamara. He maintained that he had not been the one who had pulled the trigger. He claimed to have only thrown a stone at Christopher Moran's house to lure him out on the night of the murder.

Hall pleaded guilty to the lesser charge of manslaughter, no doubt believing that this would get him a more lenient sentence. However, Mr Justice Paul Carney handed him a hefty term of 20 years' imprisonment, one of the longest-ever sentences invoked for a manslaughter conviction.

Keith Hall went to prison a marked man with rumours that a €20,000 contract had been taken out on his life. He was slashed with a makeshift 'shiv' or razor, requiring 50 stitches. Not long after, he was attacked in his cell while sleeping and a potent mixture of boiling water and sugar was poured down his throat, causing agonising injuries. He will look over his shoulder for the rest of his jail term.

The other individual arrested and charged with Melanie's murder was 17-year-old Daniel McDonnell. He had several previous convictions, including firearms possession, theft, and threatening and abusive behaviour. He didn't show a shred of remorse, but to paraphrase the character of Uncle Ben in the *Spider-Man* movie, 'With great badness comes great stupidity.'

I became involved in the periphery of the investigation due to McDonnell's bluster while in custody. He had scrawled stuff on his cell wall, bragging about Melanie's murder, and sent letters to his brother and girlfriend, again referring to his role in the slaying. Investigating gardaí asked me to compare known samples of McDonnell's handwriting to photographs of the cell wall graffiti and his letters to prove he wrote them.

It is usually quite challenging to assign authorship to graffiti. Very often, it consists of 'tagging', which is more akin to artwork and doesn't consist of traditional letter constructions. The writing surface, the posture of the author, and the writing implement used can all affect the finished article. McDonnell's writing on the cell wall was more like ordinary writing. However, its brevity prevented me from giving any strong opinion about its authorship. It consisted of a couple of lines reading: '2 in the head. Your bitch is dead ha ha.'

The two letters were another matter. McDonnell wrote them knowing full well the prison staff would intercept them. He again boasted about the murder. 'I will do 25 on the toilet while you're crying. Close range head shots. That's what I'm going for. Two in the head … your bitch is dead … little did he know had a loaded 12 gauge … left his bitch all over the Sunday World front page … I will never forget that mug crying. Best night of my life.' The letters also contained some crude drawings. As a result of my examination, I was satisfied that there was strong evidence to support the claim that Daniel McDonnell had written the two letters.

Before McDonnell's trial began, I attended a pre-trial meeting in the offices of the Criminal Courts of Justice (CCJ). In attendance were the prosecution counsel, gardaí in charge of the investigation, a colleague from the Fingerprints Section and a DNA specialist from the Forensic Science Laboratory. McDonnell's fingerprints and DNA had been identified on the letters, so along with my evidence that he had written them, the prosecution was going to use these exhibits as one of the main pillars of their case.

When it came to the actual trial, I wasn't required to give evidence because McDonnell freely admitted to having authored the letters and the writing on the cell wall. The defence argued that the letters and the graffiti were merely 'rants' and were written in the context that McDonnell was told that he would go down in history as the infamous gunman responsible for Melanie McCarthy McNamara's murder. They also stated that there wasn't a 'scintilla' of evidence against their client apart from the writing.

In summing up their case, the prosecution described the letters and graffiti as 'truly extraordinary'. They said that there was no other explanation for them other than an admission of guilt and that the jury was entitled to convict McDonnell of murder. The presiding judge, Mr Justice Paul Carney, told the jury that there was a total absence of corroboration in the case, but they were still entitled to convict if they regarded the letters and graffiti as *confessions*.

After a little over four hours of deliberation, the jury returned their unanimous verdict. They found Daniel McDonnell guilty of the murder of Melanie McCarthy McNamara. He stared straight ahead and showed no emotion as the judge handed down the mandatory life sentence.

Whatever was bad in Daniel McDonnell continued to fester. Prison staff would sometimes have to resort to wearing riot gear because of his increasingly violent outbursts. He would regularly threaten the guards, sometimes even spitting blood at them. On one occasion, he held an improvised metal shiv to his own throat before concealing it in his rear end. This led to him being hospitalised because of a serious infection. His volatile behaviour would continue. In 2021, a prison guard saw McDonnell carving into the viewing glass of his cell door with a sharpened piece of metal. When asked what he was doing, McDonnell replied: 'I'm cutting through both sides of the glass so I can spray piss and shit at whatever scumbag officer that comes near the door. See this? I'll slit your throat with this. If I can't do it, I'll get someone on the outside to do it. I can get that sorted.'

What causes a person to act this way? Is it evil? Badness? A product of circumstance? You could argue the whole nature versus nurture debate until you were blue in the face and still not get any closer to an answer. I think that some people are just rotten inside. It's like a basket of eggs, all laid by the same hen, yet one of them is just *bad*. There doesn't have to be a reason. Like bad luck, it floats around before landing on someone and soaking into their bones, tainting everything they do.

People like Daniel McDonnell don't care about the consequences of their actions. They only care about one thing: themselves. Everyone else has to pick up the pieces in their wake or bear the brunt of their deeds. Sixteen-year-old Melanie McCarthy McNamara was in the wrong place at the wrong time. She was an innocent victim of someone who won't be remembered as a cold-blooded gunman or a hardened gangster. Just ... *bad*.

People can be remarkably creative when circumstances require. I've seen all sorts of ingenious tricks employed by persons sending written communications who put that extra bit of thought into their correspondence. Sometimes, these efforts are spurred by anger, revenge, desperation or affairs of the heart that have soured. On more than one occasion, I've seen neatly addressed padded envelopes which contained heart-warming 'gifts' like dead rats, blood, semen or faeces. And sometimes, due to the need for secrecy, writers must put a little extra effort into transmitting information.

Members from the Special Detective Unit (SDU), acting on confidential information, stopped and searched a man in the car park of Portlaoise Prison. His name was Brian Kenna. He had just left the prison after visiting some inmates. Kenna had a chequered past, having previously been jailed for 10 years for his role in an attempted armed robbery at a bank in Enniscorthy, County Wexford in 1990. During the botched raid, Kenna, part of an 'active service unit' in the IRA, and his accomplices exchanged gunfire with gardaí. They surrendered when one of them was shot in the head. (The injured man later recovered from his wounds.)

When Brian Kenna was searched by the detectives in the prison car park, a small plastic package fell from one of his pockets. He denied all knowledge of it and laughed when he was quizzed about it. Inside the plastic, the gardaí found three cigarette papers stuck together and covered in tiny, neat handwriting. I was asked to compare the handwriting on the papers to the writing on several Christmas cards that were also found in the possession of Brian Kenna when he left the prison. He had been given the cards by the inmates that he visited.

A cigarette paper measures roughly 3.5 cm x 7 cm, and even three stuck together comprise a relatively small area to write. The spatial limitations most likely affected the construction of the writing, but it was also my opinion, based on previous experience, that the people sending such communiques write in a certain way to ensure anonymity and clarity in imparting the information. The result was that writing on the cigarette papers was in a neat, block style and quite different from the cursive and script handwriting on the cards.

The secret communiqué spoke about an IRA debriefing of three men who had recently been arrested after an intercepted operation in Rathkeale, County Limerick. The writer asserted that they had 'behaved as expected while in custody'. It was signed off by the commanding officer of the IRA in Portlaoise Prison.

Brian Kenna was charged with membership of an unlawful organisation, namely the IRA. He was tried before a sitting of the Special Criminal Court, which sits with three presiding judges and no jury, and tries acts of terrorism and serious organised crime offences. I gave evidence at Kenna's trial, telling the court that I could not reliably link the handwriting on the cigarette papers found on Brian Kenna to the writing on the Christmas cards. It was also my opinion that the writing was likely not a good representation of the author's normal handwriting.

Despite the fact that I could not identify the author of the intercepted communiqué, Brian Kenna was found guilty and received a 16-month sentence.

32

HOLED BELOW THE WATERLINE

Unless it is relevant and accurate, knowledge can be
the sinking ship the fool insists is sea-worthy because
knowledge often masquerades as wisdom.
Anonymous

Things were ticking along nicely as I began my second decade
working in D&HW. I was enjoying the work, particularly when
a good meaty handwriting or signature case came my way. We
were only a small section, but we got on well with each other
and ploughed through the workload like a well-oiled machine.
We kept the time between garda members submitting exhibits
for examination and our furnishing of the report as short as was
practicable.

It was all down to good management within the section. Our
detective inspector, Mick Moore, and our skipper, Ray Jackman,
kept the cogs turning and lit a fire under our arses when the pending

case file drawer started filling up. As ever, we were self-contained and largely insulated from whatever else was happening in the Bureau, and that was exactly the way we liked it. But nothing lasts forever, and certainty is the calm before the storm.

The Council of the European Union came up with a 'Framework Decision' in 2009, which decreed that all laboratories reporting on DNA and fingerprint evidence must comply with the wonderful new ISO-17025 standard. To quote from the website of the International Organisation for Standardisation, ISO-17025 'specifies the general requirements for the competence to carry out tests and/or calibrations, including sampling'.

The Bureau had already been saddled with 17025's baby brother, ISO 9001, but the decision was made to really shoot for the stars and achieve this lofty accolade. So now, to meet the new standard, mountains of new forms and process papers were conjured up. Lucky Bureau members who were picked to be internal auditors had to be trained, often resulting in their real duties being sidelined.

It seemed like every time we picked up a pen, new rules and regulations, new procedures and checks and balances all descended on us like a bad stink. To me, it only served to push the real reason for our existence – the examination of and reporting on crime scene exhibits – into the background. It was maddening, but resistance was futile. The attainment of ISO-17025 was now a priority. I just had to hunker down in my foxhole and concentrate on my work.

The new 'standard' was awarded to the Bureau with much fanfare in February 2016. Needless to say, I didn't throw any parties. As far as I was concerned, the slight list on the deck of the good ship 'Bureau' had taken on a more sinister angle. The dishes were sliding off the shelves and smashing on the galley floor.

By this time, any hint of conformity was pretty much eradicated from my mindset. Inked, bearded and stubborn, I didn't try to conceal my disdain for these extraneous endeavours. If, during the course of my duties as a documents and handwriting examiner, I was reproached for wandering 'off scope' with an exasperated, 'Sweets, what about ISO?', I would invariably reply, 'I S.O. don't give a fuck!'

Grappling with the demands of ISO-17025 was enough to contend with. However, another far-weightier bombshell was about to be dropped on the Bureau.

Changes were afoot when the chief inspector of the Garda Inspectorate, Robert K. Olson, began an examination of the force. As part of his work, he met with many gardaí from divisions and specialist units all across the country. Mr Olson had many years of policing experience behind him, including being chief of police in Minneapolis and commissioner of Yonkers, NYPD.

When Mr Olson came to the Technical Bureau to speak with members from the various sections, my colleague Geraldine and I were asked to represent the D&HW Section. I found him a pleasant and attentive man and felt comfortable chatting about the pluses and minuses of working in D&HW. He had no problem with my beard and tattoos, but after the meeting, it got back to me that certain Bureau members 'of rank' took issue with my appearance.

My response to this was two short words, and they weren't 'thank you'.

By now, Detective Inspector Mick Moore had retired, leaving Sergeant Ray Jackman as the head of our section. One day, Ray returned from the regular meeting between the chief super of the Bureau and the section heads. He had bad news. The Garda Technical Bureau, which had been in existence since 1934, was to be 'merged' with the Forensic Science Laboratory, now called Forensic Science Ireland (FSI).

The 'merge' was a result of recommendation 1.4 of the *Changing Policing in Ireland* report published by the Garda Inspectorate in November 2015. It was the death knell for the Bureau as we knew it. Serving garda members within Ballistics, Fingerprints and D&HW would be seconded to FSI in the short term. The long-term goal was to replace them with 'professional forensic science staff'. What the hell were we? Mules with ill-fitting lab coats? Glorified bottle-washers? We *were* professional forensic science staff. We were Technical Bureau *experts* with a combined pool of many decades of experience in scenes-of-crime examination, exhibit processing and evidence presentation.

The news of the proposed merger was met with shock and anger, but the die had been cast. The merger was set for the end of 2019. It loomed in the water like an iceberg, inching closer every day. At the time, I wasn't overly concerned. After all, how bad could it be? I was already working nine to five with no weekends, and my duties would remain the same. I would retain my expert allowance too. The only difference would be that my superiors would now be FSI staff instead of gardaí. Ray Jackman pulled the plug around this time, leaving Geraldine with the unenviable task of assuming the mantle of head of the D&HW Section in the run-up to the merger.

Elsewhere in the Bureau, the entire staff of the Ballistics Section dug their heels in and steadfastly refused to acquiesce to the merger. Several members of the Fingerprints Section sided with them, and something of a stand-off ensued. Two colleagues in D&HW also decided they weren't rolling over but had to pull in their horns when threatened with a transfer to a city-centre garda station. The two transferred to greener pastures instead the following year.

Before the merger, there were only five of us in the section. Perhaps if we had all stuck together, we might have been able to preserve the integrity of the Documents and Handwriting Section and remain our own entity. This eventually happened with the Ballistics Section and the few from the Fingerprints Section who went on to form the National Scenes of Crime Unit. I don't have many regrets about my years in An Garda Síochána, but that is my biggest one. I should have stood with my colleagues and said, 'No!'. I guess I didn't have the headspace for office politics around the time as Da had been diagnosed with pancreatic cancer. There were more important things on my mind.

The merger went ahead, and in December 2019, the Garda Technical Bureau ceased to be. I was now a detective garda on secondment to FSI. However, another big shake-up was looming on the horizon. A purpose-built facility was under construction in Backweston, near Celbridge in Kildare, where the State Laboratory is located.

The new building was to become the future home of the FSI Laboratory, including the Fingerprints Section and D&HW. It was a green-field site, far away from Garda HQ and the Criminal Courts of Justice. A move out there would mean a longer commute and tolls on the M50. I hoped that by the time the place was ready for us to move in, I would be near to completing my 30 years' service in An Garda Síochána. I started my countdown to retirement and planned to jump ship on 27 April 2024. What is it they say about the best-laid plans?

33

LAST WORDS

Our bodies are prisons for our souls. Our skin and blood, the iron bars of confinement. But fear not. All flesh decays. Death turns all to ash. And thus, death frees every soul.

Grand Inquisitor Silecio, The Fountain

I was early for court on 18 December 2017. Then again, I always am. I imagine I'll be early for my own funeral. I parked the state car in front of Cavan garda station and went inside. I had an upset stomach and flashed my garda ID to the mule at the front desk, asking if I could use the toilet. He buzzed me in and directed me to the loo. As soon as I mounted the throne, the world dropped out of me. Nerves. Why was I feeling like this?

By now, I was an old hand at giving evidence in court. It didn't bother me in the slightest. I was one of only two full-time handwriting experts left in the job and well-seasoned when it came to sparring with tricky defence counsel. Today, there wouldn't even *be* a defence counsel as I was attending a sitting of the Coroner's Court. I'd been to these before. They were usually short affairs; I'd normally breeze through my evidence and be gone within minutes. But this time, it would be different. The eyes and ears of the media would be zeroed in on Cavan Courthouse for the inquest into the most horrific case I would ever be involved in as a member of An Garda Síochána.

The Hawe Family Murders

Mary Coll knew that something was wrong. It was 29 August 2016, a Monday morning. Mary's daughter Clodagh Hawe had been due to drop off her two youngest boys at her mother's house in Virginia, County Cavan, before heading to work.

Thirty-nine-year-old Clodagh was due back at her teaching job at Oristown National School, near Kells, after the summer holidays. Her husband, Alan, was deputy principal of Castlerahan National School, where the boys attended.

He was due to attend a staff meeting that day, but the boys weren't starting back to school until Tuesday. So Mary had agreed to mind 11-year-old Niall and 6-year-old Ryan while the parents went to work. Clodagh and Alan's eldest boy, 14-year-old Liam, was attending secondary school that day.

However, Mary began to get worried as the clock ticked towards 9 a.m. and there was no sign of Clodagh and the boys arriving. She started calling them, but couldn't get hold of either Clodagh or Alan.

The entire family had called over to Mary the previous evening, and everything had seemed fine. Liam had been in great spirits after winning a basketball game that day. Mary was concerned because she knew it was out of character for her daughter not to phone if she was going to be delayed.

She decided to drive to the Hawes' house at Oakdene Downs, Barconey Heights. The dormer bungalow lay in a quiet country cul-de-sac, along with three other houses, all surrounded by fields. Mary pulled up outside the house and saw the couple's cars parked in the driveway and the front curtains drawn. She approached the front door with a sinking feeling in the pit of her stomach. Had there been some sort of accident? It flashed across her mind that maybe there had been a carbon monoxide leak, but when she got to the door, she saw a white note in Alan Hawe's handwriting stuck to the inside of the glass. The note read: 'Please don't come in. Please call the gardaí.' Mary later said that it was then that she knew. *He's killed them all.*

Mary dialled 999 and went to a neighbour's house to await the gardaí. Just after 11 a.m., Garda Aisling Walsh and Garda Alan Ratcliffe arrived. They told Mary to wait outside as they entered the house. The guards called out to identify themselves as they entered via the kitchen door, but they were met with a deathly silence. What greeted them afterwards was a scene straight out of a nightmare. Clodagh was wearing night clothes, lying face down dead on the couch in the living room, covered in blood. A small hand axe and a knife lay beside her on the floor. They entered the hall to find Alan Hawe's lifeless body hanging from an orange nylon rope. The two shocked gardaí then made their way upstairs. Liam and Niall's bodies were in their beds in the room they shared. Their duvets had been pulled over them. The two boys had wounds to their throats, and a bloody knife was lying on the floor. Ryan lay alone in his room. He too had suffered injuries to his throat, and a knife had been left on his pillow. A shaken Garda Walsh then had to go back outside to tell Mary Coll that nobody had been found alive.

A full-scale investigation was set in motion, and the quiet little cul-de-sac was soon swarming with gardaí and patrol cars. The Technical Bureau and deputy state pathologist, Dr Michael Curtis, were called to the scene. Dr Curtis spent 40 minutes examining the bodies in situ, and preliminary findings indicated that Alan Hawe had murdered his wife and sons before killing himself.

During the search of the interior of the house, they found several jewellery boxes neatly piled on the bed in the main bedroom. Downstairs in the kitchen, an envelope and handwritten notes were lying on the table. Dr Curtis and the Bureau team carried out their initial examination of the scene before several hearses were called to transport the bodies to the morgue for post-mortem examinations.

Two days later, on 31 August, I received the handwritten material found at the house, along with specimens of Alan Hawe's handwriting. It was another occasion where I couldn't help but be aware of the content of the pages. They were written in a neat and fluent cursive style with no signs of hesitation or duress. The pages were unlined, yet the writing remained symmetrical and aligned. Some of the pages were blood-stained, indicating that some or all of the writing had been committed to paper *after* Alan Hawe had murdered his family.

However, I was struck by how calm and pragmatic the letters appeared, listing instructions about what to do regarding Clodagh's jewellery (the boxes found on the bed) and the two cars, and where to find the children's money boxes and his wife's handbag. It reminded me of another case that I had worked on around that time.

That case also involved several letters left by a man who had died by suicide. Like the Hawe letters, the man's final writings were neat and concise. He had everything planned, including details regarding his will and bank and credit union account information. He included instructions for his funeral and advice for his family on dealing with fallout on social media after his death. There were even instructions about what to do with the car and the family dog. It's amazing how someone's mind can go into such a business-like mode before taking their life. The poor man killed himself, but the difference is he didn't take anyone else with him.

I won't go into detail about the content of the Alan Hawe letters, but they never properly explained why he murdered everyone. He alluded to some recent work-related events that he thought would come to light and disgrace him and the family. His twisted, selfish reasoning prevented him from simply killing himself. He had some warped logic that leaving his children without a father would ruin their lives. So he snuffed out those same young lives and his wife's in the most brutal way imaginable. He thought it better they were all dead so that Clodagh and the boys could be together in heaven.

In carrying out my handwriting comparisons, I had to scan over the letters again and again while comparing them with the specimen material. The specimen material consisted of work-related handwriting and, perversely, a birthday card for Clodagh, complete with a lengthy and lovingly written note inside. Again, I was struck by his neatness and attention to detail. The work-related specimen material laid out financial expenditures for the school where Alan worked, and again, it was neatly and methodically inscribed. There was also a letter regarding 'drops of water' in and around the school toilet sinks and the importance of keeping one's hands over the sink and 'shaking off excess drops carefully'. I began to build a picture of a man who was perhaps obsessed with details and perfection, always thinking about how his actions would be perceived in the community. He was someone who planned every minute detail of whatever he was involved in. Including, perhaps, murder. I got the impression that he was someone who was wound too tightly. The slightest slip-up and everything would unravel.

I had plenty of comparable material to the letters found at the murder scene and was able to give a conclusive opinion that Alan Hawe had written them in the wake of murdering his wife and kids. So, when requested, I journeyed to the Coroner's Inquest in Cavan a few days before Christmas the following year.

Before it came to my turn to give evidence, the court heard the testimony of Garda Walsh and Garda Ratcliffe, the first members to arrive at the scene. Hearing their accounts of what they had found at the house in Oakdene Downs was harrowing, and Garda Walsh needed a moment to compose herself when speaking of how she'd found the three boys in their beds. The coroner, Dr Mary Flanagan, remarked, 'No one can imagine what it was like.' Then, it was the turn of Dr Michael Curtis, who detailed the injuries that led to the deaths of Clodagh and her sons.

Clodagh Hawe had suffered multiple penetrating wounds to her head and neck. These were consistent with being made by the small axe and knife found near her body. She also had axe wounds to her hand, caused when she had tried to shield her head from the blows. She'd been stabbed in the back with such force that the blade had broken her shoulder blade.

The oldest boy, Liam, had been stabbed twice in the neck, damaging his jugular vein and carotid artery. He also had defensive wounds to his hands and forearms. He had fought back in vain. The middle child, Niall, had died from a single stab wound to his neck, which severed his windpipe. He also appeared to have a defensive wound to his right hand. Finally, the youngest, Ryan, had suffered a deep incision to his neck, cutting through his jugular and windpipe. The implement used to kill him, a Kitchen Devil-branded knife, had been laid neatly on his pillow.

Dr Curtis believed it was not coincidental that the three boys had suffered the same fate. It was apparent that, after murdering Clodagh, their father attacked them in the order of eldest to youngest, lessening the chances of any resistance. It was horrific to think about. How could a parent and a husband carry out such vicious attacks on his family? I couldn't help but think about my own kids. I could only hope that Liam, Niall and Ryan never fully comprehended what was happening when they were jolted from their sleep. It was precious little comfort to Mary Coll and family and friends when Dr Curtis stated that 'death would have ensued rapidly' following the attacks. Regarding Alan Hawe, it sounded to me that he got off easy: death by ligature strangulation.

After having listened to the harrowing evidence from the first-responding gardaí and the pathologist, it was almost a relief when I was called into the witness box. I flicked the switch and went into expert mode, informing the court of my findings about the authorship of the handwriting found at the scene. The court had a few brief questions for me. I expected to be quizzed about indications in his writing that might point to his state of mind, but this didn't happen. I was out of the box in a matter of minutes.

With my part done, I didn't stay to listen to any more evidence and left the court, glancing over at Mary Coll and her daughter Jacqueline on my way out. I wanted to stop and say something to them. Try to offer my tuppence worth of comfort, but this would have interrupted the proceedings.

The following day, as the inquest concluded, the coroner's address to Mary Coll summed up what everybody felt: 'There are no words to describe the upset that befell your family. It's unimaginable what you have had to endure.' The foreman of the jury, which comprised six women and one man, fought back emotion as she read out their findings: four counts of unlawful killing and one count of suicide.

During that second day of evidence, an attempt was made to shed some light on Alan Hawe's state of mind. Had there been any warning signs indicating what he was about to do? It emerged that he had been attending a psychotherapist, David McConnell, between March and June of 2016. Hawe had confided in McConnell that he was concerned about his position as a 'pillar of the community'. His GP stated that Alan was feeling stressed about work and was having trouble sleeping. Professor Harry Kennedy, clinical director at the Central Mental Hospital, had reviewed both the GP's notes and the letters left at the scene and surmised that Hawe was subject to delusional beliefs, such as catastrophising that some terrible event was going to happen, from which there could be no recovery. He had suffered a severe depressive episode with psychotic symptoms. Mary Coll put it to Professor Kennedy: how could he comment on someone he had never met? She had known Alan for 20 years but still didn't *really* know him.

The most frustrating thing for Mary Coll and her family, even after the inquest, was that they still didn't know the *why*. A seemingly loving and devoted husband and father had wiped out his whole family that August night. The letters Alan Hawe left behind indicated he had killed them all out of 'love', but it was really the ultimate act of selfishness. Clodagh, Liam, Niall and little Ryan had their futures snatched from them by the very person who should have protected them from harm.

Mary chooses to remember her daughter and her three grandsons as the smiling, happy people in the photographs that were taken during the family's holiday in Italy, just weeks before they were killed. I was moved to hear she keeps an empty packet of Hunky Dorys salt and vinegar crisps in a drawer in the kitchen. They were the last thing Ryan had eaten at her house on the evening of 28 August.

The Hawe case would stay with me. However, I got off lightly compared to my Bureau colleagues, who had to process that horrendous scene. It is said that nobody knows what goes on behind closed doors. I try not to think about what went on behind the door at Oakdene Downs, Barconey Heights, that night in August 2016. However, the more time passes since the event, the more it pops up, like a handwritten note stuck inside my mind.

34

EXODUS

I started out pretty strong and fast. But it's beginning
to get to me.
Luke Jackson, Cool Hand Luke

Married couple Nicholas and Hilary Smith moved to Ireland
from the UK in 2006, eventually settling in Rossane, Cloneen in
County Tipperary in 2009. 82-year-old Nicholas and 79-year-old
Hilary were quiet people, tending to keep to themselves. No one
had seen them for over 18 months, by the time neighbours became
concerned. When gardaí gained entry to the Smiths' house in June
2022, they found the bodies of the couple in an advanced state of
decomposition.

Nicholas was found in his bed, covered by a duvet, and Hilary's
body was sitting upright in an armchair in another part of the
house. Post-mortem examinations determined that Nicholas
had died from coronary artery disease, but it wasn't possible to

definitively ascertain how Hilary had died due to the condition of her remains.

A torn-up letter found in their kitchen bin was forwarded to D&HW to be reassembled. I was able to piece it back together and read the content. It appeared that Hilary had written it in December 2020, 18 months before the bodies were discovered. No envelope was found, and I don't remember if it was addressed to anyone in particular. It was a rather rambling letter, but in it, she criticised the Irish healthcare system and regretted ever coming to Ireland: 'We were both so perfectly healthy before we came to Ireland. We should never, ever have set foot in Ireland. So sad and cruel to end this way.'

She stated how weak she was and how difficult she was finding it to write because of her arthritis, but there was nothing in the letter to indicate that anything untoward had occurred. The torn-up letter helped to shed some light on what had happened. The Smiths' deaths were sad and lonely but ultimately deemed *not* to be suspicious. Foul play was ruled out.

The case had garnered a lot of attention in the media, and the investigating gardaí were under pressure to be seen to be actively determining the details of what had happened; therefore, I was contacted about sending my report. Unfortunately, for one reason or another, there were very few staff in D&HW around that time, so the FSI double-peer review and final review couldn't be carried out. I made the decision that since there was nothing contentious about the content of the letter, I would send a preliminary report so that the investigating member could close off that particular line of inquiry. *Big* mistake. I ended up in a lot of hot water, and it resulted in my departure from D&HW.

When the Bureau merged with FSI in December of 2019, there were five of us mules. Immediately, three new 'civilian' FSI staff were added to the section. Within the year, I would be one of only two garda members left in the office, along with Detective Garda Jer Moloney.

Two new additions, Jonathan and Ciaran, shared Jer's and my mule-like sense of humour, so we got on like a house on fire. However, we had another less welcome office interloper in the guise of a new 'state-of-the-art' computer system.

The Exhibit Tracking System, which was tasked over many years with logging all exhibits received for examination, was to be replaced. It was a hard-working and dependable system that wasn't cumbersome or difficult to use and didn't complicate matters. For years, it diligently worked away in the background, content in providing assistance in its straightforward way. In short, it wasn't broken. But nonetheless, senior management insisted it needed to be fixed, and there was only one show in town to do this: PEMS.

The Property and Exhibits Management System (PEMS) was to be the new kid on the block. There was a collective cry of 'Surely not!' from the mules, but PEMS had its foot in the door and wasn't budging. No more would there be a smooth and painless method for logging exhibits. Now, every item received for examination had to have a bar code, and every time an exhibit changed hands, there was much scanning and cursing. PEMS had been born out of the need to track property and exhibits at a *station level*, not in an environment like the Bureau, where exhibits were frequently moving between sections and members. The air was now full of the beep-beep-beep of bar-code scanners, trying to keep tabs on the current locations of the thousands of exhibits ferrying between offices and examination rooms.

An Garda Síochána loved its bar codes. Everything got one, not just exhibits: tables, chairs, monitors, microscopes, sets of drawers, folders, folders within folders and so on, ad nauseam. PEMS multiplied bar codes a thousand-fold and more. A D&HW file, such as a cheque fraud case, would now have a bar code for each exhibit, so you can imagine the amount of incessant beeping that would occur if you had a hundred or more individual cheques. Remember, these had to be scanned *each time* they changed custody. I came to dread the days when it was my turn to take in exhibits. There would always be some sort of cock-up. Maybe a bar code had been duplicated, or an exhibit was still recorded as being in someone else's custody, and PEMS wouldn't allow you to change its status.

Maybe the delivering member hadn't scanned the exhibits when removing them from the station's exhibits storage, or perhaps the right bar codes were on the wrong exhibit bags. The old Tracking System wouldn't have concerned itself with this stuff. It had still relied on good old dependable pen and paper to back it up. All we had to do was input the exhibits on the computer and have whoever was taking possession of them sign the accompanying C56 form. Easy-peasy. But PEMS was here to stay, so we just had to grin and bear it and factor in extra time for PEMS-related problems when processing case files.

If the Exhibit Tracking System had been a straight, two-lane highway, and PEMS was an awkward roundabout, what came next was a complete spaghetti junction mind-fuck. Along with the merger came the Laboratory Information Management

System (LIMS), and out the door went common sense. It was new to everyone, not just the gardaí that had seconded, but to many FSI personnel. Its selling point was that it would 'streamline lab operations, increase efficiency, and speed up research outcomes'. Somewhere out among the stars, there may be a planet where these promises would ring true, but not in garda headquarters. The delivery of exhibits from SOCOs and exhibit officers became a nightmare, as the PEMS system was still in use in every garda station. PEMS and LIMS were not compatible, so everything would have to be re-entered on the LIMS system, turning a simple handover of exhibits into a long and laborious task.

Seconded mules like myself would also have to use two computers, one with access to the garda Pulse system and garda email and the other for LIMS and any FSI-related work. I used Photoshop when putting together charts and reports, so I had to do these tasks on my garda computer and then email my work to my FSI inbox to attach them to the case on LIMS.

LIMS retained the bar code scanning of exhibits, but these were all new bar codes, which had to be generated and allocated to each exhibit, thereby doubling the amount of scanning to be done. We even had to scan a bar code on whatever drawer we took pending case files from. But the counter-intuitiveness didn't end there.

In the old days, a case would come in, exhibits would be entered into the Tracking System, and a case number would be generated. Now, with both PEMS and LIMS in operation, the amount of generated information went through the roof. For example, say you had an exhibit labelled JS1 on the bag that contained it. PEMS would need to generate a seven-digit *object* number. So now JS1 would have a second identifier, say OBJ1234567. When the exhibit was logged into LIMS, yet another number would be conjured up. JS1 would now be also identified as OBJ1234567 and C23-12345-01. Now, imagine if you had dozens of exhibits in a case. It became mind-boggling and sometimes very confusing when compiling statements for court, as the investigating member or SOCO would likely refer to JS1 when giving evidence, which might then be identified under its PEMS or LIMS number by someone who examined that particular exhibit.

Nobody liked using LIMS. Trying to get it to do what you wanted was akin to shovelling sand with a fork. It made simple, straightforward cases, such as questioned driving licences or currency, into needlessly long-winded affairs. It now took at least twice as long to put a report together on LIMS than it took to examine the questioned exhibit.

Any completed cases then had to be peer-reviewed (on LIMS) by at least two other people before a report could be dispatched to the investigating member. The awkwardness of LIMS and the loss of fully trained staff meant that the backlog of pending cases grew exponentially. When D&HW was an all-garda affair, an investigating member could expect to wait a few months at most for a report to be issued. When I left D&HW, less than three years after the merger, the backlog of pending files was more than two years. It was the same story in Fingerprints. As far as I was concerned, this was a totally unacceptable level of service.

If only the good old Garda Inspectorate could have seen what their recommendations would lead to. It was a long way away from the model of efficiency and effectiveness they had envisaged when they proposed the disbanding of the Technical Bureau.

My last few years in An Garda Síochána were by far the most frustrating. The LIMS debacle was compounded by the continued adherence to the ISO-17025 protocol. All I wanted to do was work, as did the other seconded garda members, but there was a severe culture clash between us and FSI.

As mules, our purpose was to assist in the investigation of crime and to prepare evidence for court. Everything else should have been secondary to this, but our primary function was being pushed aside in favour of long-winded and counter-intuitive procedures. Our expertise and experience didn't seem to count.

In D&HW, I now had people who were not document or handwriting experts, yet had final approval of my reports before they went out. When I voiced my concerns about this, I was told that they had many years' experience working in the Forensic Science Laboratory. I pointed out that none of those years were spent processing questioned documents or handwriting and signature files. I had over 25 years under my belt in the Bureau, but I would never consider myself qualified to walk into the DNA or Drugs sections and start processing cases.

Further frustrations came along with the whole Covid pandemic. We had to split the number of staff working in the office at any one time, so every second week, I had to work from home. This was pointless, as you weren't allowed to take exhibits home to examine them, and if it was your turn to be in the office, then there was rarely enough staff around to carry out the LIMS verifications on completed files.

This was the situation I was faced with when the preliminary report on the deaths of Nicholas and Hilary Smith was completed. The LIMS double-peer review couldn't be carried out as there were very few staff around. This meant the report was just sitting on my desk while the investigating gardaí were under pressure to release it. So I took the initiative and gave it to the investigating members. As I said, there was nothing contentious in it. But as a result, I was hauled in and reprimanded for blatantly disregarding protocol.

I was told LIMS procedure was sacrosanct and should be adhered to at all times. In my defence, I pointed out that we were not providing a timely service to investigating gardaí because of all the hoops that had to be jumped through with LIMS and ISO. I was a sworn member of An Garda Síochána; therefore, my primary duty was the investigation of crime and not the slavish adherence to time-consuming and counter-intuitive checks and balances, the existence of which only served to push actual tangible work ever further into the background.

Unsurprisingly, my views fell on deaf ears, and it was the beginning of the end for me. From the start, 2022 had been a stressful year. My heightened frustrations with work were compounded by other events in my life. Da passed away in late 2020, and I still hadn't adjusted to his loss. There were also other family matters compounding the stress that I felt. Probably due to all this, another old companion, the tiger, was back.

I began to take a lot of sick leave and contacted the Garda Welfare Service, who put me in touch with a counsellor with whom I could voice my frustrations. However, I knew that my position within D&HW was no longer tenable. I was the most qualified documents and handwriting member in the section, but my expertise and opinions no longer counted for what they had. It was my view that FSI policy trumped garda experience and procedures. I was no longer a mule; I felt more like the last of the woolly mammoths, wandering aimlessly around my shrinking environment. When I requested a transfer back to the Fingerprints Section, it was immediately agreed. I was responsible for processing practically all the handwriting and signature cases, yet I was able to leave D&HW almost straight away. In my opinion, they were glad to be rid of an independently minded, old-school garda.

The Fingerprints Section was also under FSI governance, but at least the head of the section was still a garda member, Richie. My old pal Allen was also a detective inspector in Fingerprints, and I knew all of the other mules still working there, so we could still have a bit of banter. Although I was still a fully qualified fingerprint expert, FSI management insisted I undergo 'training'. I spent my first few weeks reviewing stuff that I already knew and doing quality control on fingerprints sets on AFIS. However, by Christmas 2022, I was back searching cases and getting a few idents. Even though it had been 15 years since I'd searched case files, I got back into the flow quickly and still got that buzz from getting 'hits'.

With just one year until I reached the 30-year finish line and retirement, I kept my head down and counted off the days until I could retire. With luck, I would get there before the proposed move out to Backweston because I had no interest in a longer commute. I also reckoned that whatever autonomy the seconded garda members still retained would quickly evaporate once we were isolated at the new campus. However, things did not go according to plan.

In the closing months of 2022, my depression brought me down lower than snake shit. Unresolved grief over Da's death and other stressful events at home put me in the blackest place that I had ever known. I didn't realise just how bad things were until one day when Richie sat down for a chat with me, I found myself conversing with him at the same time as searching the internet to find out which arteries were closest to the skin's surface.

Even though I was plagued by suicidal ideation, I never acted on any of my impulses. I was aware what effect such actions would have on my family and knew my kids needed me. But I found myself reaching for blades so that I could self-harm. It was a way to release some of the pent-up feelings of dread that always seemed to be racing around in my head.

I was living on my nerves and fighting off the fear of living. It felt like I had to battle just to get through each day. I was like a rat dodging traffic crossing a busy road. Every night, when I crawled into bed, it felt like I had barely survived the day. If it so happened that I didn't wake up, then that would have been fine by me. I needed help.

Over Christmas, my GP decided I should spend time in St Patrick's mental hospital. A garda colleague who had done two stints in St Pat's also thought it would help. So, in January 2023, I went on sick leave again and entered the hospital for what turned out to be a period of eight weeks. While it served as some respite, I became frustrated with the lack of real constructive help. It was six weeks before I even got to see a psychiatrist. 'Staff shortages' were cited as the reason for this. As well as the many in-patients in the hospital, there were many more being treated under homecare plans and daily clinics were also running for out-patients. The healthcare professionals were stretched thin. It was still extremely frustrating for me as the weeks passed by without any *Eureka!*

moment. During this time the seed became planted in my mind that I might not be able to return to work at all.

I was still in turmoil, but I explained to my medical team that not wanting to live differs greatly from wanting to kill yourself. I knew that ending my pain would only cause immeasurable pain for those who loved me.

When I was finally discharged from the hospital, I was put into the care of a local HSE mental health service. Through them and my garda welfare officer, I came to the decision that I would look for early retirement on medical grounds. If it was granted, I wouldn't lose anything from my pension, and my gratuity lump sum would also not be affected.

I didn't realise that this would be the beginning of a very long and frustrating process. The chief medical officer of An Garda Síochána would ultimately decide if I met the requirements for medical discharge. They performed the same role as the old garda surgeon, so it was like when I was awaiting the decision as to whether I was suitable to join the job 30 years previously.

I thought that I had a good chance of getting early retirement. I had been tentatively diagnosed as suffering from 'adjustment disorder', which was explained to me as having excessive reactions to stressful events or experiencing more intense feelings than would typically be expected. I was still unwell and had lost a considerable amount of weight because I would sometimes go for days without eating much at all.

But as the summer came around, I still didn't know if my request for early retirement would be granted. It was a perfect storm of delays, red tape and unfortunate occurrences. The doctor whom I had been attending in the HSE left the practice, so a report for the chief medical officer had to be compiled by another consultant I never met. Also, even though I made myself available for face-to-face meetings with the chief medical officer, I never met him either. I only had two brief conversations with him over the phone from the time I applied for a medical discharge to when I received the decision six months later.

At the end of August, I was informed that the chief medical officer was not endorsing my application for early retirement. This even though he noted that I would be unfit for work for a period of up to six months, and I only had seven months left to serve.

I was devastated. I had known other members with much more time left to do who got early retirement on medical grounds. Many were not suffering from anything as serious. My future in the job had been decided by a consultant and a chief medical officer who had never even met me face-to-face. I now had to choose between going back to work, which I knew I wasn't in a fit state to do, or pulling the plug.

Although I was told by my welfare officer I could appeal the chief medical officer's decision, I knew that it would take months, and he was unlikely to change his mind. Also, I was now on less than half pay and no longer accruing any reckonable service as I'd been out sick for so long.

I said, 'Fuck it' and decided to take the only real option that I felt was left for me. I was done. The clock had ground to a halt a mere seven months before the finish line. I would take what is called 'cost-neutral early retirement'. This would mean I would only get around 60 per cent of my pension and a reduced gratuity payment. The day after I received confirmation of the chief medical officer's rebuttal, I put in my papers. I would retire from An Garda Síochána at midnight on 30 September 2023.

EPILOGUE

Rehabilitated? It's just a bullshit word. So you go on and stamp your form, sonny, and stop wastin' my time. Because, to tell you the truth, I don't give a shit.
Red, The Shawshank Redemption

Garda headquarters was empty when I arrived just before 7 a.m. on a Sunday in early September 2023. At that hour, no one was ever around, which was the way I wanted it. I still had my access card, so I was able to swipe through the various doors and corridors and head up to the first floor and the D&HW office. I flicked on the lights as I entered and, for the last time, walked to my old desk in the far left corner of the room. It had been the nerve centre of my working life for most of the last 15 years, and now it was bare, with just a few scattered bits lying around like pieces of bone after a carrion feast. Some of the wallpaper had peeled away behind my old chair and was drooping down like dead flesh. It was sad to see.

I'd brought a hold-all to pick up any last bits of stuff I might want to take home, but there was precious little to take. When I'd moved back to the Fingerprints Section the previous year, I had thrown out everything I didn't need and had boxed up anything else for storage, either in the archives at Santry or wherever FSI files go to sleep. My stereo-microscope sat on the bench behind my desk, covered with a thin layer of dust, and my old fingerprint examination kit was still where I'd put it, tucked away under the bench, where it had been since 2007. I wouldn't be needing any of it now. I'd never open the kit again or look through the twin viewfinders of the microscope, scrutinising a questioned document or interesting handwriting feature. It was all over.

I hadn't worked for the better part of a year and was coming to terms with the end of my career in An Garda Síochána. That sad, quiet corner of D&HW where, in better times, I had spent the longest single period of my time in the job now seemed like a snapshot from a different life. Someone else's life.

I didn't stay in the empty office for long. I knew that I'd only get upset. So, for the last time, I switched off the lights and let the heavy outer door swing shut behind me. Then I called up to the equally quiet and empty Fingerprints Section to carry out one final task. Although I had a desk in the section, there wasn't much to collect as I'd only been working there a few months before I'd gone on sick leave. One thing I wanted to pick up was my old hand magnifier that I'd had throughout my time in the Bureau. I'd made many idents with it, and it had accompanied me to all the crime scenes I'd visited over the years. I also collected my old steel ruler, which still had my name and '1989' on it, the year I'd first used it for my Leaving Certificate. I was always fond of keeping quotes that I found inspiring, and over the years, I'd added one I liked, printed in small, neat lettering along the spine of the ruler. It was a quote by Alex 'Hurricane' Higgins: 'Visualize it. And if you believe it, you can do all sorts.' I had visualised myself as a fingerprint expert and later as a handwriting expert, and I had accomplished both. As Da used to say, 'John, you'll always land on your feet.'

My final task was a small but significant one. I went into Allen's office and left a little envelope on his desk. Inside was my garda identity badge, which had been with me since I was sworn in as a member of An Garda Síochána in October 1994. I'd carried it with me nearly every day since then. Now, I had to surrender it before I retired. I felt it fitting to leave it with the very person I started with in the Bureau in 1997. I included a short note thanking Allen and the rest of my colleagues for their friendship and support over the years.

I didn't want any retirement party. No fuss. I just wanted to go quietly, and that's what I did. I took one last look at the AFIS suite, where I'd spent many happy years doing fingerprint work, surrounded by a very talented and professional bunch of mules. Good friends. I knew everyone else in the room would soon be gone too, as the move to Backweston loomed.

It seemed to me that everything was coming to an end. Not just my career but also what was left of the Technical Bureau. I had been so lucky and privileged to have worked within its walls. I can confidently say that everyone who had worked in Fingerprints, Ballistics, Photography, Mapping and D&HW was part of something special. They were easily among the best in the world at what they did, and, for a while, I was a little part of that. But, once again to paraphrase good ol' Doctor Who, times change, and now, so must I. I left the office and garda headquarters for the last time as a serving member.

The day back in 1993, when I walked through the gates of Templemore, seemed like a long time ago. I could hardly believe I had been a garda for over half my life. Truth be told, throughout all those years, I hardly even considered myself a garda. Not a good *garda* at any rate, but I do think I was good at being an *expert*, be it in Fingerprints or D&HW. Ultimately, that is for others to decide, most notably the tireless and professional members of the force whom I hope I was able to assist in some small way over the years.

So, 30 September came and went. There was no seismic shift. No final regrets. At 51 years of age, I was once more a civilian. I still had my demons, the tiger was still on my back. But once again, I found the best thing was to keep busy. To keep my mind occupied. Depression is like asthma or diabetes. It doesn't just get better and go away. You try to live with it. I had spent most of the year doing odd jobs around the house and tending to the garden. I was back dabbling in art and doing portraits for people. I would also occasionally be called to give evidence in court for a few cases still knocking around in the system. I had one other thing to think about, a certain little writing project I was contemplating. Maybe I had a few interesting stories to tell. Stories about my time identifying people from their fingerprints and handwriting, and the story about trying to find my place in an organisation like An Garda Síochána. The story of finding my own identity.

ACKNOWLEDGEMENTS

When I sat down to write about my career in An Garda Síochána, I naively thought that it would be a solitary endeavour, but hammering out an acceptable finished product was an experience built on a solid foundation of collaboration. I owe a debt of gratitude to Ciara Considine at Hachette for taking a chance on this cynical old mule. Many thanks also to Kathryn Rogers for helping to polish and shape the manuscript and ensuring its accuracy.

I'd like to thank my mam Anne, my brother James and my sisters Mary and Bernie for their support and encouragement. Bernie provided much-needed feedback as she read through the first draft of *Identity*.

Many thanks to my kids, Orin and Aleisha, for putting up with me hogging the kitchen table with all my writing stuff! And thanks to Orlagh for the kind words of encouragement.

To my good mates Sean, John and Ben. Thanks for the laughs (and the pints!).

I would have had no stories to tell without having had the privilege of working with the many supremely professional and knowledgeable men and women of the Garda Technical Bureau, in particular my good friends Glenn Ryan, Jim Cunningham and

Niall Dean of the Fingerprints Section. Thanks also to my old partner in training, Allen Slevin.

Many thanks too to retired Detective Inspector Michael Moore and all my colleagues in the Documents and Handwriting Examination Section, with a special mention to 'Baldy', 'Dr Jon' and 'Zendaya'.

Special thanks to Sergeant Colin O'Leary for his invaluable assistance with regard to the 'midlands letters' investigation.

Finally, I would like to thank the thousands of men and women of An Garda Síochána who on a daily basis carry out an often challenging and stressful service on behalf of the public. It has been an honour to have been able to assist our frontline guardians of the peace, even if only in a small way. So, the next time you find yourself grumpy or impatient while stuck at a garda checkpoint, or in a traffic jam caused by an accident on the motorway, spare a thought for the ordinary people behind those flashing blue lights who dedicate their working lives to an often extraordinary job.